The Amish on the Iowa Prairie, 1840 to 1910

Published in cooperation with The Center for American Places,
Santa Fe, New Mexico, and Harrisonburg, Virginia

Steven D. Reschly

The Amish on the Iowa Prairie, 1840 to 1910

The Johns Hopkins University Press | Baltimore and London

Unless indicated otherwise, all photographs are from the Mennonite Historical Society of Iowa, Kalona, Iowa.
Figures 2.3–2.5 are from *Combination Atlas Map of Johnson County, Iowa.* Geneva, Ill: Thompson & Everts, 1870.

Printed in the United States of America on acid-free paper
9 8 7 6 5 4 3 2 1

The Johns Hopkins University Press
2715 North Charles Street
Baltimore, Maryland 21218-4363
www. Press.jhu.edu

Library of Congress Cataloging-in-Publication Data
will be found at the end of this book.
A catalog record for this book is available from the British Library.

ISBN 0-8018-6388-0

To Nancy

Contents

Acknowledgments

The winding road of a study, when completed, seems shorter in retrospect than it did in prospect—and much shorter than it seemed while in transit. Still, a long list of colleagues to whom one is indebted reminds one of the long journey one has taken. Even though the trip often seemed lonely and solitary, in no way did I traverse it alone.

My thanks for help along the way go to my major dissertation advisors at the University of Iowa, Shelton Stromquist and Malcolm Rohrbough. Their scholarly talents and ability to complement each other always inspired me. Linda Kerber, my third reader, offered excellent advice and guidance. A collegial cohort of graduate students made my graduate education more pleasant than I expected. Several read and critiqued my research at many stages along the way. Thanks in particular go to Katherine Jellison, Barbara Handy-Marchello, Kevin Neuberger, and John Taylor.

This study began as a master's thesis at the University of Northern Iowa, where Chuck Quirk guided my research and encouraged me to set out on an academic path.

Professional research assistance from numerous librarians and archivists deserves special praise. At the Iowa Mennonite Historical Society archives in Kalona, Lois Gugel, Neva Lou Hershberger, and Lester J. Miller were endlessly generous with access times and assistance. The staff at the Archives of the Mennonite Church in Goshen, Indiana, helped me find and use the important collections held there from the Amish in Iowa. My thanks to Leonard Gross, Levi Miller, and Dennis Stoesz.

Thanks also go to the staff of public offices and institutions who generously gave their time to help me find county records. These offices include the County Clerk's Office in the Bee County Courthouse in Beeville, Texas; the Barker Center of Texas History in Austin, Texas; the County Clerk's Office in Wright County, Iowa; the County Clerk's Office in Somerset County, Pennsylvania; and the County Clerk's Office in Johnson County, Iowa.

Participants in the Newberry Seminar in Rural History at the Newberry Library in Chicago challenged me to keep up with rural scholarship. Their reading and discussion of several of my chapters were particularly astute. My thanks to Kathleen Neils Conzen and James Grossman for supporting the Seminar.

For expert reading and marvelous comments, thanks especially to Stacy Cordery, Julia Kasdorf, Royden Loewen, Frank Yoder, David Zercher, Kimberly Schmidt, Rachel Waltner Goossen, Gertrude Enders Huntington, anonymous readers for the University of Illinois Press and the Johns Hopkins University Press, and several Amish readers who wish to remain anonymous. Several colleagues at Truman State University offered perspectives from other times and other disciplines—my thanks to Sally West, Julia DeLancey, Janet Davis, Mike Ashcraft, Sara Orel, Cole Woodcox, and Christine Harker. Special appreciation goes to my wife, Martha Edwards, for many hours spent reading this manuscript and for generous support. Her commitment to combining scholarship with teaching never fails to amaze me.

Financial support from several sources helped keep this project alive. In particular, the Iowa Fellowship at the University of Iowa helped me survive graduate school with a family. The Pew Program in Religion and American History provided a Faculty Fellowship and a precious year for additional study and revision. The Mennonite Historical Society of Goshen, Indiana, awarded a grant to support publication. Truman State University provided several generous research grants and valuable student assistants.

Finally, thanks to my beloved children—Leah, Jessica, and Joel—for their patience and tolerance as I researched and wrote this book.

The Amish on the Iowa Prairie, 1840 to 1910

Introduction

Looking back more than a half century after Amish settlers reached Iowa, the first historian of the community, Samuel D. Guengerich, recalled two main reasons for the migration. The migrants sought good, cheap land "so that persons with small means could procure homes," and they wanted to "colonize close together" in hopes of organizing an Amish church.[1] Guengerich had inside information. His parents, Daniel P. and Susanna Miller Guengerich, were among the first Amish newcomers to Johnson County, Iowa, in 1846, when Samuel was ten years old. He observed firsthand the development of a thriving rural settlement, the most enduring and largest Amish community west of the Mississippi River.

The simultaneous quest for economic security and ethnoreligious association, recalled in Iowa by an elderly S. D. Guengerich in 1929, has led Amish families and individuals to an astonishing number of locations, from western North America to western Russia. Their quest has stretched over four centuries, from seventeenth-century expulsions from Switzerland to twentieth-century choices to settle in Central America and most American states and Canadian provinces. Amish people migrated for many reasons: to escape persecution, to manage internal conflicts, to flee the devastation wrought by Europe's wars, to find better farmland, and to gratify the spirit of adventure. As they traveled, Amish migrants carried with them the habits of consciousness and lifestyle that reproduced their cherished shared existence. These strategies and behaviors constitute the unique repertoire of Amish community, a configuration of generative internalized principles and preferred ways of confronting both familiar and unfamiliar circumstances. What are the historical sources for the distinctive Amish approach to ethnicity and community?

Interpreting Amish History

Social theory and studies of rural immigration have often proven inadequate to interpret Amish historical experience. Theories of social structure and change, steeped in the individualistic and behaviorist assumptions of nineteenth-century liberalism, tend to focus on static systems or predestined courses of social evolution. Students of immigration tend to assume the existence of self-contained social units without reference to social context or external influences. Definitions of community presuppose unitary, all-inclusive societies without recognizing discrete, smaller ethnic communities within a larger society or the existence of multiple social identities.[2] Scholarly literature on the Amish has been oriented to the present, asking how the Amish got here (the late twentieth century) rather than viewing them as historical actors in past times.[3] The static term *boundary maintenance* is ubiquitous in descriptions of Amish ethnicity. The rhetoric of boundary is a convenient fiction used by Amish insiders to mystify selective appropriation of the surrounding culture. Scholars seem taken in by this language of entire detachment, whereas the lived experience of Amish history is far more complex and dynamic.[4]

Worse, social theory in general is bedeviled by dichotomous oppositions: primitive-modern, with a linear progression called modernization; inside versus outside, implied by boundary maintenance; assimilation versus persistence; the gemeinschaft-gesellschaft contrast drawn by Ferdinand Tönnies; the church-sect cycle of Ernst Troeltsch; Redfield's folk society versus mass culture; precapitalist and capitalist economies in the capitalist transformation debate; and many others. Dichotomous theories are pervasive in studies of the Amish, with predictable and simplistic results. Stereotypically, the Amish are a premodern, unassimilated sect that practices gemeinschaft by relying on strict social boundaries to remain separate from the modern world. The tip-off to problems with these approaches should be that several of the most obvious Amish distinctives in the twentieth century, such as technological limits and peculiar clothing, played little part in nineteenth-century Amish history. In contrast to wallowing in dichotomies, anthropologist James Clifford proposed forsaking such oppositional typologies in order to conceive identity not so much as a "boundary to be maintained," but as a "nexus of relations and transactions actively engaging a subject." This would make for less linear and more complex stories of cultural interactions.[5] The lived experience of Amish community demands such complexity and subtlety of description.

Social theorists and historians alike have long sought ways to explain both social systems and historical change, and to reconcile social structure and human agency. One promising approach is to locate social reproduction, including class inequalities, at the intersection of shared external conditions of existence and shared internalized dispositions.[6] French sociologist Pierre Bourdieu named this intersection *habitus,* or "the practical mastery of a small number of implicit principles that have spawned an infinite number of practices."[7]

Peter Burke interpreted Bourdieu's *habitus* as "regulated improvisation," an alternative to the rigid cultural rules of structuralism and structural-functionalism.[8] However, *habitus* does not exist in isolation. Bourdieu placed the system of essential principles in dialectical relationship with a complementary concept, "field." *Habitus* is a structuring mechanism that operates from *within* agents, "though it is neither strictly individual nor in itself fully determinative of conduct."[9] It is "the strategy-generating principle enabling agents to cope with unforeseen and ever-changing situations."[10] Field, on the other hand, is a patterned system of objective forces (analogous to a magnetic field) imposed on agents by external reality. The field imposes "a structure of probabilities," but at the same time "always implies a measure of indeterminacy. People play according to rules and regulations, but also play with the rules themselves."[11] *Habitus* and field function only in relation to one another, offering a way to recognize both internal mental structures and external economic and social conditions.

However, Bourdieu lacks a theory of community as a mediating agent between individual and society in the field; he depends solely on class and class *habitus.* His two poles of analysis are the individual and society, with little attention to the possibility of ethnic communities as mediating agents of *habitus.* I have coined the term *repertoire of community* to describe shared ethnoreligious *habitus,* which becomes visible when an Amish community is compared with several other ethnoreligious communities in the same geographic location. Most students of rural communities situate themselves in a homogeneous world or in a setting where one group dominates. This monoculture is similar to the locations where Bourdieu has developed his methodology of "generative structuralism." However, there is a need for study of heterogeneous cultural settings. Since the Amish rarely dominate their local communities, even at the township level, they can offer an alternative perspective to homogeneity.

In addition, Bourdieu's methodology does not account for fields in which multiple ethnic groups contend for material and symbolic capital and thereby create a shared *habitus* that differs from any one community's *habitus. The Middle Ground,* in which Richard White described the creation of shared cultural space between Native Americans and white Europeans, comes closer to this sense of groups, not just individuals, contesting in Bourdieu's field. In White's reading, several groups created a shared common culture in a historically contingent process of conflict and cooperation.[12]

The Repertoire in Practice

Bourdieu's own formula for his research praxis, lifted from *Distinction,* can be expressed as an equation: (*Habitus* × Capital) + Field = Practice. Practice, or cultural production and reproduction, occurs in the mutual interpenetration of objective and subjective structures. The interaction between *habitus* and capital within a given field demarcates the cultural practice of those influenced by a given *habitus.*[13] As a research agenda, the formula reads from right to left. Bourdieu begins with actual practices within fields of economic and social forces, and infers the operation of generalized sets of dispositions from these observations. However, the dialectic of individual and society theorized by Bourdieu should explicitly include "community" as a mediating agent between the one and the many.

Just as a theater company can perform several plays on demand, so a community finds mental dispositions and behavioral tendencies already available through group processes in the familiar and unfamiliar situations of life. However, the analogy of repertory theater is too mechanical to fit lived reality. Members of a community experience life more like an athlete who has many set plays available but finally relies on semiconscious and trained attitudes and actions to achieve general goals. Bourdieu called this sports analogy a "feel for the game," the intuitions of unselfconsciousness in adapting behavior to any given situation.[14] The goals, the rationale for action, can remain stable even as the means adjust and transmute. For a community, the rationale of life together can remain relatively stable, while systems to actualize the rationale can change over time. In community theory, a "repertoire" concept offers a delicate balance between channels of consciousness and established patterns of individual and communal behavior, and between static social structures and historical change. A community member can almost always answer the question "What is the commonsense response to this situation?"

Community occurs in the interchange of consciousness and action, and in the melding of set patterns and free agency. Every community, and every member of a community, generates a repertoire of actions and attitudes that can be called upon as needed. Principles of adaptation grow from previous experiences, with memories and institutions available as infrastructure for innovation and identity continuity in the community's life. Communal principles and applications are contextually activated components of socioreligious identity, creating possible options to meet unfamiliar situations. Communities must sometimes preserve themselves in the acute crises of wars and depressions, sometimes in the gradual crises of assimilation and generational reproduction. The specific attitude or behavior may be conscious and carefully chosen, or it may be a result of group processes of socialization and selected unselfconsciously. A community is a group of persons sharing a similar repertoire of generative principles to meet external, internal, and personal challenges. These principles may be termed *collective memory,* not collective consciousness in the Jungian sense, but rather shared memories and recognition of commonality as a basis for shared action. Any given response or pattern of life may be shared with other communities, but the repertoire itself, the total configuration, is always unique.

A repertoire of community consists of channels of consciousness and habits of behavior. These generative principles guide and limit the possible range of attitudes and actions available to individuals in any given situation. However, individuals and entire societies are not the only possible units of analysis. We may also posit the idea of community-in-society as an alternative to a unitary view of society that automatically encompasses all individuals. The lived experience of community may be different from both individual existence and participation in a large society. Principles of behavior can be both individual and communal, opposing the hegemony of the larger social structures within which the community exists. A repertoire of community reflects the realities of individual-in-community-in-society.

How does this "system of strategies" concept, what I am calling the *repertoire of community,* illuminate the historical experience of a particular community? A repertoire is unknowable apart from historical experience. Contingencies of behavior and emotion reveal the purposefulness of human community. As a community deploys its shared repertoire in response to specific historical events, the responses must reveal the repertoire. As a community enacts cherished principles, members may produce novel responses to unique historical circumstances. The interplay of individual choice with community principles, and the interaction of one community's principles with those of other social groups, may produce alternative strategies in the attempt to preserve core communal identity. These contingencies and reactions unfold a repertoire of community and modify it over time. Therefore, the chapters of this study are organized around narratives that illustrate continuity and transformation, in order to gain access to the specific configuration of the Amish repertoire of community.

The Amish repertoire has proven effective in preserving a particular quality of rural, ethnic community through changing historical circumstances. Amish polity is decentralized and nonhierarchical, consensual in making decisions, and flexible in filtering cultural environments. The nexus of individual, family, and community traced by historians of ethnicity features the community among the Amish, especially through submission of the individual to community imperatives. The balance of individual and community interests is crucial in Amish history.

The community mediates between Amish individuals and larger social, political, and economic structures. The Amish person's responses to wars, economic upheavals, and social trends are affected by community guidance in direct and indirect ways. At the same time, the *habitus* itself is hardly immutable. Community values and intracommunal power relations are themselves contested according to differences in age, gender, household position, economic wealth, relations with the larger world, and other factors. Among the Amish, conflict is seldom strictly doctrinal, but rather it is related to individual behavior as it affects communal wholeness. That the Amish consider community worth fighting over indicates the importance of the communal repertoire to their lives.

This Amish repertoire of community allowed the establishment, growth, and persistence of an Amish settlement in Iowa. The Amish live within an untidy congeries of ethnic and religious groups in rural Johnson County, mainly in Washington and Sharon townships in the southwest corner of the county. They maintain relationships with other Amish communities scattered across several states and nations. They were never dominant numerically, and it was not obvious in the nineteenth century which ethnic community would retain its unique cultural configuration most tenaciously. Meeting new challenges to the existence of an Amish version of rural community was not so much a matter of creative individuals as it was the application and adaptation of a repertoire of community developed historically and situationally. The specific repertoire of flexible and constrained choices has not worked for all Amish individuals, but the community itself has met all challenges and still flourishes at the beginning of the twenty-first century.

The Old Order Amish component of these townships still maintains a rural community at variance with the dominant urban industrial and postindustrial mainstream culture of contemporary North America. The Amish are distinguished by simple technology; local control; face-to-face relationships; small scale family farming; and relative independence from market forces. A particular configuration of strategies differentiated the Amish from their neighbors. Many other rural ethnic communities were fully committed to reproducing themselves in the next generation. Initially, differences between the Amish and their neighbors were not great. However, cumulative subtle differences collectively produced the stubborn allegiance to rural primary community that outsiders still associate most often with the Old Order Amish. While it is difficult to describe any one of these aspects of the Amish communal repertoire in isolation from the others, since they do reinforce one another and the effect is cumulative, the components of an Amish repertoire become clear as they are activated by historical events.

In this book, discrete narratives of a small Amish community in nineteenth-century Iowa illuminate generative principles of Amish life. Several narratives employ a reverse strategy, showing the existence of an element in the Amish composition of community by examining a case of its breakdown or traumatic modification. The early chapters stretch far into the European and early American past. Amish householders imposed habits of mind developed in Europe and the eastern United States on the Iowa landscape with relative ease and success. The antecedents become shorter and shorter in subsequent chapters until the Sleeping Preacher of chapter 6, a moment the past could not predict and a moment that could not predict the future. Chapters 7 and 8 strain toward the future in their implicit acceptance of religious pluralism and a capitalist marketplace. Chapter 6, then, serves as a fulcrum where tradition and transformation meet. This sequence of revealing moments unfolds across eight chapters.

In chapter 1 I trace how Anabaptists and their Amish and Mennonite descendants developed specific attitudes and institutions necessary for survival in a hostile environment. They experienced marginality and persecution in early modern Europe and therefore developed mentalities and social structures of separation and autonomy. The Anabaptists dissociated themselves from civil government during the Reformation after disastrous experiences in which they tried to Christianize civil society in Zürich, the Peasants' War, and Münster.

The Amish renewal movement a century and a half later occurred in reaction to Pietism, confirming a worldview of concrete, visible, minority religious community rather than a universal spiritual and inner religion. And both Amish and Mennonites learned to consider their community portable as they migrated to preserve religious autonomy and economic survival. Amish religious convictions, arising from their roots in Reformation Europe, emphasize separation from, and nonconformity to, the world. These convictions were expressed in social and political refusals: military service, oaths of loyalty, coercive police power, and spiritualized religion. Avoiding any likeness to "the world" was and is a positive value in the Amish paradigm of faith community.

In chapter 2 I discuss the Amish agricultural system. The Amish employ a particular approach to agricultural production, rooted in the early modern European agricultural revolution. The Amish who settled in Iowa brought a highly developed and coherent system of agriculture from Europe, Pennsylvania, and other eastern Amish communities. This system emphasized subsistence with some market participation, the maintenance of soil fertility through legumes and manure, crop diversification, and keeping large numbers of animals. Expert farming methods amount to cultural capital, giving Amish farmers an advantage in competing with other ethnic groups. The close connection of this agricultural system with the structure of Amish community made it an efficient means of forming new communities in suitable locations, but less efficient in adjusting to environments not suited to diversified production. This aspect of the Amish repertoire functioned almost without change in Iowa.

In chapter 3 I show how male Amish leaders increasingly relied on paternal household authority to preserve communal separation. Borrowing from early modern central European culture, the male household head was always part of Amish family structure. Under rising pressure to assimilate in North America during the early nineteenth century, Amish leaders sought to strengthen this component of the Amish repertoire. Clarifying lines of household authority enabled Amish household heads to exercise greater control over family labor resources, inheritance practices, migration decisions, farming systems, and other aspects of communal coherence. Women and children contested the limitations imposed on them by paternal authority. Nevertheless, in response to the freedom and individualism of North America, Amish leaders strengthened their household authority and constructed a preservationist patriarchy, a stable structure of female subordination to male household heads on behalf of the community.

In chapter 4 I discuss the Amish attempt to limit their relationship to the modern nation-state. Social patterns of nonconformity and separation from the world, incorporated from Anabaptist theology, enabled the Amish community to escape the worst effects of the American Civil War and the resulting economic upheavals. But the intensity of separation had to be clarified in the turmoil of war and the pressures for home-front participation. By not fully accepting the exercise of statist or legal coercive power and hence refusing to use political activism to protect their pacifism, they avoided the assimilating tendencies of political involvement. Their nonparticipation in the military during the Civil War—only one Amish youth from Johnson County fought in the war—served to accentuate their differences from surrounding ethnic communities, which strengthened internal cohesion as well. A surge in land purchases by Amish buyers immediately after the Civil War suggests an ability to benefit from wartime conditions. By 1870 the Amish were well established and growing in comparison with the other ethnic communities in southwestern Johnson County.

In chapter 5 I examine how the Amish in Iowa created strategies of land ownership and inheritance to fulfill their practice of modified community of goods. No established pattern developed in Europe, where Amish farmers were prohibited by civil governments from land ownership, and the Amish in America had to find appropriate communal structures for individual property holding. Rather than renouncing private property, like the Hutterites, the Amish emphasized the responsibility of each individual and family to use material wealth for community good. They practiced fraternal mutual aid through institutions such as barn raisings, insurance societies, and food-preserving "frolics." Ideologies of economic individualism and private use of property, especially land, could threaten this component of the Amish repertoire. The inheritance controversy centered on Moses Kauffman reveals communal concern over the holding and disposition of private property. Stewardship of a widow's inheritance demonstrates the special male responsibility for property relations. The Amish combined private property with communal responsibility.

In chapter 6 I tell the story of how a sleeping preacher, Noah Troyer, disrupted a critical strategy of the Amish and how their ability to satisfy individual, family, and community needs was challenged and nearly destroyed during the 1870s and 1880s. Due in part to strains within the established communal consensus and in part to newer strands of market orientation and individual self-assertion, the Amish community began to fragment and divide.

Some migrated, some joined other churches, some became Amish-Mennonite and eventually Mennonite. Other ethnic groups offered alternate approaches to community.

In a setting of rural depression and discontent, the internal Amish conflict came to center on Noah Troyer. His trance sermons challenged the Amish approach to communal consensus by taking place apart from sanctioned religious leadership. Troyer offered a new balance of communal submission and individual self-assertion, raising new questions about leadership, ordination, and gender roles. He shifted the traditional binary worldview of church versus world to a new binary structure, heaven versus hell. His visions of Amish identity made "the world" seem less dangerous than spiritual dissolution and thereby threatened the established autonomous communal order.

In chapter 7 I follow one result of Troyer's activity, the gradual separation of religion and social reality in parts of the Amish community. After Troyer, the Amish developed divergent but complementary paths. By 1890 the Amish community had divided into tradition-minded, or Old Order Amish, and change-minded, or Amish-Mennonite, denominations. Old Order Amish sought to preserve the traditional repertoire of community with as little change as possible, while Amish-Mennonites began to practice "defensive structuration." Amish-Mennonites exhibited a new openness to influence from American varieties of Protestant activism and began to seek recourse within the American political system to ensure their survival instead of focusing exclusively on household and communal reproduction. However, even during this initial period of internal differentiation, both Amish communities continued to follow the Amish agricultural and household systems in comparison to their rural neighbors. Despite internal conflict, between 1880 and 1895 the ethnic Amish formed more new households than any other ethnic community in Washington and Sharon townships. Both Old Order Amish and Amish-Mennonite farmers continued to practice diversified agriculture. In this case, religious assimilation preceded economic and social acculturation.

In chapter 8 I discuss changes in Amish migration strategies. The Amish in Iowa preserved their communal identity by modifying the principle of portable community to include movement to other groups. Both spatial migration and conversion to more liberal Amish identities occurred. Amish pioneers established many new communities during the 1890s, including settlements in Oregon, Texas, Arizona, and most other states of the trans-Mississippi West. Most of these settlements failed, but geographic mobility helped dissipate conflict in many established communities by allowing dissenters to move elsewhere. Conflict and economic stress activated the migration system. The younger age of Amish household heads in 1870 and 1880 indicates not only early inheritance but also replenishment of the community by immigration from eastern Amish settlements. In addition, the possibility of migrating to an Amish community farther west or of returning to an eastern community alleviated the shortage of available land. Daughter colonies in north central Iowa, Missouri, and Texas illustrate the economic usefulness and the absorbing dangers associated with the Amish migration system.

By the early twentieth century, the Amish repertoire of community had differentiated the Amish from their neighbors in southwestern Johnson County, Iowa. Washington and Sharon townships were hosts to Old Order Amish, Amish-Mennonite, German Lutheran, German Evangelical, Irish Catholic, and Welsh Congregational communities. These several groups had successfully recreated ethnic communities on the Iowa prairie, each with a unique repertoire. Many elements in these repertoires were shared, although the contour was unique in each case. The Amish repertoire consisted of separation and autonomy; visible religious community; portability; agriculture; household patriarchy; distance from the nation-state; modified common property; balancing individual, family, and community; unifying religion and social system; and spatial and affiliative migration. These are hardly the only components in the Amish repertoire of community. The rhetoric of boundaries is surely to be included, as is the assumption of continuity, age hierarchy, German language, and much more. The repertoire I have identified became visible in historical interactions and contingent situations during the nineteenth century in Iowa.

The repertoire itself is subject to change and adjustment, of course. At times internal and external circumstances stretched the configured features of Amish historical experience to the breaking point, and many individual members left the faith or migrated to new locations. Nonetheless, the Amish lived experience and hard-won insight into the essential coherence of community stimulated a dynamic social generativity resistant to simple assimilation. Amish communities were never stagnant and unchanging, as the following chapters will make evident.

> True believing Christians are sheep among wolves, sheep for the slaughter. They must be baptized in anguish and tribulation, persecution, suffering, and death, tried in fire, and must reach the fatherland of eternal rest not by slaying the physical but the spiritual.
>
> —Conrad Grebel, 1524

Chapter 1

Configuring Amish Historical Experience

The Amish of Johnson County, Iowa, in the company of Mennonites, Hutterites, and other groups, count the Anabaptists of sixteenth-century Europe their direct ancestors. The violence and repression of the Reformation and early modern state building imprinted a deep consciousness of mutual hostility between creators of the resulting social order and members of the dissident religious movements that produced the several Mennonite and Amish traditions. Anabaptists of the sixteenth century, associated by authorities with social revolution and religious heresy, were persecuted and suppressed with the full combined weight of state and church, whether in Catholic or Protestant regions. State builders marginalized and excluded those who did not fit their vision of a homogeneous, unified, and disciplined polity, symbolized by obedience to centralized authority, military service, and religious uniformity. Several of the most consistent and important tendencies in the Amish repertoire—suspicion of civil society, assertion of communal autonomy, and the expectation of moving to form new communities—developed in early modern

Europe.[1] Through martyr literature and hymnody, the Amish kept alive the memory of persecution and the consciousness of disengagement from civil society. Their *mentalité* (core consciousness) of estrangement reflected and was reinforced by symbolic and structural institutions of autonomous community. These patterns stemmed from several critical challenges faced by Anabaptists and their Amish and Mennonite offshoots in Europe.

The Problem of Civil Society

Sixteenth-century Anabaptists developed a suspicious and distant relationship with civil society. Anabaptism had its roots in a broad popular movement of radical resistance and revolt against the church-state synthesis of early modern Europe. The diverse and polyglot set of movements that fall under the umbrella term *Anabaptism* originated in at least three places and represented competing theologies and practices.[2]

Historians have revised scholarly opinion of the Anabaptist movement during the past two decades. Harold S. Bender in 1943 sought to combat polemics against Anabaptism as a revolutionary movement associated with the violence and polygamy of Münster by proposing a normative "Evangelical Anabaptism" with one historical origin and three coherent emphases. Bender considered urban humanism in Zürich the seedbed of Anabaptism, and discipleship, brotherhood, and an ethic of love and nonresistance as the essential theological criteria of a mainstream "Anabaptist Movement."[3] Recent studies of the German Peasants' War of 1525; Thomas Müntzer, the anti-Luther visionary and military leader of a peasant army in Thuringia; and Anabaptist leaders previously labeled "fringe" have chipped away the clarity of Bender's "Anabaptist Vision."[4] It is difficult, apart from confessional purposes, to identify a normative Anabaptist theology.

Anabaptism as a religious movement resulted from three failed attempts to impose a radical version of Christianity on the entire social order. First, a group of young urban humanists in Zürich, early supporters of Ulrich Zwingli and his reform preaching, attempted to take over the city's Council by legal election in 1524. They believed reform, hindered by the cautious town fathers, was moving too slowly. Second, many leaders of the failed German Peasants' War of 1525 became Anabaptists after imperial forces crushed the attempt to establish a Christian social order through peasant revolution. Finally, many Anabaptists attempted to realize the apocalyptic visions of Melchior Hofmann by organizing a political revolution in the Westphalian city of Münster in 1534. Believing themselves to be in the vanguard of a more just and Christian social order, they expected divine action to bring the rest of humankind into the kingdom of God. Combined Catholic and Protestant armies crushed the Münsterite New Jerusalem in 1536. Klaus Deppermann has argued that leaders of Anabaptist movements in Switzerland and Strasbourg did not accept pacifism at first and claimed the necessity of self-defense and the possibility of a Christian society.[5] Reaction to these three disasters—Zürich reform, Peasants' War, and Münster—produced a pacifist, apolitical variety of Anabaptism.

Ulrich Zwingli began preaching at the Großmünster in Zürich in 1519. He soon gathered a group of enthusiastic young humanists to support his reform movement, among them Conrad Grebel and Felix Manz. Grebel's father sat on the Council of Two Hundred, the governing body of the city, and Manz was the son of a canon at the Großmünster. Grebel's sister Martha married Vadian, the Swiss humanist; correspondence between Grebel and Vadian preserves key pieces of the Zürich story in the early 1520s.[6] Grebel was well positioned to influence events in the newly Protestant city.

Grebel and Zwingli came to disagree on the pace and control of reform. Although Zwingli preached against the Roman Catholic mass and in favor of an evangelical communion service, the Council hesitated to make fundamental changes. At a disputation in October 1523, Grebel demanded immediate action, and Zwingli deferred to the Council to decide the timing of reform. In December, despite Zwingli's initial plan to celebrate a Protestant communion on Christmas Day, the Council delayed indefinitely any change in the mass, and Zwingli acquiesced.

At first, Grebel and Manz plotted to replace the recalcitrant Council. They approached Zwingli sometime in early 1524 with a plan to make the Reformation a political party. They proposed that Zwingli issue a public challenge to the people of Zürich to choose for or against the Word of God, as preached by Zwingli. Confident that the majority would side with reform, this majority could then elect a Council more disposed to immediate reform, and Zwingli could continue to work with the state without slowing change to a crawl. Zwingli refused, confident that the Council would move ahead in time. He feared dividing the populace by instituting a "Reformation Party" that might destroy the symbiosis of church and state.

Later in 1524, the issue became focused on infant baptism, symbolic of the Constantinian synthesis of religion and civil society. Grebel wrote to Thomas

Müntzer in September in hopes of finding a revolutionary ally, but unlike Müntzer, Grebel rejected both violence and infant baptism. At a public meeting on 17 January 1525, the Council threatened banishment for any parents who refused to baptize their children. The circle of dissidents met in the home of Felix Manz on the evening of January 21. A priest, George Blaurock, asked Grebel to baptize him. In effect, this act was a rebaptism and rejection of his infant baptism by the state church. Grebel or Blaurock then baptized the others, symbolizing their renunciation of the state as an instrument of religious faith.[7]

Another area of disagreement was the issue of violence. Article 6, the longest article in the Schleitheim Confession of Faith (1527), written by Michael Sattler and reflecting an attempt to unify factious impulses in Anabaptism, stated, "The sword is an ordering of God outside the perfection of Christ [the church]." Within the church, only excommunication could be used to keep order. Christians might not take up the sword of war or internal judicial order. Schleitheim made an absolute distinction between church and world.[8]

A similar structural effect on Anabaptism—pessimism about reforming an entire society—resulted from the German Peasants' War of 1525. Historian James M. Stayer has concluded that while one can understand the Peasants' War without Anabaptism, the reverse is not equally true.[9] Anabaptist religious radicals shared many goals with the authors of peasant manifestos: a nonhierarchical social order, common access to resources, communal claims on private property, communal autonomy, obedience to divine law rather than religious tradition, and a society based on Scripture, not on human inventions.

Following the defeat of peasant armies at the battle of Frankenhausen and the execution of Thomas Müntzer, some leaders of the socioreligious revolution transferred their allegiance to the religiosocial revolution of Anabaptism. They still sought an egalitarian social order, but they no longer counted on violence to overcome ongoing persecution. Several peasant leaders became Anabaptists. Stayer identified Hans Hut, Melchior Rinck, Hans Römer, probably Hans Denck, and several other veterans of the Peasants' War who "had all sorts of important roles in central German Anabaptism." Many fought in the same vicinity as Müntzer, sometimes as his colleagues and companions.[10] The communitarian ideals and critique of private property in peasant manifestos such as the Twelve Articles were preserved by the Hutterian Brethren in Moravia.[11]

Münster represents a third formative influence on Anabaptism. Itinerant preacher Melchior Hofmann prophesied millennial fulfillment in the 1530s in northern Germany.[12] After Hofmann sought imprisonment in Strasbourg in 1533 to hasten the Second Coming, a baker from Haarlem, Jan Matthijs, claimed leadership of the Melchiorite movement. Matthijs moved to Münster in 1534 and proclaimed it the New Jerusalem, teaching violent revolution to prepare the way for Christ's return. Anabaptist governments ruled the major city of Westphalia from February 1534 to June 1535, under siege the entire time by Protestant and Catholic armies gathered by the displaced bishop of Münster. After Matthijs died in battle on Easter Sunday in 1534 (he had predicted the end of the world for that day), Jan van Leyden named himself a new David, instituted polygamy, and enforced common ownership of property. The city fell on 24 June 1535, and all Anabaptists were henceforth labeled visionaries and revolutionaries.[13] Exact numbers are difficult to establish, but estimates of those executed run into the thousands. Perhaps as many as four thousand Anabaptists were executed by 1600.[14]

Dirk and Obbe Philips and Menno Simons attempted to reconstitute the movement by advocating a peaceful Anabaptism. The Philips brothers were baptized by apostles sent to Leeuwarden by Jan Matthijs, but they rejected the use of force. Menno probably lost a brother to the Münster massacre. He resigned his priesthood in his home village of Witmarsum in Friesland on 30 January 1536 and went into hiding to shepherd the peaceful Anabaptist movement. Obbe Philips baptized Menno and later ordained him a minister of the outlaw religious group.

These three events—Zürich, the Peasants' War, and Münster—profoundly affected the early course of Anabaptist history. Taken together, they contributed to selective memory. The negative events—Peasants' War and Münster—were denied, while Zürich and heroic martyrdom were celebrated in Anabaptist hymns and stories. Decades of persecution forced Anabaptists to hide in the countryside or migrate to the rare regions of Europe that allowed limited toleration of heretics and dissidents. During the next century and a half, until the Swiss Brethren division, Anabaptist writers produced a common fund of literature available to both Amish and Mennonites: the *Ausbund,* containing a core of hymns composed by Anabaptists imprisoned at Passau along the Danube River;[15] the writings of Menno Simons and Dirk Philips;[16] *Martyrs Mirror,* written by a Dutch Mennonite in 1660;[17] and several confessions of faith and congregational disciplines. Their writings reflected an identity of innocent martyrdom, not aggressive revolution.

The Challenge of Pietism

The principle of communal autonomy appears again in the complex relationship between German Pietism and Anabaptism. The connections, if any, have long presented nearly insoluble difficulties for historians and theologians. For one thing, neither movement was either monolithic or easily classifiable. The publication in 1675 of Philipp Jakob Spener's *Pia Desideria* (*Desires of the Heart*), written as a postil to Johann Arndt's *Wahres Christentum* (*True Christianity*), usually serves to date the beginning of Pietism as a historical phenomenon.[18]

In religious terms, Pietism arose out of the moral and spiritual chaos that followed the Thirty Years' War; the sterility of neoscholastic Lutheran and Reformed orthodoxy, emphasizing pure doctrine and sacraments at the expense of warm, personal, and lay piety; and the mystical-evangelical tradition represented in Puritanism (John Bunyan, and Lewis Bayly's *The Practice of Pietie*), Quakerism, Judaism (Hasidism), and Lutheranism (Johann Arndt).[19] Out of this crisis, Spener called for thorough and practical piety (*gründliche und würckliche Gottseligkeit*), church discipline, and greater openness to the Holy Spirit.[20] He offered six proposals toward reforming the church: intensive Bible reading; practicing the priesthood of all believers, as mentioned by Luther; convincing the people that faith consists of lifestyle and not mere knowledge; pursuing ecumenical harmony to avoid offending unbelievers; ensuring that only qualified men were called to the ministry; and encouraging practical sermons.[21] Spener directed his suggestions toward the clergy for application, and he especially promoted small group/conventicle Bible study for lay members.

Swiss Brethren[22] read Arndt, and they likely read Spener's introduction as well. Spener was a native of the Alsatian village of Rappoltstein near Strasbourg, and many Alsatian nobles and landowners were attracted to the *collegia pietatis* in the years after 1675. In fact, County Rappoltstein included the areas of Amish settlement in Alsace, especially the village of Markirch (Sainte-Marie-aux-Mines), where Jakob Ammann lived part of his life. These facts offer a striking geographic, temporal, and theological proximity to the Swiss Brethren division of 1693.

Pietism ranged from attempts to deepen spirituality within the state churches to questioning the state-church synthesis or rejecting it altogether. Nicholas Ludwig, Count von Zinzendorf, and the Moravians; the Schwarzenau Movement of Alexander Mack that developed into the Church of the

Brethren; and the Community of True Inspiration that produced Iowa's Amana Colonies were all radical versions of Pietism. These radical movements often considered Anabaptism their precursor and even sought contact and mutual support.

Across the spectrum of movements that took inspiration from Spener and his follower, August Hermann Franke, several central tendencies are discernible. Pietists generally sought to make religious faith a matter of experience and practice more than of intellectual assent to doctrine or obedience to hierarchical leadership. Stressing personal experience and each individual's immediacy to God meant less need for ordained clergy to mediate faith. For historian F. Ernest Stoeffler, the central characteristic of the pietistic impulse was reform of the Christian life. The magisterial Reformation transformed doctrine and polity; the "second phase of the Reformation" sought to apply the transformation to behavior.[23]

These emphases, on the surface, are not incompatible with Anabaptism. Anabaptist writers also stressed change of life and nonhierarchical leadership. However, to some Anabaptists chosen by later Amish and Mennonites as normative, faith was a matter of personal and communal will, a decision to "follow after Christ" (*Nachfolge Christi*) in costly discipleship and responsible commitment to a religious community. The Anabaptist worldview was decisively dualistic, making a radical distinction between church and world. Anabaptists were not at all ecumenical or willing to set aside "nonessentials" in matters of faith and practice. Whatever direct connections can or cannot be made, issues of purity and separation informed the movement led by Jacob Ammann in Alsace and Switzerland during the 1690s.

The Swiss Brethren division of 1693 can be viewed as a result of the powerful new Pietist ideas. The renewal movement led by Jacob Ammann expressed extreme caution toward Pietism, especially when "heart religion" seemed to threaten a visible, concrete, and communal expression of faith. Historian Leo Schelbert has suggested that Amish origins were a case of outright rejection of Pietism. His provocative piece may oversimplify a complex historical relationship, but Schelbert's thesis has proven difficult to refute.[24]

Swiss persecution and suppression had crushed Anabaptism in urban areas by the mid-sixteenth century, but not in rural areas. Swiss Brethren families lived in the Swiss back country, in the highlands and isolated river valleys, especially in Canton Bern and the Emme Valley (Emmental). The Brethren faced continual mandates from the authorities threatening banishment, fines, slavery, or execution.[25] However, the local populace and Reformed pastors often accepted their presence or even supported them in times of persecution; the Swiss Brethren called these secret supporters the Truehearted (*Treuherzigen*) or Half-Anabaptists (*Halbtäufer*). Bernese authorities mounted new campaigns to eradicate the tiny sect in the 1660s and again in the early 1690s. For example, a mandate dated 8 September 1670 demanded a general oath of allegiance on pain of expulsion within two weeks. Those who refused the oath were to be whipped, led to the border under armed guard, and branded with hot irons; if they returned, the result was summary execution.[26] At least six Swiss Brethren men were subsequently sent to Venice as galley slaves.

Some Swiss Brethren complied with the mandates, trying to get by until the wave of persecution died down and even allowing their infants to be baptized. Many others migrated to Alsace or down the Rhine River to the Palatinate region, where, in the aftermath of rural depopulation wrought by the Thirty Years' War, landholders often tolerated the heretical sect in return for their farming skills. In 1671 some seven hundred Swiss Brethren moved to the Palatinate, and perhaps another four hundred went to Alsace in the early 1690s. In Alsace there were Swiss Brethren congregations in Markirch, Jebsheim, and Ohnenheim. Other Swiss Brethren stayed, and despite the severe persecution, they saw their congregations grow rapidly with converts from Reformed villages. Frustrated Reformed pastors sent reports to Bern indicating rapid Swiss Brethren growth despite official repression. The combination of persecution, emigration, and new converts created confusion in the Swiss Brethren congregations of Alsace and Switzerland.

Swiss Brethren in Alsace lived under a more tolerant regime and sensed a need to maintain rigorous social barriers against the outside world in the absence of official persecution. The Swiss Brethren in Switzerland experienced the world's hostility all too clearly and were reluctant to condemn the supportive Truehearted, although they were not baptized as adults and therefore not members of any Brethren congregation. As the Alsatian and Swiss congregations debated the salvation of the Truehearted, other issues came to the fore, especially shunning (*Meidung*), or social avoidance of excommunicated former church members.[27] Excommunication and shunning appear in Articles 16 and 17 of the Dordrecht Confession of Faith, written in 1632 by Dutch Mennonites following the teachings of Menno Simons.[28] Swiss Brethren ministers accepted Dordrecht in 1660 in a meeting at Ohnenheim in Alsace.[29]

Three decades later, the newer Swiss Brethren congregations in Alsace commissioned Jacob Ammann, a minister from Markirch, to visit the Swiss Brethren in the Emmental to investigate questions of church discipline and order, or *Ordnung*. Ammann tirelessly advocated footwashing, more frequent communion, and strict shunning in faithfulness to the Dordrecht Confession. Hans Reist, a senior minister in the Emmental, delayed attending a meeting set up by Ammann and dismissed his concerns. In a dramatic meeting at Niklaus Moser's barn, Ammann banned several ministers who refused to agree with him and returned to Alsace. Attempts to mediate the rift failed, and the disagreement hardened. In 1700 the "Ammansch" group admitted making mistakes from hasty and rash methods, revoked the excommunication of the "Reistisch" group, and even excommunicated themselves in hopes of reconciliation; but the animosity continued. In 1711, during yet another forced expulsion from Switzerland (the Bernese government hired the Ritter Company to ship Swiss Brethren and other undesirables down the Rhine), the *Häftler* (Hook-users, or Amish) and the *Knöpfler* (Buttoners, or Mennonites) did not want to travel together on the same vessel. Most of the Mennonites left the shipment along the way to stay with coreligionists in the Palatinate.[30]

Past analyses of the Swiss Brethren division have focused on the personality of Ammann, who did act aggressively and confidently in his demands for immediate responses from the ministers he visited.[31] Ammann was born on 12 February 1644 in Erlenbach, Switzerland. His father and grandfather were tailors in Steffisburg. He resided in Steffisburg until about 1693 and likely developed a strong following within the Swiss Brethren renewal movement before moving to Alsace. From 1693 to 1695 Ammann lived at Heidolsheim in Alsace, in the Rhine plain. At this time, fifty-two Swiss Brethren families lived in the plain and only ten in the valley of Sainte-Marie-aux-Mines. Jacob's father, Michael, died in April 1695 and had to be buried in the Protestant village of Baldenheim, a privilege denied him in Heidolsheim because of his Anabaptist membership. After his father died, Jacob moved into the Vosges Mountains, into the Val d'Argent (Valley of Silver) above Sainte-Marie-aux-Mines, where he lived until 1712. Some sixty Swiss Brethren families arrived in the valley between 1694 and 1696, forming as much as a quarter of the total population. The newcomers invested heavily in abandoned lodgings and businesses, vacant because of a decrease in silver mining activity. They bought estates, controlled the production of wood with a sawmill, and built several mills. Robert Baecher has estimated the value of their goods at twelve million francs, or about two million dollars today. There were three groups of Swiss Brethren in the valley, none having anything to do with the others: the Amish, led by Jacob Ammann; the Mennonites, led by Roudolph Houser; and later arrivals from Switzerland, who belonged to neither group.

Ammann acted aggressively to shepherd his people and protect them from state interference. In February 1696 he petitioned for exemption from militia service and the function of *Heimburg,* an elected position responsible for collecting taxes. A pattern developed in which the local population protested Anabaptist exemption, and the Amish paid sums of money for the relief to continue. In a petition to Duke Christian III of Birkenfeld, Jacob Ammann offered to appoint a person "of their religion" to be the accountant and collect the tax. Ammann also had several public conflicts with the local priest, once even threatening the curate in the street for putting pressure on the Anabaptists. Jacob Ammann virtually disappears after 1712, when he moved to Zellwiller, still in Alsace. He must have died sometime before 1730, for when his daughter reconverted to the state church at Erlenbach in that year, she testified that her father had died.

In the painful events of the 1690s, Jacob Ammann and his followers asserted the social reality of religion versus the individualistic, internal heart religion of Pietism. They sought to avoid assimilation to Alsatian culture and to preserve the dualism of Schleitheim. The consciousness of keeping internal and external life in harmony was reinforced by the Swiss Brethren division, as were the social institutions of visible difference, such as simple clothing and untrimmed beards.

The Compulsion of Portable Community

Anabaptists and their Amish and Mennonite descendants expressed their quest for autonomy through constant movement. They migrated continually to avoid persecution, to form new communities, and to seek new economic opportunities.[32] After being pushed out of Switzerland into Alsace and the Palatinate, many Amish families were also expelled from Alsace and migrated southward to Montbéliard or northward to Lorraine. The expulsion from Canton Bern in 1711 resulted in several settlements in the Netherlands. A number of families moved from Alsace and the Palatinate to other German territories, including Hesse, Bavaria, and onward to Galicia (now western Ukraine) and Volhynia (now southeastern Poland). The Galician Amish eventually moved to western Russia and joined a Hutterite community, while the Volhynian Amish merged with nearby Mennonites and joined a migration to North America.[33] However, no matter how scattered, most of the Amish refugees and migrants managed to maintain a sense of ethnic and religious difference from whatever larger culture in which they established themselves.

The Amish who migrated to the north central German principalities of Waldeck and Wittgenstein are of particular interest because several of these families and individuals moved to North America and later joined the new settlement in frontier Iowa. (Amish family names were similar to those found in Johnson County, Iowa: Bender, Brenneman, Guengerich, Roth, Schlabach, Shetler, and Swartzendruber.) Amish refugees from Switzerland entered these regions, located in the present German states of Hessen and Nordrhein-Westfalen, in the early eighteenth century, often after sojourns in Alsace or the Palatinate. The rulers of Waldeck and Wittgenstein allowed religious minorities, including Pietists and Spiritualists, to settle in their regions. In Waldeck, the Amish mainly lived as *conductoren* (tenant-managers with long-term leases) on noble estates and royal dairy farms. While inhabitants of villages were still obliged to do compulsory work for the count, the *conductoren* contracts required them to act as "suppliers to the Court" for meat, butter, cheese, and wool. One clause in a 1741 lease contract for the Netze dairy farm with Swartzendruber tenants reads: "The *conductoren* as well as their wives and children shall be exempt from all official obligations and consequently liable directly and only to the royal jurisdiction. The rest of the servants and domestics however are subjected to the official obligations like all other subjects."[34] Regular congregational worship services took place on several estates, and the Amish kept peace with local state church pastors by paying the required church fees. However, the Amish had large families, and there were few estates available for lease; thus, there were mass emigrations to America after 1830.[35]

Jacob Swartzendruber, the first Amish bishop in Iowa, was born in Waldeck in 1800. His grandfather, Christian, was co-tenant at Netze in 1741. His father, Christian, operated the Hafersack mill, and married Catharina Roth, whose family operated the Gallows Mill (*Galgenmühle*, later the *Luisenmühle*). Both mills were located near the village of Mengeringhausen. Jacob married a widow, Barbara Oesch, in 1821 and moved to the Gallows Mill, where they had six children of their own.[36] Oesch had been the third wife of Peter Guengerich, who died in 1816; she brought two sons from the previous marriage, Jacob P. (b. 1811) and Daniel P. (b. 1813). The family also included John P. (b. 1791), a son of Peter's by his second wife, who also emigrated to Iowa. John P. Guengerich

1.1. Site of the Gallows Mill near Mengeringhausen, Germany. Jacob Swartzendruber, later the first Amish bishop in Johnson County, Iowa, operated this mill before emigrating to Pennsylvania in 1833.

and Jacob Swartzendruber were both ordained to the Amish ministry by the Mengeringhausen congregation (Figure 1.1). Swartzendruber's church letter, for transfer of membership to another Amish congregation, was dated 10 April 1833. The letter, signed by Bishop Daniel Schlabach, stated that Swartzendruber was a minister in good standing and should be allowed to continue his office where he settled. The letter was also signed by John P. Guengerich, stepson of Swartzendruber's wife.[37]

The blended family headed by Jacob Swartzendruber emigrated to America in 1833, when the stepsons reached military age and became subject to compulsory military service.[38] All the Amish eventually left Waldeck for America or for Hesse-Cassel. A diary of the ocean crossing to America kept by 20-year-old Daniel P. Guengerich, Jacob's stepson, records the emotional farewell received by the Amish party from the local populace. On May 9, the group planned to leave at 8 A.M., but the many good-byes prevented their departure until 2 P.M. Guengerich described the parting scene in his diary:

> The wagon with mother, children, and baggage drove off and went through Mengeringhausen, where a curious crowd stood there and looked out the win-

> dows, calling out yet another very sincere "Farewell and happy journey!" And one can easily understand how, when one has stood so long in such intimate association with the people as we did at the Gallows Mill, this would perhaps arouse a great sensation at the permanent parting.[39]

Leaving behind a family business and familiar community was not so easy, but the pull of migration was stronger still. The passage should also temper the impression that the Amish faced unremitting hostility at every turn. Persecution in Europe arose mostly from official sources, while local populations often got along quite well with Amish farmers and business people.

Guengerich's diary describes the journey down the Weser River to Bremen, where the party boarded a ship on May 29. Through difficult wind conditions and storms, bad water, stale food, and overcrowded living quarters, Guengerich maintained a sense of humor. "Seasickness is simply customary and all appetite goes away," he wrote on June 3. He described a funeral at sea on June 25. The captain gave such a beautiful message that many hearers cried. Later, however, the diarist noted, "The Captain doesn't always tell the truth" when he declared the ship was not in the gulf stream.

Guengerich recorded three dreams from the Atlantic crossing, two of his own and one dreamed by his mother.[40] Two consecutive nights, June 25 and 26, Guengerich dreamed of the Gallows Mill. The first night, a flock of birds flew out of an apple tree. They were not flying high or properly, but he could not catch any, though he jumped over ditches along the way. Everything was in the most beautiful meadow, with long grass. Wild plums were ripe, so heavy on the trees that the branches bent, beautiful to look at but not to enjoy. The sense of loss and inaccessibility is palpable. The second night, Guengerich dreamed he was sitting on a beam above the thresher in the Gallows Mill, and second-growth hay on the beam caught fire. The fire burned so brightly that he snatched at the blaze. "How it would have gone after that I don't know," he commented. In both dreams, Guengerich found himself back in the home his family had just left, with food just out of reach, surrounded by a sense of impending disaster.

Daniel Guengerich's mother, Jacob Swartzendruber's wife, had her dream on the night of July 21. Barbara's dream had to do with drinks, and she was busy trying to come up with some. A few days later, on July 28, the ship's passengers put containers on deck during a rainstorm because they were suffering from lack of water. She found being unable to provide for her family frustrating. The difficult ocean voyage produced musings of anxiety and regret as the Swartzendrubers and Guengerichs transferred their community allegiance from Europe to America, but the party survived the journey and landed at Philadelphia September 11.

Of necessity, the Amish in Europe experienced their community life as mobile. Amishness was not dependent on a certain location or a particular region, and Amish migrants maintained a communal identity in a bewildering number of European principalities. Many, to be sure, lost their lives to persecution or galley slavery, and others rejoined their Mennonite cousins or simply faded into the state churches. Still, after the compulsion of persecution ended, the Amish continued to move with enthusiasm, and North America offered inviting opportunities to form new communities.

Mennonites had reached Germantown, near Philadelphia, in 1683, and the first Amish arrived several decades later. A passenger list for the *Adventure,* arriving in Philadelphia on 2 October 1727, contains several Amish names, although their identity remains uncertain. The first documented Amish immigrants arrived on 8 October 1737 on the ship *Charming Nancy,* with twenty-one Amish families.[41] The first Amish migrants to Pennsylvania created the Northkill Settlement in north-central Berks County. Amish families soon reached Lancaster and Somerset counties farther west and Mifflin County in 1791. Before 1800, the principal concentrations of Amish population were in Berks and Chester counties and the eastern parts of Lancaster and Lebanon counties. Migration from Europe occurred in two waves, the first lasting until about 1770—interrupted by the American and French revolutions—and the second from 1815 to 1860. Perhaps one hundred families, about five hundred people, moved to North America before 1800, producing an Amish population in colonial America of under a thousand persons.[42]

After the American Revolution and the opening of the trans-Appalachian frontier to white settlement, Amish pioneers followed the westward push of American civilization. The colonial Amish settlements, especially those in central and western Pennsylvania, often served as bases for further migration to the West. Families from Somerset County, Pennsylvania, founded Amish communities in Tuscarawas and Holmes counties in Ohio; emigrants from Mifflin County moved to Logan, Champaign, and Stark counties in Ohio; these settlements, in their turn, produced further migrations to Indiana, Illinois, and Iowa.[43]

The second wave of European Amish migration to North America, 1816 to

1860, numbered about three thousand persons.[44] The later Amish immigrants typically formed new communities, although sometimes they settled in established Amish locations. Immigrants of the second wave formed settlements in Butler, Stark, and Fulton counties in Ohio; Adams, Allen, and Daviess counties in Indiana; several counties in central Illinois; Lewis County, New York; and Waterloo County, Ontario. Generally, second-wave and first-wave communities maintained fellowship with one another, although a Hessian Amish settlement in Butler County, Ohio, was viewed with suspicion because members used buttons on clothing and played musical instruments.

Jacob and Barbara Swartzendruber with their children settled first in Somerset County, Pennsylvania, where he served as minister in the Glades Amish congregation until 1840. He represented the Glades congregation at the 1837 regional ministers meeting and signed the discipline produced there. Then the family moved to New Germany, near Grantsville, Maryland, and Swartzendruber built a sawmill and grist mill.[45] But soon the Swartzendruber family contracted the strange malady known as "western fever."

Movable to Iowa

Relative freedom of movement and the chance to create communities without fear of persecution or limitations on their economic activity encouraged extensive migration by Amish and Mennonites in North America. Amish and Mennonite families sometimes settled close to each other, seeking the same kind of land and following German migration streams. Members of both groups seemed to think of themselves as interchangeable parts in the task of creating rural communities. Amish families, for example, expected to gather from disparate locations and distinctive experiences and develop workable congregations wherever they lived. Nothing demonstrates more powerfully the internal Amish map of portable community than their willingness to move about and mingle with other Amish families at the drop of the proverbial hat.

By 1840 the westward Amish and Mennonite migration in North America had reached Iowa. Mennonite John Carl Krehbiel arrived in Lee County on 1 November 1839; Amish settlers followed shortly thereafter. In 1846, after his first wife died in 1840, Krehbiel married Catharine Raber, daughter of Amish preacher Christian Raber.[46] A second Amish community developed in Jefferson, Henry, and Washington counties after 1841. Eventually, the settlement centered on the town of Wayland in northern Henry and southern Washington counties. Several Amish families left Lee County and settled in Davis County in 1854, seeking inexpensive government land.[47] However, the largest Amish settlement in Iowa began in 1846, in Johnson County and in neighboring Washington and Iowa counties.[48]

Already in 1840, four Amish "land scouts" had set out from Somerset County, Pennsylvania, to investigate western land. They skipped Ohio, where several younger settlements were underway, and instead traveled by riverboat down the Ohio River, then up the Mississippi to Burlington, Iowa, in Des Moines County, which was the territorial capital of Iowa.[49] From Burlington, the party walked to Iowa City, through Des Moines, Henry, Washington, and Johnson counties. They liked this country "quite well," especially a hickory tree grove along Deer Creek in southwestern Johnson County. However, reports of ague discouraged the scouts, and they resolved to see Indiana before deciding. They returned East via Chicago, crossed Lake Michigan, and went up the St. Joseph River. The prairie land in Elkhart County suited them "very well," and the first Amish families removed to Indiana the following spring. The first Amish settlement in Indiana, begun in 1841, is now the third largest, following Holmes County, Ohio, and Lancaster County, Pennsylvania. Echoing S. D. Guengerich's observation about the first Amish migrants to Iowa, Hansi Bontrager, age 4 in 1841 when his parents moved to Indiana, wrote in 1907 that his parents did not merely decide to settle in Indiana because of land, but "to make this the future home for their congregation."[50]

During the summer of 1845, Daniel P. Guengerich of Fairfield County, Ohio, and his half-brother, Joseph J. Swartzendruber of Allegheny (now Garrett) County, Maryland, investigated Iowa Territory. Swartzendruber, nicknamed "Hickory Joe," was the eldest son of Jacob Swartzendruber; Guengerich was his stepson. They traveled by water to Keokuk and visited the Lee County Amish settlement. Because the land titles were in question, they traveled on to Henry, Washington, and Johnson counties and selected claims along Deer Creek in what became Washington Township, Johnson County. Swartzendruber selected the same hickory grove that had appealed to his Pennsylvania coreligionists in 1840.

This land attracted the Amish land scouts because of its potential for diverse agriculture: fertile soil, rich timber, and running water. But they also sought commercial potential. Southwestern Johnson County was close to Iowa City, then the capital of Iowa Territory. Steamboats had been coming to Iowa City since 1841, when the territorial capital moved from Burlington, and they believed it offered exceptional opportunities for selling agricultural products.[51] The characteristic combination of Amish migration reappears in these travelers to Johnson County: protecting Amish ties, maintaining an intertwined kinship network, finding suitable land for diverse agriculture, meeting pioneer needs for wood and running water, avoiding flat undrained land, and developing commercial potential.

In April of 1846, Daniel P. Guengerich and family, William Wertz and family, and Joseph J. Swartzendruber came to Bloomington (Muscatine) by river transportation. Their household goods went by wagon to Iowa City, and they rented a small house for a week while the men hunted a place to plant a few acres of potatoes and corn. Guengerich found a small cabin near the present village of Joetown, and William Wertz moved in with John Lammert. Wertz and Swartzendruber walked to Dubuque to enter their claims along Deer Creek, and Guengerich also entered a claim, as did Lammert. Guengerich bought 120 acres of government land along the creek at $1.25 per acre. Local resident Daniel K. Shaver related a story at the dedication of Lower Deer Creek Church in 1890, claiming credit as the Moses who led the Amish to their promised land since he helped settle these first migrants to Johnson County.

In 1846, Jacob Swartzendruber visited his son and stepson in Iowa. Impressed by the rich farm land, he wrote in his notebook:

> If I mistake not that country has a great future in store. The soil is very rich black loam, and has no stones or gravel on the fields. The land is timbered and prairie land mixed. The timber and brush lands seem to be the richest. It is cleared off and plowed with a very sharp steel plow, which cuts the roots as it strikes them. The land raises enormous crops of wheat and corn the first year, without any fertilizers. The wild Grasses on the Prairies and the sloughs make good hay for the stock, but cattle feed on the prairies all winter unless there is too much snow on the ground.[52]

Swartzendruber was considered a truthful man, but his neighbors in Maryland would hardly believe the story of fields so free from stones that farmers could use steel plows. Swartzendruber also saw disadvantages: the Indians were possibly dangerous, there were few opportunities for cash income, and there was illness.

While Swartzendruber was visiting, Christina Guengerich, daughter of Daniel and Susanna Miller Guengerich, died two weeks shy of her first birthday. As the only Amish minister available, Swartzendruber preached the funeral sermon. Then the entire Guengerich family became ill with fevers, which lasted until late in the fall. Joseph J. Swartzendruber, also ill with the ague, became discouraged and started back for Maryland. He stopped awhile in Lee County and worked as his health permitted. He married Barbara Brenneman in Maryland and did not return to Iowa until 1856. Joseph was ordained as a preacher in Iowa in 1860, having been ordained as a deacon in Maryland in 1853; he was later ordained bishop of Deer Creek district in 1869, a year after his father died.

Reports of ague slowed migration to Johnson County between 1846 and 1849. Only two Amish families remained, facing illness and poverty. Daniel P. Guengerich built a log cabin north of Kalona in Washington County in 1847. To his 4-year-old son, it looked like a stable, and the building did not have a single iron nail.[53] The families would have left had they had the means to do so. Their team of horses died, and Guengerich traded his pocket knife to have a patch of corn plowed.[54]

Settlement of German immigrants with reputations as aggressive farmers did not occur entirely without opposition. False reports circulated in rural Johnson County that one hundred Dutch families were coming with plenty of money to claim jump the squatter lands. One rumor connected the Amish with the Mormon movement, understandable since the Mormon Trek had left Iowa City only a few years earlier. A local vigilante committee raised an armed mob, surrounded both Amish log cabins, and sent their spokesman to the door with the message, "If you do not have peace with God, better make peace." The newcomers hastily explained that they had settled in good faith and had no intention of claiming the land the squatters had improved, and the vigilantes rode away without further incident. The spokesman later became one of the staunchest supporters of the "hook and eye Dutch," and considered them a guarantee for honesty.[55]

William Wertz was a blacksmith, a desirable trade on the frontier. Locals tried to convince him to settle in West Liberty, Iowa, on his way to his claim in Johnson County. But he had promised his bishop, David Zook of Fairfield County, Ohio, that he and Guengerich would settle in the same neighborhood and attempt to build a church. He was also offered a blacksmith job in Iowa City, but he decided to stay in the country. The Peter B. Miller family joined the colony in 1846; Miller was a brother of Susanna Miller Guengerich, Daniel's wife. They moved to Iowa from Knox County, Ohio.

In the fall of 1849, two Amish bishops from Lee County, Joseph Goldsmith

Table 1.1. New Amish Households in Johnson, Washington, and Iowa Counties in the State of Iowa, 1846–1869

Year	*New Households*	*Year*	*New Households*	*Year*	*New Households*
1846	3	1856	6	1863	7
1850	5	1857	6	1864	12
1851	12	1858	5	1865	5
1852	3	1859	5	1866	4
1853	3	1860	2	1867	2
1854	2	1861	5	1868	8
1855	7	1862	6	1869	9

Source: Katie Yoder Lind, *From Hazelbrush to Cornfields: The First One Hundred Years of the Amish-Memmonites in Johnson, Washington and Iowa Counties* (Kalona: Mennonite Historical Society of Iowa, 1994).

and Christian Swartzendruber, visited the small group in Johnson County. The two families and visiting ministers assembled in the Guengerich home, a 14 by 16 foot log cabin, and held the first religious service with six adult participants.[56] No more Amish migrants moved to Johnson County until 1850, when five families arrived from Indiana and Ohio. Twelve more moved to the community in 1851, and thereafter a steady stream of immigrants joined the group, forming at least two new households per year over the next twenty years. Table 1.1 depicts the consistent flow of in-migration, with another surge toward the end of the American Civil War. One of the families moving to Iowa in 1851 was that of Jacob Swartzendruber, who wanted to join his stepson on the frontier.

Despite his wife's opposition, Jacob Swartzendruber decided to move west in 1851 and "grow up with the country," and Barbara "finally yielded."[57] Counting the ocean crossing in 1833 and the move from Pennsylvania to Maryland in 1840, this would be their third and final migration. They converted their possessions to money, Barbara received her patrimonial inheritance of several hundred dollars in twenty-dollar gold pieces, and they left Maryland on 14 April 1851. The company numbered six: Jacob and Barbara; their youngest son, George, age 20; another son and daughter-in-law, Frederick and Sarah Yoder Swartzendruber, with their 15-month-old daughter Barbara. Sarah was pregnant during the journey with Jacob Frederick, born in October. After another emotional farewell to their friends at Grantsville, Maryland, they traveled by land on the National Turnpike to Brownsville, Pennsylvania, where they boarded a steamboat to Pittsburgh, then went down the Ohio to St. Louis, up the Mississippi to Muscatine, and overland with two hired teamsters to Iowa City and rural Johnson County. Barbara Swartzendruber found it appalling to take leave again from friends and relatives, and she felt they were going to a dreary land of poverty "where they were likely to be massacred by the Indians."[58] The party arrived in Johnson County on 4 May 1851.

The Peter B. Miller farm in Washington Township was the first reached by the Jacob and Barbara Swartzendruber family during their trek from Maryland to Iowa. Jacob Frederick Swartzendruber, Jacob's grandson, wrote of the Miller family:

> This family consisted of father and mother, two girls in their teens, and seven boys. Several of the older children were of age, yet they were contented in the paternal home. The youngest was five years old. They were a jolly set of boys, always in good humor. There was apparently no end of vocal music and whistling. Their needs were but few and easily supplied, and I dare say, as I have known them since, they lived more contented than the ordinary person does to-day with all the improvements and modern conveniences.

The morning after Jacob's arrival, while making breakfast, Catherine Miller found Peter's lost hat in her wheat flour barrel: "The hat was removed rather on the sly and taken out and given a hasty dusting."[59] Swartzendruber described a two-story house with two rooms on the first floor, a kitchen, and an all-purpose living and dining room. A ladder served as stairway to the second floor. The girls slept in a lean-to on one of the long sides, a sod addition with dirt floor. After cleaning up the next day, Sunday morning, Jacob and Barbara continued their journey to the farmstead of Daniel P. Guengerich.

The early settlers soon saw their dream of an Amish church come to fruition. Joseph Goldsmith returned in 1851 and organized the first Amish congregation in Johnson County, a dozen families and twenty-seven members, with Jacob Swartzendruber and John P. Gingerich as resident ministers. The first communion took place during the spring of 1852 at the home of Daniel J. Gingerich, with Joseph Goldsmith in charge. Frederick Swartzendruber, son of Jacob and brother of Joseph J., was ordained deacon. The ministers held church services every three weeks the first year and every two weeks thereafter. Jacob Swartzendruber was ordained elder, or bishop, in 1852. In 1855 Joseph Keim was ordained preacher, and bishop in 1858, to assist Jacob Swartzendruber.

1.2. The Shetler Cemetery, first burial in 1863, overlooking Deer Creek Valley near the site of the first Amish farmsteads in Johnson County.

Joseph J. Swartzendruber, who had been ordained a deacon in Maryland and a minister in 1860 in Iowa, was ordained as bishop in 1869.

There were four categories of ordained men in the Amish church, all based on the fundamental term, *Diener* (Servant); *voelliger Diener* or *Aeltester* (full minister or elder); *Diener des Worts* or *Diener zum Buch* (servant of the word or book, or minister); *voelliger Armendiener* (full deacon); and *Armendiener* (minister to the poor, or deacon). All these offices were unpaid positions.[60] The "full deacon" office was later dropped because of controversies over duties.[61] Ordained men were expected to "keep house" by maintaining the discipline and purity of Amish congregations, and to "hold the line" in keeping the Amish separate from the world.[62]

By 1863 the settlement had divided into Deer Creek and Sharon districts, since the membership had grown too large to meet in one home (Figure 1.2). By 1877 both districts had divided further into Upper and Lower Deer Creek, and North and South Sharon districts. The Amish in Johnson County maintained close ties with other Amish communities. Individuals and families constantly joined the community and left the community as new migrants arrived from the East and others left to establish more settlements farther West.

Contacts with older and newer communities could be painful, however, as the Amish in North America experienced a protracted divisiveness during the second half of the nineteenth century. The slow wave of consensus breakdown washed over the Amish in northern Indiana as early as the 1850s, and over the Amish in Ontario and Iowa as late as the 1880s and 1890s.[63] It may be considered a phenomenon of "sorting out" between Amish leaders and members opposed to change and those more open to controlled change.[64] By the end of the nineteenth century, two larger denominations, the Old Order Amish and the Amish-Mennonites, and several smaller groups had resulted from the splintering of mid-century Amish communities.

The stresses and strains in the Johnson County, Iowa, Amish settlement did not reach the breaking point for several decades. The issues that caused trouble in other locales, such as mode of baptism, never appeared in Iowa. Nevertheless, in the chapters that follow issues such as household authority, relationship to the American government, and private property illuminate one part of this "sorting out" process in the wider Amish world as the Amish in Iowa attempted to adjust and recreate their repertoire of community on the Iowa prairie.

The most deeply rooted component of the Amish configuration of community was their agricultural system. Amish settlers in Iowa constructed a successful ethnic agricultural community on the foundation of their considerable farming skills.

> [Mennonites] introduced the Palatines to clover culture, were considered the most skillful farmers, raised the most livestock, and distinguished themselves in all branches of agriculture.
>
> —Werner Weidmann, 1968

> Where the plow goes through golden meadows, there the Mennonite raises also his house of prayer.
>
> —Wilhelm Riehl, 1857

Chapter 2

The Amish Agricultural System

Anabaptist farmers and their Amish and Mennonite descendants acquired effective methods of agriculture in the midst of their persecution and marginality in early modern Europe. The Amish who settled in Iowa brought with them a coherent system of agriculture and transplanted it to North American farms in Pennsylvania, Ohio, Maryland, Ontario, and other eastern locations. This system, often identified as "Pennsylvania Dutch," emphasized self-sufficient subsistence balanced with commodity market participation, maintenance of soil fertility through use of manure and natural fertilizers, cultivation of clover meadows and forage products, diversity and rotation of crops, and large herds of livestock. These agricultural methods were deeply ingrained in Amish consciousness and became part of Amish commonsense understandings of how the world should work. Their farming habits became the most programmed corner of the Amish repertoire of community, so entrenched that Jacob Swartzendruber once dreamed of hauling manure to his fields as he reflected on incidents of communal disharmony.

On 21 January 1860, Amish Bishop Jacob Swartzendruber and Assistant Bishop Joseph Keim met together at the elder Conrad's house to help arbitrate a conflict. Later that night, Swartzendruber dreamed he was driving a load of manure with four horses, steering without trouble on a rather good road but concentrating intensely. The road became more and more slanted until finally it became so tilted that the wagon started to turn over, since the lower wheels cut in too deeply. He held on while the horses pulled hard, but the wagon would not budge. Upon careful reflection he saw it was hopeless, and he hurriedly turned and tried to make two loads from the one. Then the team could go forward, and the way would become smooth. The wagon fell over, but no harm was done. Then Swartzendruber awoke, perhaps about four o'clock, and could sleep no more.[1]

In his dream, Jacob Swartzendruber associated communal conflict with one of the most fundamental Amish farm activities: hauling manure to the fields. The dream road may have been twisted and the wagon unstable, and the offal of religious conflict may have seemed similar to livestock waste at times, but the Amish bishop still wanted to help his congregation grow. Sometimes it takes manure to fertilize a field or a fight. Swartzendruber wished for the golden qualities of manure—restoration, fecundity, and even the intimacy of working with living, breathing beings—for his religious field as well as for his farm. The powerful dream illustrates concern for maintaining and enhancing soil fertility, the most characteristic aspect of the agricultural system Amish pioneers dreamed of reproducing in Iowa. This component of the Amish repertoire of community transferred virtually unchanged to North America and served as a powerful economic base for Amish ethnoreligious identity.

Amish and Mennonite Agriculture in Europe

Jacob Swartzendruber learned Amish farming methods as a farmer and miller in the German principality of Waldeck, where the Swartzendrubers and other Amish families had migrated to escape religious persecution. The Swiss Confederation had suppressed and expelled Anabaptists during the seventeenth and eighteenth centuries, and many moved to Alsace and Lorraine, to the

Palatinate region, and to many other principalities of central Europe. After the Treaty of Westphalia gave Alsace to France in 1648, Swiss Bernese Anabaptists, fleeing an expulsion order in 1670 to 1671, moved into Alsace in "something resembling a small-scale organized migration." They were welcomed by a few individual families who earlier had moved from Switzerland to Alsace, and a trickle of migration has continued almost to the present. By 1780 there were about fifteen hundred Mennonites living in France; the number peaked at more than five thousand in 1850.[2]

The first Alsatian refuge for Swiss Anabaptists was in the Rhine plain, near Heidolsheim. When their presence became uncomfortable there, they moved into the Vosges mountains, especially the valley above Sainte-Marie-aux-Mines (Markirch). The lords of Sainte-Marie-aux-Mines acknowledged the French throne after the 1648 annexation of Alsace by the French crown. Much of the Rhine Valley had been devastated and depopulated by the Thirty Years' War, so rulers tolerated the presence of Bernese Anabaptists because of their farming prowess.[3]

In order to farm at all, Anabaptists and their descendants had to rent land from large landowners since, as religious dissidents, they were usually prohibited from owning land. Their agricultural success soon made them desirable tenants. Ironically, their position outside the established social and religious order enabled Anabaptist farmers to innovate and position themselves in the forefront of the eighteenth-century agricultural revolution. As historian Georg Schmidt observed in 1932, "In the same way that they cut themselves off from political association, from both the authority of the State and the community, so also they went their own way economically."[4] Schmidt credited Anabaptists with freeing Swiss peasants from tradition and helping them acquire a willingness to try new agricultural methods. The Anabaptists and their Amish and Mennonite descendants practiced agricultural innovation in the interstices between state and church authority, whether by retiring to the Jura highlands within Switzerland or by migrating to more tolerant regions of Europe.

Perhaps as a result of coerced migration, the Swiss Brethren division of 1693 separated the Swiss Anabaptists into Amish and Mennonite groupings. Most members in Alsace followed the teachings of Jakob Ammann, while those in South Germany and Switzerland, led by Swiss elder Hans Reist, opposed Ammann. Despite religious differences, most Amish and Mennonites continued to farm, and few socioeconomic distinctions can be made between the two groups in Europe. In 1712 Louis XIV ordered the immediate expulsion of all Anabaptists from his realm. The Brethren moved to tiny independent principalities such as Salm and Montbéliard; some moved on to Lorraine. They had worked exclusively on the domains of local nobility before 1712, but their uncertain legal status after 1712 limited their economic and social activities; "implicitly they were supposed to remain farmers or practice rural activities connected with farming," such as milling or weaving.[5] Anabaptists living in Alsace faced additional expulsion orders in 1744, 1766, and 1780. Most stayed and continued to farm despite restrictions on owning land and limitations on other political and civil rights.

In Alsace, Amish and Mennonite farmers garnered a reputation for expert farming. From about 1700 to about 1850, French authorities considered them models of efficient agriculture. Landowners sought them because of their innovative methods and reliable payment of taxes and rents. Toward the end of the *ancien régime,* the Marquis Masson de Pezay praised Mennonite agriculture in these words: "It was by their more careful and better understood cultivation that I could distinguish the valleys inhabited by Anabaptists in Alsace. I would look at the hills before entering the cottages; and when the hills were better cultivated, even before seeing the shoes without buckles and the clothes without buttons, I said to myself: there are Anabaptists here."[6] He specifically discussed one Anabaptist farm in Waldeck, where Jacob Swartzendruber's Gallows Mill was located, and recommended that the entire realm adopt Amish and Mennonite levée and irrigation systems.[7]

Angelus, a traveler who described the newly German province of Lorraine in 1880, noted the Amish and Mennonite reputation for livestock and meadow farming on isolated farms, as well as their work in mills. He reported that "their diligence, their honesty and sobriety gain them the respect of all."[8] Contemporary observers often credited them with spreading the "new agriculture" in the eighteenth century, whose features were rationalization of method, insistence upon animal husbandry, use of natural fertilizer, and artificial pastures.[9]

The Dutch economic historian, B. H. Slicher van Bath, described the development of the "new husbandry" in early modern Europe. He identified several different systems in the varied regions of northwestern Europe, characterized by intensive tillage, disappearance of the fallow, use of manure, reliance on fodder crops for soil fertility, and livestock. Among the regions with highly developed agriculture in the eighteenth century were the Palatinate, Rhineland, Baden, and Alsace.[10] Within this general system of livestock and fodder agriculture, an identifiable Amish and Mennonite style can be distinguished, composed of seven elements:[11]

1. Tenant farming (*fermage*). Since they were only allowed to own land after the French Revolution, Amish and Mennonite farmers learned to combine animal husbandry with intensive cultivation of large tracts of land. Of necessity, they invested in animals rather than land. Tenancy and long-term leases allowed Anabaptists to treat farming as a way of life, focused on family labor, relative isolation, and separation from the larger culture.
2. Family labor. Mennonites tended to marry young, and the parents "divided up their savings early in life." Hired labor was usually supposed to be Mennonite as well. They emphasized self-sufficiency in both labor and subsistence, allowing greater control over socialization of their children.
3. Innovation. Mennonite farmers developed methodical, intensive, and varied techniques of cultivation. Particular skills associated with the Mennonites were improved methods of clearing land, using natural fertilizer and manure, breeding cattle, rotating crops instead of allowing land to lie fallow, improving tools, and cultivating artificial meadows. A legend that they introduced the potato to eastern France enhances their reputation as expert farmers.
4. Livestock and dairy farming, including hogs and sheep. Mennonites and Amish imported Swiss cattle and worked at breeding better varieties. They reinvested profits in livestock, not land.
5. Agricultural leadership. Jacques Klopfenstein (1763–1841), an expert Mennonite farmer living near Belfort, started publishing a rural almanac in 1812, one of several successful agricultural journals associated with the Anabaptists.[12] One historian stated that the collection of Anabaptist agricultural almanacs at the University of Strasbourg "constitutes a small encyclopedia of popular agronomy."[13]
6. Some diversification of vocation. After 1712, Anabaptists often worked as millers in rented mills, as weavers, and in various commercial trades.
7. Veterinary medicine. The healing arts were an Anabaptist specialty, and they even developed a reputation as counter-sorcerers.

This coherent agricultural system—a communal economic system—allowed the "Anabaptist nation" in eastern France to function as a subsociety within the larger culture. Many scholars have noted the isolation of Amish and Mennonite families on estates of large landowners who preferred Anabaptist farmers.[14]

The French Revolution broke up the large estates and otherwise changed the social and economic conditions within which the Amish and Mennonites had found a niche. Leaders of the Revolution removed civil restrictions and ended active persecution, using the legal status of Jews as an analogy.[15] However, the Revolution also served as the occasion for dividing large landholdings, and due to their history of successfully farming large estates, the Anabaptists found themselves caught between peasants and landholders. They were also foreign farmers to whom the landowners had entrusted their estates, and conflicts of tenure led some local leaders to pursue a "struggle against Anabaptism" in the revolutionary atmosphere.[16]

In 1793 the French Revolutionary government annexed the formerly independent principalities where the Anabaptists had found refuge. French historian Jean Séguy noted the mixed results: "The principle of equality that inspired the new republican legislation entailed, in its everyday application, that the Anabaptists should behave like other French citizens"—they were granted freedom of conscience, but they were also expected to take oaths and bear arms. Many did serve in the Napoleonic wars, although they were granted the right to make a solemn pledge rather than take an oath.[17] Leaders of the other democratic revolutions during the same era also struggled with the meaning of citizenship for pacifist religious groups.[18] Many Amish families migrated from France after the Napoleonic era, driven partly by a demographic boom from 1789 to 1852 and an increase in small estates.

In nineteenth century France, Amish and Mennonite farmers faced the possibility of land ownership for the first time. The Revolutionary government nationalized the properties of those bourgeois or noble families who had emigrated and created from these estates tracts of land that were known as the *Biens Nationaux*. Despite their new access to land ownership, most Amish and Mennonite farm families kept to tenant farming instead of rushing to buy farms, probably because of their uncertain legal status. In addition, there were economic advantages to renting rather than tying up capital in land. Tenancy based on long-term leases allowed continued agricultural experimentation and innovation, combining intensive with extensive farming. They tended natural meadows, supplemented field agriculture with cattle breeding and dairy farming, and produced and marketed cheese. Quite a number of Mennonite and Amish farmers lived in "privileged economic circumstances" as relatively well-to-do small-scale agricultural entrepreneurs, according to Jean Séguy. "That this resulted partly, indirectly, and most unexpectedly from the legal incapacity of purchasing land suffered by the Brethren, has to be counted one of the ironies of their history."[19] However, with the onset of universal military conscription in the Napoleonic era, many Amish and Mennonites emigrated to protect pacifist principles. There were difficult linguistic changes as Alsace bounced between German and French ownership, making stability almost impossible to achieve. By the late twentieth century, there were no more Amish in Alsace, but Mennonite farmers continued to own and farm fairly large tracts of land.

The story in the Palatinate is similar and is important for Amish and Mennonite communities in North America because the Palatinate region was the source of much of the Pennsylvania Dutch culture. The local nobility invited Anabaptist agriculturists to help rebuild their region after the devastation wrought by the Thirty Years' War (1618–48) and the War of the Palatinate (1688–97). During the latter conflict, Louis XIV of France ordered his generals to devastate the area as part of his military strategy. Many Palatinate Germans emigrated to North America during the first decades of the eighteenth century to escape the ravaged region. Mennonites and Amish had responded to a proclamation by the elector, Karl Ludwig (1648–80), issued on 4 August 1664, granting a general concession for the Mennonites of the Palatinate: "We have urgent need of subjects who will restore the ruined land"; therefore, the Mennonites could stay by paying extra taxes.[20]

During the eighteenth century, especially in the decades after 1760, members of the Palatinate nobility founded a number of new estates (*Höfe,* singular *Hof*) to promote the desired recovery of agriculture. Villagers continued to practice traditional *Dreifelderwirtschaft* (three-field agriculture, in which one field always lies fallow); the first residents of the new *Höfe* were too poor to construct buildings or invest in livestock. Mennonites tended to take over leases since they possessed capital for investment in agricultural innovation on the isolated tracts of land, and the petty nobles preferred their agricultural expertise and secure rent payments. By 1780 Mennonite *Höfe* already stood as "islands of 'modern' agriculture," surrounded by the "old routine" village three-field agriculture. As in Alsace and Lorraine, Mennonite and Amish farmers functioned as isolated individualists economically, in powerful alliance with capitalist landowners, although they were also members of a coherent and disciplined religious faith. Their outsider status vis-à-vis local society allowed the combination of separate ethnoreligious identity with mainstream economic revolution.[21]

Gerhard Hard listed several characteristics of Mennonite agriculture in the Palatinate, compared with village *Dreifelderwirtschaft* with its one-fourth to one-third fallow land: intensive wheat cultivation, stall-feeding of livestock, artificial clover meadows supported by lime fertilizer, field irrigation, liquid manure, reforestation of marginal land or transforming poor land to permanent meadow, distilling alcohol from potato crops, intensive crop rotation with manure fertilizer, and plowing immediately after a grain rotation. To an objection from poor renters that clover agriculture robbed them of bread, a noble replied in 1774 with the cycle introduced by Mennonite farmers: first clover, then forage, livestock, manure for fertilizer, and finally more grain for all.[22] Leaders of the late twentieth-century sustainable agriculture movement show interest in reviving this same agricultural chain as a foundation for social stability and rural development. Several scholars are paying new attention to the Amish experience of cultural persistence supported by clover and livestock agriculture.[23]

Although the *Knöpfler* (Buttoners, or Mennonites) and *Häftler* (Hook-users, or Amish) wanted nothing to do with each other after their bitter division in the 1690s in Alsace and Switzerland—they lived on separate *Höfe* in the Palatinate—both groups enjoyed spectacular reputations for agricultural prowess.[24] Mennonite David Möllinger (1709–87) is often named the "father of Palatinate agriculture" due to his agricultural innovations, imitated by other farmers in the region. Möllinger and fellow Mennonite Johann Dettweiler (b. 1739) played important roles in the transition from feudal *Dreifelderwirtschaft* to an agricultural system oriented to market production and replenishing soil fertility. Dettweiler, in fact, built the first Palatinate potato distillery in 1770 at the Hornbacher Unterhof. In addition to increasing the market value of potatoes by turning them into alcohol, the byproducts served as especially good animal feed, producing even more field fertilizer.[25]

Mennonites and Amish stood at the forefront of innovation and developed the same reputation as expert farmers and desirable tenants as they had in Alsace and Lorraine. F. C. Medicus emphasized their manure usage in 1771:

> The anabaptists practiced until now copious fertilizing and for that reason people declare them to be masters in farming but without determining the reason of their greater success. Fertilizer was the main-spring of the zeal with which they raised cattle, which created for them abundant manure. With the manure they constantly maintained their fields, but our usual farming only robbed the soil.

State economist Christian W. Dohn wrote in 1778, "Germany's most accomplished farmers are the palatine Mennonites."[26]

By the nineteenth century, Mennonite farmers became an artistic symbol of the idyllic peasant, "almost more than Jacobins of the agricultural revolution, almost more than saints of the new agriculture, a rural reincarnation of the primitive Christian lifestyle, and a living genre stereotype of archaic charm," wrote Gerhard Hard.[27] And Wilhelm Riehl wrote this lapidary observation in 1857: "Where the plow goes through golden meadows, there the Mennonite raises also his house of prayer."[28] The excesses of Romanticism apparently extended to plowshares.

Elsewhere in central Europe, Amish migrations led to small settlements in Hesse, Bavaria, Saarland, and other small principalities. The Amish usually did not own land but rented it from the estates of the nobility.[29] Absolute rulers such as the eighteenth-century Prussian king, Frederick the Great (1712–86), and Tsar Catharine the Great (1729–96) of Russia granted exemptions from military service to Amish and Mennonites in return for their agricultural skills.[30] After the French Revolution, liberal governments under constitutional monarchs instituted universal military training to defend revolutionary achievements, and nonresistant Amish and Mennonite groups found less space for their minority views. They often tried to retain French citizenship in German territories and thus take their military exemptions along as baggage, but they had limited success.[31] Migration became a consistent pattern in the quest for religious toleration, exemption from military service, and economic opportunity.

At the beginning of the eighteenth century, there were thirteen Amish congregations in Europe: eight in Alsace, three in Bern, one in the Palatinate, and one in Lorraine.[32] The small Amish community in Waldeck in central Germany, now part of Hesse, accommodated many of the families who later found their way to Iowa. Jacob Swartzendruber worked as a miller in the village of Mengeringhausen; and Gingerich, Bender, Shetler, and Brenneman family members migrated to Pennsylvania and Ohio and some on to Iowa.

Amish and Mennonite farmers may have been in the vanguard of agricultural change, but all large farmers sought to practice the new agriculture. There was an element of popular culture in the agricultural revolution, as individual peasants developed new methods and taught them to others. Amish and Mennonites in particular found themselves free to experiment in social isolation from village agriculture. But the new agriculture was also an aspect of early modern state building, and a stable food supply was associated with centralizing and consolidating political power. State officials and agrarian reformers encouraged the intensification and expansion of agriculture, and they found Amish and Mennonite farmers to be willing participants and effective models.[33] Eventually, all Palatinate farmers used artificial meadows, crop rotation, livestock, and manure in combination; and the various German-speaking religious groups that settled in Pennsylvania during the seventeenth and eighteenth centuries brought the new agriculture with them. Amish and Mennonite farmers added their particular experiences of tenancy, innovation, and reliance on family labor in isolation from rural society.

Amish and Mennonite Agriculture in North America

Amish immigrants to North America found sustenance in the coherent system of agriculture developed in their various European homelands. Amish pioneers tended to select environments adaptable to their system rather than adapting their system to a strange environment or alien culture. Pennsylvania offered a combination of climate, soil, and tolerant political system where the Amish and Mennonites could own land and build contiguous settlements rather than living on rented isolated farms as in Europe. German immigrants soon found their way to the rich limestone soils of Lancaster County, and Amish and Mennonite farmers flourished in the congenial atmosphere of colonial Pennsylvania. The mutual support of German communities can be summarized with a Schwenkfelder leader's comment in a letter to friends in Europe in 1768: "We are all going to and fro like fish in water."[34]

Most important for this narrative, Pennsylvania Dutch agriculture inherited aspects of the early modern European agricultural revolution. Contemporary descriptions of colonial German agriculture sound nearly identical to accounts of Amish and Mennonite farming in central Europe. Dr. Benjamin Rush reported on German farmers of Pennsylvania in 1789, noting their good fences, extensive orchards, fertile soil, productive fields, and luxurious meadows. Rush gave special attention to their treatment of horses and cattle, commenting that German farmers feed horses and cows so well that horses could do twice the labor and cows yield twice the milk as ill-fed animals (Fig. 2.1). Others remarked on field irrigation, use of gypsum as fertilizer, family labor and the industriousness of German farm wives, diversity of crops, and, of course, the omnipresent attention to soil fertility with large quantities of manure.[35]

2.1. Amish farmers in Iowa with horse teams.

Observers have detected a distinctive German style of agriculture among the Pennsylvania Dutch from colonial times to the present.[36] Pennsylvania Dutch culture was shared by three general groups: "church people," members of established state churches such as Lutheran and Reformed; Moravians; and "plain people," so named because of their plainness in dress. The plain people included Mennonites, Amish, Dunkards (Church of the Brethren), Brethren in Christ, Schwenckfelders, and other sects. Perhaps only 10 to 15 percent of all Pennsylvania Dutch were members of the smaller groups. Pennsylvania Germans as a cultural group are credited with introducing the willow tree to North America, developing many varieties of fruit, rotating crops, building "bank" barns, inventing the Conestoga wagon, burning lime to support red clover, and many additional practices associated with advanced pre-twentieth-century agriculture.[37]

During the twentieth century, many Pennsylvania Dutch groups gradually assimilated to the dominant American culture. The pressure of two wars with Germany and the opportunities offered by urban America have made the larger Pennsylvania German culture much less visible.[38] Only Old Order Amish and Old Order Mennonite communities still retain the Pennsylvania Dutch language and now serve to represent all of Pennsylvania Dutch culture.[39]

The Amish who migrated from the Pennsylvania German cultural hearth during the eighteenth and nineteenth centuries attempted to reestablish the Pennsylvania Dutch system of agriculture wherever they settled. Sometimes it did not fit the environment, as on the Great Plains and much of the West, where Amish settlers experienced difficulty in adapting to dry land farming and new crops. Those who wished to remain Amish moved to other environments.[40] But Amish agriculture worked well in post-frontier Iowa.

Amish Agriculture in Iowa

White settlement of Iowa began in earnest after the Black Hawk War of 1832. The Winnebago, Sauk, and Fox agreed to vacate land just west of the Mississippi River in return for small amounts of cash and provisions. Some 10,531 white people lived in the area by 1836 as part of Michigan Territory (1833–36). What became Iowa was shifted to Wisconsin Territory in 1836, and a separate Iowa Territory was formed by Congress in 1838. Small family farmers, mainly from states between Pennsylvania and Illinois, settled rural Iowa with an eye toward subsistence and future market opportunities. Early farmers grew wheat for grain, and corn for cattle and hog feed.[41]

It is not without irony that Amish farmers participated in the same geopolitical process that had served them so well in Europe: securing conquered space to stabilize a growing nation-state and feeding industrializing cities through incorporating grassland regions into capitalist markets like the Chicago grain market in the 1850s.[42] However, even as most Midwestern farmers moved inexorably toward a corn-hogs agricultural system, Amish farmers retained an orientation to subsistence and diverse agriculture rather than exclusive reliance on cash crops and market livestock.[43] They practiced a safety-first style of farming, honed during centuries of insecurity in Europe.

The earliest Mennonite and Amish families in Iowa arrived in 1839 and settled in Lee County, part of the so-called Half-Breed Tract. The first Amish settlers in Johnson County arrived in the southwest corner of the county in 1846, relocating from Somerset County, Pennsylvania; Fairfield County, Ohio; and other eastern communities. In the 1850 federal population census, there were only three Amish households in Washington Township and none at all in Sharon; four more Amish families lived across the county line in Washington County.[44] As shown in Appendix Table 1, just about 3 percent of the 107 households in Washington and Sharon townships were Amish in 1850, all of these in Washington Township: William and Helen Wertz and their two children lived on 240 acres of land in section 20; Daniel and Laura Shetler with eight children and one boarder bought 160 acres later that year in Sections 29 and 30; and Peter and Catharine Miller with nine children owned 320 acres in section 32. By 1860 there were 40 Amish households, or 17 percent of the population in the two townships; in 1870, 85 households and 24.4 percent; and by 1880, 115 households and 30.3 percent.[45]

Appendix Tables 1 and 2 show the marked increase in the number of Amish households during the 1860s. The number of Amish households grew rapidly from 1850 to 1880, but the largest increase occurred between 1860 and 1870 and continued at nearly the same pace between 1870 and 1880. German households also increased in number between 1860 and 1870, due in part to an influx of German Lutherans into Sharon Township, but the growth stopped in 1870. Native-born households also increased in number between 1860 and 1870 but actually declined slightly during the following decade. Average age of household heads shows a steady increase as the frontier recedes, except Amish farm households during the 1860s. A large number of young Amish men, both new immigrants and local sons, established themselves in farming in Johnson County between 1860 and 1870.

These immigrants and new householders established an Amish system of agricultural production in southwestern Johnson County. The 1860s were a crucial decade in the process. The Amish were typical frontier farmers in the 1840s and 1850s, but they gradually shifted to an identifiable Pennsylvania German style of agriculture in the years following 1860. This distinction took place, of course, within the larger pattern of Midwestern corn belt creation during the late nineteenth century. The Amish became relatively distinct from their German, native-born American, Welsh, and Irish neighbors by pursuing their unique combination of livestock, meadows and hay harvesting, innovation with new technologies, efficient use of household labor resources, market participation balanced with an orientation to diverse crop production and subsistence, passing on farms to children, and shared communal responsibility in holding property and wealth.

First, Amish farmers were renowned in Europe and Pennsylvania for their innovative combining of field agriculture with livestock raising, and for their pioneering use of manure to restore soil fertility. Amish household heads listed higher than average values for livestock in Washington and Sharon townships for every census year between 1850 and 1880. In 1880, for example, Amish farmers reported an average of $1,096 in livestock, while the average farmer raised $962 worth of livestock. Animals are a distinguishing feature of Amish agriculture.

Second, Amish and Mennonite farmers were well known in Europe for innovations in meadow cultivation and hay. Amish farmers in Johnson county produced more than the average tons of hay grown by their neighbors in every agricultural census year. In 1880 the figures were 33.8 tons versus 29.7 tons of hay.

Third, innovation was a crucial part of the Amish farming system. Amish ownership of agricultural implements increased rapidly between 1860 and 1870, from an average of $87.60 per household in 1860 to $320 in 1870, larger than the average increase of $84.60 to $252.60. Until the advent of the tractor, Amish farmers positioned themselves at the cutting edge of innovation and adaptation of new agricultural technology. According to local lore, Jacob Swartzendruber's son Frederick, who also became a bishop in the Amish church (actually a full deacon, though he functioned as a bishop),[46] was especially eager to acquire new implements. Swartzendruber "owned the first McCormick reaper in the community. The same was true of the table rake, the Marsh Harvester, the self-binder, the hayrake, the corn planter, and the checkrow."[47] The image of an Amish farmer eagerly collecting all the latest agricultural implements contradicts most stereotypes of their twentieth-century backwardness and conservatism. Melvin Gingerich noted in 1939 that the Old Order Amish used the latest farm machinery even though they eschewed automobiles, musical instruments, telephones, electric lights, and furnaces (Figure 2.2.)[48]

Fourth, Amish farmers used all available household labor resources, something for which German farmers were also justly famous. Amish women churned more butter than township averages, indicating a strong value of mobilizing household labor resources on behalf of the agricultural enterprise. In 1880 the figures were 438 pounds versus 370, a statistically significant difference. Butter is often used as a proxy for female labor in nineteenth-century farming.[49] Amish farmers utilized their children as labor and paid few wages to hired hands.

Fifth, Amish farmers produced commodities for the market at normal rates for all farmers in Washington and Sharon townships. In producing corn, hogs, cattle, and wheat, the Amish were similar to their neighbors. There is no statistically significant difference in the value of market production among the several ethnic communities.[50] Amish farmers lagged behind in 1850 and 1860, but they ranked slightly ahead of their neighbors in 1870 and 1880. In any case,

2.2. Amish threshing crew. Until tractors and automobiles changed the scale of rural life, Amish farmers participated enthusiastically in the early mechanization of farming.

after a period characterized by frontier subsistence, all farmers in the townships experienced more opportunities to market their products by 1870.

Sixth, Amish farmers were committed to passing farms to their children. From 1860 to 1880, the household heads in all other ethnic groupings became older, while Amish farmers remained young in comparison. In 1870 Amish household heads averaged 40.5 years of age, while the mean for all farmers was 42.5. Amish farmers typically pass land on to the next generation at an early age to help their children establish economically viable households. The difference in age indicates a fundamental commitment to reproduce the Amish farming system and maintain a long-term community on the land. By 1880 Amish household heads were a full three years younger than the average of all farmers in Washington and Sharon townships.

Seventh, communal responsibility for property required keeping land inside the group. Acquiring land, making the commodity available to children, and thus founding a base for community are important values for Amish household heads. Amish farmers came to own the highest average number of acres by 1870. The difference in 1860 was only 172.9 acres for Amish farmers and 169.7 acres for all farmers. By 1870 the difference was much greater, 169 acres on average for Amish farmers and 149.4 acres for all farmers. Amish farmers were somewhat more able to maintain a stable farm size during the Civil War decade, and they continued to own the most acres in 1880.

The Amish farming system survived and thrived during the disruptions of the Civil War decade as the Amish began to differentiate from their neighbors and establish their particular balance of market-orientation and subsistence food production. This balance can be seen in representative Amish and non-Amish farmsteads in southwestern Johnson County.

Farms can be compared in three different ways: first, two farms of similar size (Samuel D. Guengerich and Lafayette DeFrance); second, two farms appearing in all four agricultural censuses, 1850 to 1880 (Peter B. Miller and Robert Roup); and third, farms from several ethnic groups in the two townships (Frederick Swartzendruber, Amish; David H. Jones, Welsh; Gottlieb F. Roessler, German; and Ellias B. Howell and Corbly Snyder, native-born American).

Two Farms of Similar Size

Amish farmer Samuel D. Guengerich and native-born American farmer Lafayette DeFrance both owned small farms in Washington Township. DeFrance (1825–1907) resided on Section 9 in Washington Township in 1869. He appears in the 1860 census with his wife, Martha Ellen (1835–1906); two children, William Allen, age 3, and Leonard, age 1; and a brother, Martin Van Buren DeFrance (1840–92). Lafayette and Martha Ellen are buried in the Frank Pierce (Frytown) Congregational Church cemetery, and Martin in the Pleasant Hill (town of Amish, now Joetown) Methodist cemetery. All three were born in Pennsylvania. Although the household is listed on the 1860 population census as owning $1,600 in real estate and $400 in personal wealth, DeFrance does not appear in the manuscript agricultural census. Plat maps, such as the details from Washington and Sharon townships in 1869 (Figures 2.3 and 2.4), locate the farms in relation to each other and thus provide a control for geographical difference.

In 1870 Lafayette DeFrance headed a household composed of his wife and two sons. He owned 136 acres, close to the average size of farms in Washing-

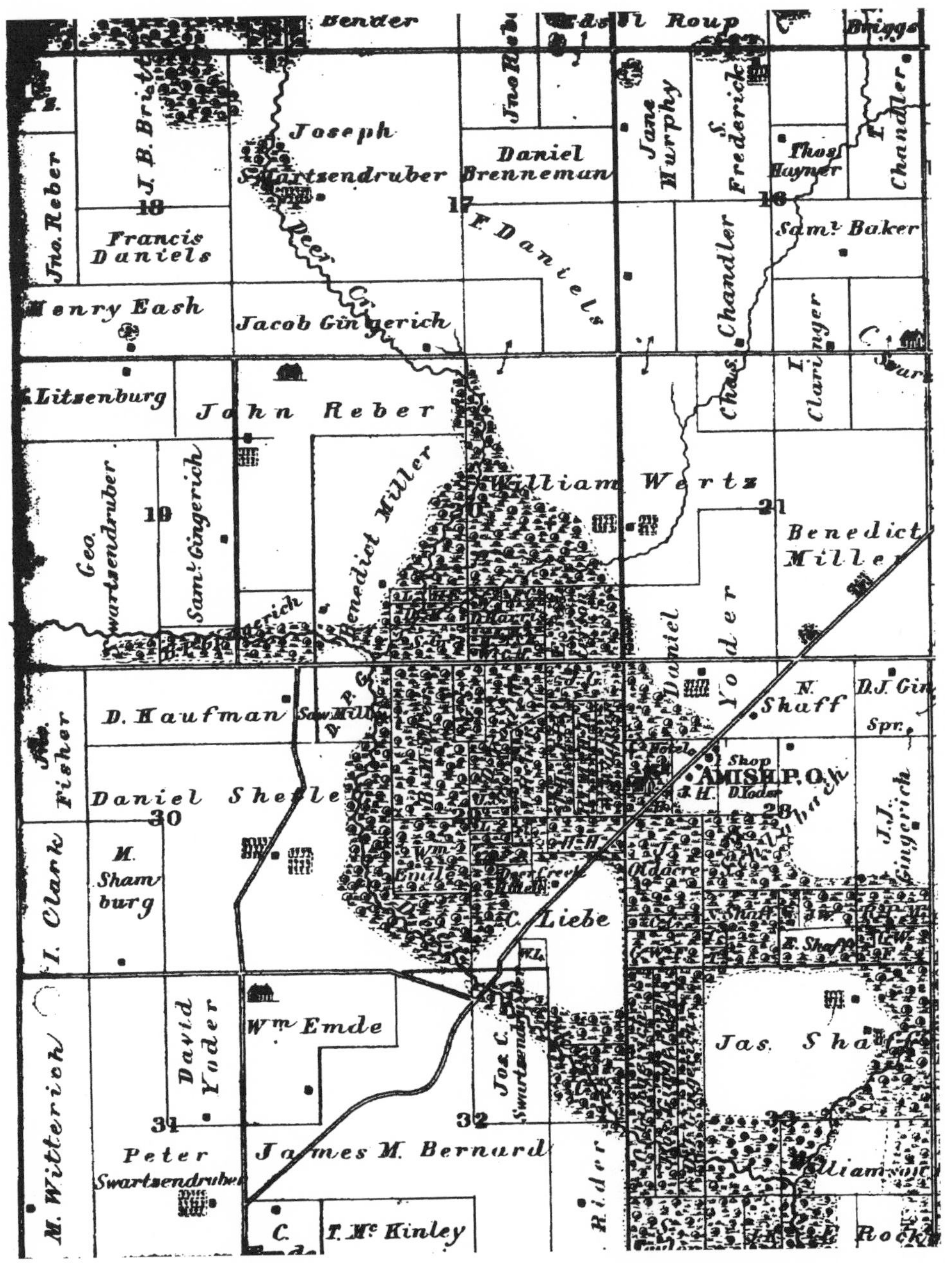

2.3. Plat map of Washington Township, Johnson County, Iowa, 1869.

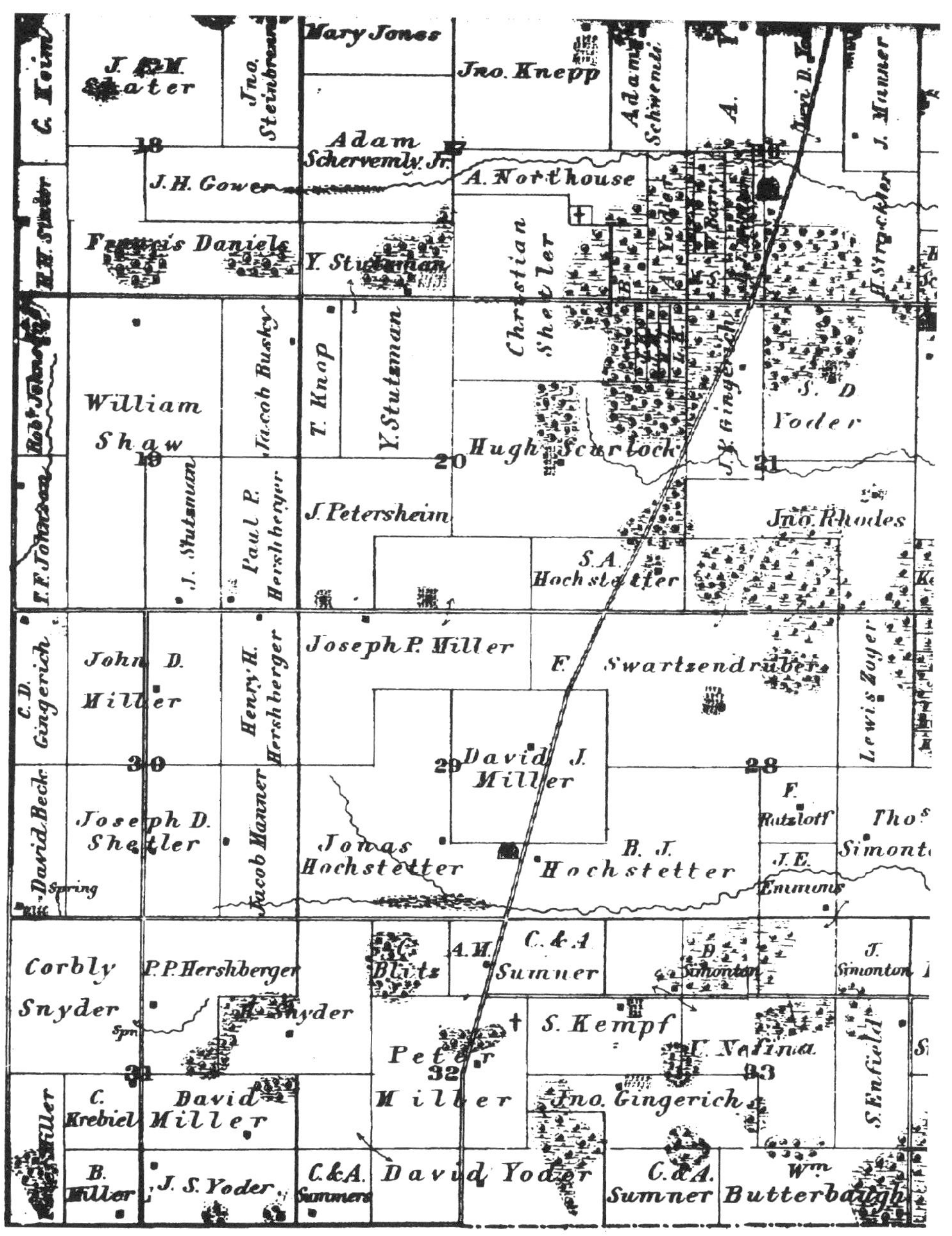

2.4. Plat map of Sharon Township, Johnson County, Iowa, 1869.

2.5A. Residence of Lafayette DeFrance.

ton and Sharon townships as well as to the average size of native-born acreages (150 and 151 respectively). He listed $800 worth of livestock, produced 20 tons of hay, and owned $400 in agricultural implements. Martha Ellen produced 400 pounds of butter. In his fields, DeFrance harvested 800 bushels of corn, 100 of wheat, 300 of oats, and 30 of potatoes; and he made 38 gallons of sorghum molasses. He listed the value of his farm as $6,000.

The 1870 atlas drawing (Figure 2.5A) depicts their two-story frame house surrounded by a few trees, with a small livestock barn across the road. No garden appears beside the house, and the overall impression is one of a modest farm operation.

In the 1880 census, Lafayette DeFrance continued to reside with his wife and two sons, although the older son, William Allen, had married, and the newlyweds were living with the groom's parents. DeFrance's brother, Martin, was living with Daniel and Anne Yoder as a hired hand. DeFrance owned 133 acres of land, but only $575 worth of livestock, compared to the overall average of $962 in the two townships. His farm produced 25 tons of hay. He owned only $75 in agricultural implements and kept only 4 cows, producing 150 pounds of butter worth $16.50, and 75 dozen eggs. In his fields, DeFrance harvested 1,500 bushels of corn, 40 of wheat, 300 of oats, and 25 of potatoes; and he made 100 gallons of sorghum molasses. The value of his farm was $4,000. He also tended 2 acres of apple trees, which produced 60 bushels of apples. DeFrance kept no sheep and grew no barley, rye, or buckwheat.

The farm of Samuel D. Guengerich can be compared to the homestead of Lafayette DeFrance in size and age, since both farms appear for the first time on the 1870 agricultural census, although DeFrance was 45 years old and Guengerich was 34 years old. Samuel D. Guengerich (1836–1929), son of Daniel P. Guengerich, a stepson of Jacob Swartzendruber, came to Johnson County with his parents in 1846. Daniel Guengerich had first staked a claim along Deer Creek in Washington Township, but he soon moved across the county line into northern Washington County. His son S. D. returned to Pennsylvania and acquired a teaching certificate from Millersville Normal School in 1864, married Barbara Beachy (1843–1938), paid a $300 commutation fee for exemption from military duty in 1865, and returned to Iowa to farm after the Civil War.[51] Guengerich was born in Pennsylvania, and his wife, Barbara, was born in Maryland.

In 1870 Guengerich headed a household located on section 19 comprised of his wife; two children, Elizabeth, age 2, and Daniel, age 1; and two other household members, housekeeper Barbara Kinsinger, age 30, and farm worker William H. Harvey, age 23. He owned 122 acres on a rise above Deer Creek, far below the Amish average farm size of 168 acres in the 1870 census, although it was comparable to the 136 acres of fellow farm newcomer DeFrance. He listed $700 worth of livestock, quite comparable to the DeFrance farm operation, except for 9 sheep. His farm produced 20 tons of hay, and he owned $200 in agricultural implements. Barbara produced 300 pounds of butter. In his fields, Guengerich harvested 1,200 bushels of corn, 200 of wheat, 100 of oats, 100 of rye, 12 of buckwheat, and 30 of potatoes; and he raised no sorghum. He gave the value of his farm as $4,500.

The 1870 atlas drawing (Figure 2.5B) depicts a two-story frame house with a porch, surrounded by a cluster of farm buildings. Daniel P. Guengerich had moved into a "Grossdoddy house" (Grandpa house, for retirement) on his son's

2.5B. Residence of Samuel Guengerich.

property, which may be the building to the right of Guengerich's house, or it may be the print shop that Guengerich opened. The tidy fences, apple orchard, and garden convey an impression of an orderly and productive farm. In 1870 DeFrance and Guengerich both operated small farms with about the same balance of livestock and crop production, although Guengerich could afford more hired help in household and field.

In the 1880 census, S. D. Guengerich continued to own 120 acres. He resided with Barbara and five children and no other household members. He owned $600 in livestock, quite a few more animals than DeFrance. His farm produced 60 tons of hay, far above the average in Washington and Sharon townships. He owned $300 in agricultural implements, a 50 percent increase over 1870, the same period when all the ethnic averages in the two townships declined; DeFrance actually dropped from $400 to $75 in value of implements.

Barbara produced 400 pounds of butter, just below the Amish average of $48, and 300 dozen eggs. In his fields, Guengerich harvested 1,400 bushels of corn, 100 of wheat, 400 of oats, no rye, 60 bushels of potatoes; and he made 40 gallons of molasses. The value of the farm was $6,500, and of all farm production, $1,200. He also tended 2 acres of apple trees, which produced 40 bushels of apples.

On a farm slightly smaller than Lafayette DeFrance's, S. D. Guengerich produced more agricultural commodities and kept more animals. DeFrance paid no farm labor in 1880, likely because his sons were old enough to help, and Guengerich paid $280 in wages, his oldest child being 12. The Amish agricultural system appears more firmly established in 1880 than 1870 on Guengerich's farm, probably because he only started farming in the late 1860s. Guengerich purchased 92 acres from his father in August 1859 in sections 19 and 20 for $640, or $7 per acre, and another 30 in sections 19 and 29 in November 1868 for $480, or $16 per acre.

DeFrance and Guengerich provide a good comparison of similar-sized farm enterprises. They were almost exactly the same in 1870, but Guengerich had moved to a more identifiable Amish system by 1880. In 1880 Guengerich and his family owned a large number of animals and agricultural implements; produced large quantities of hay, butter, and eggs; and planted a diverse selection of field crops.

Guengerich and DeFrance could be compared in only two censuses. Two farms that appear in all four nineteenth-century agricultural censuses, from 1850 to 1880, offer a longer-term perspective to show that an Amish agricultural system became more firmly entrenched during the 1860s. Robert Roup farmed in sections 8 and 9 of Washington Township, and Peter B. Miller in section 32 of Sharon Township.

Two Households in Four Censuses

Robert and Edsel Roup moved to Johnson County in 1840 with their parents, Christian and Ruth Roup. Christian died in 1843 and Ruth in 1859; both are buried in the Bethel Methodist Church graveyard in section 8. In the 1850 census, Ruth was listed as household head; and Edsel, the elder brother, appears on the agricultural census. Edsel and Robert were born in New York, Ruth in Pennsylvania. The 1850 census shows the household with 20 acres of tilled land and 180 acres unimproved, very close to the 197 acre average for all farms in

Washington and Sharon townships in 1850 and also close to the 210 acre average for native-born household heads. Edsel listed $307 worth of livestock and 10 tons of hay, and he owned $75 in agricultural implements. Ruth produced 100 pounds of butter. In his fields, Roup harvested 350 bushels of corn, 60 of wheat, 95 of oats, but no potatoes or sorghum. He listed the value of his farm as $800, which matches the figure for real estate owned on the population census.

The Peter B. Miller (1805–79) family moved to Johnson County from Knox County, Ohio, in the fall of 1846. Miller was a brother to Susanna, Daniel P. Guengerich's wife, hence an uncle of Samuel D. Guengerich. Peter B.'s father, Benedict Miller (1781–1837), was an Amish bishop in Maryland and Pennsylvania. Peter B. married Catherine Yoder in Maryland, and their first six children were born there. In about 1841, the Miller family moved to Ohio, where two more children were born, then on to Iowa. The 1850 population census shows Peter and Catherine Miller living in Washington Township (probably a mistake, since they settled in Sharon Township and the other censuses show them living there), with two daughters and seven sons ranging in age from 1 to 20, one of only three Amish families in Washington and Sharon townships.

In the 1850 agricultural census, Peter Miller owned 30 acres of tilled land and 290 acres of unimproved land. Miller listed $267 worth of livestock and 18 tons of hay, and he owned $100 in agricultural implements. Catherine churned 150 pounds of butter. In his fields, Miller harvested 250 bushels of corn and 150 of wheat, but no oats, rye, potatoes, or sorghum. Miller also reported 100 pounds of honey and eight oxen. He listed the value of his farm as $1,000. Peter Miller produced more hay than Robert Roup, but owned less livestock; and Miller grew only corn and wheat, while Roup added oats to his crop mixture.

By 1860 Robert and Edsel Roup both headed farm households in Washington Township, on neighboring farms in sections 8 and 9. Both had married, Robert to Margaret Montgomery, born in Pennsylvania, and Edsel to Elizabeth, born in Ohio. Robert had three young children. Also in the Robert Roup household were James, Henry, and Olive Montgomery and James Wilkins. Peter B. and Catherine Miller headed a large household in 1860, with six sons still at home, plus Catharine Summers (a domestic born in Switzerland), George Randal (a farm hand born in Illinois), and Charles Mentyor (born in New York). Their two daughters had married, Sarah to Daniel Stemler, born in Germany, and Anna to Solomon Harger, born in Ohio; another son, David P., had married Barbara Kempf.

The 1860 agricultural census shows Robert Roup with 140 tilled acres and none unimproved, while Edsel owned 140 tilled and 40 unimproved acres. Peter B. Miller owned 100 tilled acres and 60 unimproved; he bought the center quarter of section 32 from Benjamin H. Buckingham on 6 February 1850, which he still owned on the 1870 map of Sharon Township in the Johnson County Atlas.[52] Roup listed $400 worth of livestock, while Miller listed $800, mostly more sheep (Roup kept none) and hogs. Both farms produced 25 tons of hay, and both farmers owned $75 in agricultural implements; Edsel owned $100 in implements, and the brothers may have shared tools. Margaret Roup produced 300 pounds of butter, and Catherine Miller 500 pounds; the average in the two townships was 220 pounds, 296 for Amish farms. In the fields, Miller grew twice as much corn, less wheat, but added oats and barley; Roup grew neither. Miller also owned two oxen and harvested 100 pounds of honey. On similar sized farms, Peter Miller in 1860 had moved to farming with more livestock, more diverse field crops, and more extensive use of family labor in comparison with Robert Roup.

In 1870 Robert and Margaret Roup lived with six children and a hired hand, David Leawald, as neighbors to Edsel and Elizabeth, who also hosted a hired man, George Wimer. Peter B. and Catherine Miller lived with Mary Yoder in Sharon Township, but no other children still lived at home. Roup owned 220 acres, 130 tilled, 40 woodland, and 50 unimproved. In addition to his land in sections 8 and 9, 20 acres of his woodland lay in section 5. Miller owned the same 160 acres as in 1860, with 120 tilled, 10 woodland, and 30 unimproved. Roup listed $2,000 worth of livestock, while Miller listed $1,600; and Roup had added sheep since 1860 to his animal stock. His farm produced 60 tons of hay, and Miller cut 30 tons of hay. Roup owned $500 in agricultural implements; Edsel owned another $400 in implements. Miller owned $400 worth of implements. Margaret Roup produced 500 pounds of butter, as did Catherine Miller. Roup grew more corn, less wheat, and more oats; but Miller also planted barley and rye. Like Roup, Miller paid $200 in farm labor wages. Roup also harvested 50 bushels of grass seed, 1,000 pounds of flax, and 120 bushels of flax seed.

The 1870 Johnson County Atlas depicts the Roup farmstead as a two-story frame house with a columned and balconied entrance (Figure 2.5C). An apple orchard and barn lie across the road, but there is no garden. Similar to Lafayette DeFrance's farmstead, farm buildings lie across the road from the main house. There was no depiction of Peter Miller's farm in the atlas.

Peter Miller had passed the point of peak agricultural production in his life cycle. In 1870 he was 65 years old and nearing retirement, while Roup was age

2.5C. Residence of Robert Roup.

45 and in the prime of life. Other than greater diversity of field crops, his farm operation in 1870 was not substantially different from Roup's; the peak of his "Amish system" had been reached in the 1860 census.

By 1880 Robert Roup owned 325 acres of land, 230 tilled, 10 meadow, 25 woodland, and 60 unimproved; he was one of the wealthiest farmers in Washington Township. He lived with Margaret and four children; Edsel lived with Elizabeth and five children. Peter B. Miller died in 1879 and was buried in the Peter Miller cemetery, which he had ceded to the Amish Church of Sharon Township in 1869, one acre in section 32.[53] Catherine lived with her son and daughter-in-law, Abraham and Emma Miller, and a nephew, Samuel B. Miller, son of Peter's younger brother, Benedict. On the agricultural census, the farm is listed in the name of Catherine and heirs. Catherine then owned 159 acres, minus the one acre for the cemetery where her late husband rested, all tilled, plus 40 acres woodland. Robert Roup owned 13 horses, 12 milk cows, 22 cattle, 108 sheep, and 120 hogs; while Catherine Miller listed 6 horses, 4 milk cows, 4 cattle, 61 sheep, and 60 hogs. Roup produced 75 tons of hay, and the Miller farm produced only 25 tons. Roup owned $200 in agricultural implements, and Miller $100. Margaret Roup produced 200 pounds of butter and 125 dozen eggs, while the Miller women produced 250 pounds of butter and 700 dozen eggs. The Millers relied even more heavily on female labor for income in 1880. Roup harvested almost four times as much corn as Miller, less wheat, more oats, and some barley; while Miller planted a small amount of rye. Roup paid $75 in farm labor wages, and Miller paid none. Roup planted a more diverse mix of crops in 1880 than in 1870, and he even tended a quarter-acre vineyard and four acres of apple trees, yielding 25 bushels of apples.

Robert Roup and Peter B. Miller are slightly out of phase in their life courses, although it is worth comparing them because they reach across all four censuses. Miller reached the peak of agricultural production in 1860, and Roup in 1880. There are limitations in comparing the stories of individual households as illustrations of aggregate trends. Patterns of agriculture seem most visible at the peak of a farmer's life cycle, between the ages of 35 and 45, when the household has accumulated sufficient capital for investment in land and implements and has access to the greatest quantity of family labor.

Five Farmers in One Cohort

The final comparative framework of ethnic farming examines five different farmers in the same age cohort. Farmsteads occupied by Corbly Snyder, section 36, and Elias B. Howell, section 13, appear as drawings in the 1870 atlas (Figures 2.5D and 2.5E). Snyder was age 44 and Howell age 45 in 1870, in the same cohort as the 45-year-old Robert Roup. Their farmsteads are depicted as somewhat opulent, with columned porches, large farm buildings, and neat fenced yards. In the same comparative cohort are Frederick Swartzendruber (1825–95), born in Germany to Jacob Swartzendruber; Welsh immigrant David H. Jones (1817–93); and German Lutheran immigrant Gottlieb F. Roessler (1821–89). Without comparing each household in each census year, comparisons for 1870 will illustrate each ethnic group with a farmer in his prime.

All five farmers owned a farm worth more than $10,000 in 1870. Snyder owned 456 acres; Howell owned 240; Swartzendruber, 310; Roessler, 500; and

2.5D. Residence of Corbly Snyder.

Jones, 320—the latter three in Sharon Township. Differences among the five farmsteads are subtle. For example, Snyder, Roessler, and Swartzendruber all owned $2,600 worth of livestock; Roessler cut the most hay, 80 tons; Mrs. Jones churned the most butter, 900 pounds; Swartzendruber owned the most woodland, 80 acres; all owned between $300 and $400 in agricultural implements; and Howell owned 100 sheep, the highest figure among these five farms. Snyder tilled 300 acres, 66 percent of his land; Howell tilled 160 acres, 67 percent of his total acreage; Swartzendruber tilled 200 acres, or 65 percent; Roessler tilled 340 acres, or 68 percent; and Jones tilled 200 acres, 63 percent of his land.

Despite the similarities among the five ethnic farmsteads, close examination reveals more balance in Swartzendruber's farm, while each of the other farms was weak in at least one area. First, Swartzendruber owned $2,600 in livestock, and Jones held only $1,400 and Howell $2,000; Roessler held fewer milk cows and sheep. Only one farmer owned less land than Swartzendruber, making the high commodity and livestock figures the more significant by comparison. Second, Swartzendruber cut 50 tons of hay, far above the 22 ton average for all farmers in Washington and Sharon townships. Roessler cut 80 tons of hay, and Jones cut 65, but Howell cut only 12 tons. Third, agricultural implements were equivalent in value, with each farmer holding $400, except Howell with $300. Fourth, butter production was also roughly equal, about 500 pounds, except the 900 pounds churned by Jones. Fifth, Swartzendruber harvested 3,000 bushels of corn and 1,000 bushels of wheat, and raised 25 cattle and 60 hogs, a total value in 1869 of $2,040; while the average for all farmers was $1,113. Roessler and Jones produced about the same value of marketable grains and livestock, but Howell produced $1,220 and Snyder $1,360. The other German farmer in this sample was most similar to Swartzendruber.

The differences become clearer in the 1880 agricultural census. Swartzendruber maintained about the same balance, while Roessler and Snyder moved into specialized large-scale cattle and hog production, and Jones and Howell conducted smaller farming operations. Amish farmers consistently practiced a system of agriculture in which livestock, meadows, innovative technology, family labor, and production for the marketplace all played significant roles. The balance among these five elements was seldom tilted toward cash grain farming or livestock production, to cite the most usual specializations among

2.5E. Residence of E. B. Howell.

their Iowa neighbors, to the detriment of attention to soil fertility or female production, represented by butter and eggs.

Farming for Good

Armed with a sustainable agricultural system developed in Europe and transplanted to Pennsylvania, Amish pioneers selected a congenial environment and re-created that system in Johnson County, Iowa. They chose a diverse landscape with woods, streams, and rolling prairie, suitable for subsistence agriculture; they also chose a locale with market access and raised a healthy variety of marketable crops. Amish farmers sustained a system of farming, not mere ethnic tendencies, and the system contributed to communal survival and expansion. The author of the 1870 Washington Township map in the Johnson County Atlas recognized the distinctive quality of the Amish agricultural settlement. After listing the earliest settlers in the township, including Robert and Edsel Roup and several members of the Fry family, the author remarked, "The Township is now quite thickly settled, having a population of eight hundred and ninety-one (891) of which quite a number are Amish Germans, a thrifty class of people, who work hard, and make their land produce all it is capable of."

During the three decades following 1850, a Pennsylvania Dutch way of farming became increasingly distinct in comparison with surrounding ethnic and religious communities in southwestern Johnson County. In particular, Amish economic foundations became stronger during and after the American Civil War. Amish families acquired land, established new households, diversified field crop production, and raised livestock. These long-term trends began to take shape during the 1860s.

But there is more to community building than economic systems. During the 1860s, the Amish community experienced intra-community conflict, competition with other ethnic groups for land and resources, and the social and economic disruptions of the Civil War. The Amish almost split in 1863 over the dissent of Preacher Joseph Keim. As he dreamed of hauling manure to his field, Swartzendruber may have considered it simpler at one point to divide the load and carry on, rather than to pull forever on one load under difficult conditions. Keim could have his load and Swartzendruber his, and the way would become smooth again. But the elderly bishop continued to struggle to keep his community unified, and when dissenting leaders such as Joseph Keim and Deacon

John Mishler moved away, the load remained together, albeit somewhat precariously.

In order to steady the load of maintaining community unity, Swartzendruber and other Amish leaders wished to place the burden of Amish continuity on male household heads. Strengthening male household authority would help maintain the re-created agricultural system and enhance community coherence, and Jacob Swartzendruber dreamed of making familial responsibility central again to the Amish way of life.

> With regard to the excesses practiced among the youth, namely that the youth take the liberty to sleep or lie together without any fear or shame, such things shall not be tolerated at all. And when it takes place with the knowledge of the parents and something bad happens on account of it [that is, a pregnancy], the parents shall not go unpunished.
>
> —1837 Amish Discipline

Chapter 3

Preservationist Patriarchy

The problematic relationship of household and community has exercised religious and political leaders across centuries of Western history. Male authority has most often served to correlate and articulate segments of an idealized social order—individual, family, household, church, community, state. In particular, during times of instability (and what situation cannot be portrayed as unstable?), male authority has fixed social relations and assuaged anxieties. Puritans named family a "little commonwealth." State builders in early modern France formulated a "family-state compact" of mutual patriarchal support. Stabilizers of revolutionary ideology in the early American nation were well served by "Republican Motherhood," giving women a crucial role while retaining political authority in male hands.[1] The problems of instability, nevertheless, failed to stay fixed in each case; and movements ranging from revivalism, proslavery and antislavery, utopianism, and many others have been credited with addressing gendered insecurity.[2]

Amish immigrants from Europe to eighteenth- and nineteenth-century America, confronted by nearly insoluble dangers to their mere survival, developed their own version of preservationist patriarchy. Immigration from Europe in the early eighteenth century had resulted in scattered clusters of Amish families in the English colonies, leading to intermarriage with non-Amish neighbors and to variations in prescribed and proscribed behavior—for example, the nontraditional building of an Amish meetinghouse in Chester County, Pennsylvania.[3] It seemed clear to Amish leaders that their communities were in danger of losing their distinctive identity. The environment of colonial politics, particularly the hostility toward pacifist Quakers and their supporters during the French and Indian War and the Revolutionary War, made the relatively isolated Amish communities vulnerable to external pressures toward acculturation to the new American nation.[4]

The early American republic, wracked by a powerful market revolution, presented a difficult environment for the survival of patriarchal rural producer communities.[5] One cluster of responses to the new urban marketplace and resulting anxieties about the patriarchal household centered around religious revival and reform, often led and shaped by women. Another cluster focused on patriarchal preservation, attempting to preserve an ancient order in the face of change perceived to be out of control. The commonsense repertoire of national and communal identity made appeal to paternal authority virtually instinctive as the preferred means of connecting individuals-in-households with the communal sense of itself. The Amish joined in the cultural recovery of male leadership in their repertoire of community.

Their own search for means of self-preservation in the early nineteenth century led Amish religious and social leaders in the United States to strengthen the household, and paternal authority within the household, as the core of Amish community. These leaders, including Jacob Swartzendruber, first Amish bishop in Iowa, were able to call on a long-standing tradition of patriarchal household authority in European Christianity, a legacy left unchallenged by the social radicalism of the Anabaptist movement.[6] This pattern of male leadership made sense within the Amish repertoire of community when leaders found it necessary to clarify communal distinctiveness against American society.

The Amish Tradition and Patriarchy

Research on women and the family in Anabaptist traditions continues to be sketchy. However, a consensus is emerging on an overall hypothesis: Despite a general position of religious and social radicalism, Anabaptists did little to challenge the patriarchal Western family. The first religious group to offer a sustained alternative vision of women was the English Quakers of the seventeenth century. Joyce Irwin, on the basis of limited evidence, suggested in her 1979 book, *Womanhood in Radical Protestantism, 1525–1675,* that Anabaptists were essentially conservative when it came to gender.[7] More specific research on Anabaptist women, especially their depiction in *Martyrs Mirror* and their experience in Hutterite colonies, has supported Irwin's hypothesis.

Women found Anabaptism attractive, and under the press of persecution they often acted outside traditional roles, but "they did not consciously question the subordinate role assigned to them as women."[8] Keith Sprunger traced a prominent place for women in the Anabaptist movement as they helped to carry the momentum in the midst of fierce repression. Anabaptism did challenge Protestant and Catholic society in the spheres of religion (voluntarism and believer's baptism), economics (attacks on usury and limits on the use of private property), and politics (withdrawal from the magistracy and refusal to participate in wars). Nevertheless, despite some glib statements by earlier historians about a revolution in the status of women, Sprunger concluded, "There was no sixteenth-century Anabaptist women's or sexual revolution, nor did Anabaptist women seem to be calling for one."[9]

Anabaptists and their descendants accepted the European tradition of "housefather" dominion in the family. The term *hausvater* entered German theological rhetoric through Martin Luther's translation of the Greek term *oikodespotēs,* 'house despot.' The Latin Vulgate translated the term *paterfamilias,* following Roman family law. Luther used *hausvater* in the Synoptic Gospel householder parables but translated the same Greek term as *haushalten,* 'keep house,' in 1 Timothy 5:14, where Paul instructs young widows to remarry, bear children, and rule their households. In Luther's translation, men were "housefathers" and women were "housekeepers." The Froschauer Bible, a 1536 German translation used most often by Anabaptists, followed the same distinction. Thus, Anabaptists followed with little alteration the principle and practice of father rule that was deeply embedded in European culture.[10]

In the three centuries following the Reformation, an extensive literature instructed housefathers in their duties and responsibilities. "Housebook literature" made explicit connections among the household, the state, and the church. Writers referred to God as "the heavenly housefather." Above all, housefathers and "property owners" (*Gutsherrn*) were virtually synonymous.[11] The early modern state began to exercise its centralizing authority by reinforcing and acting through housefather rule, thus gaining more direct access to the production and consumption of economic households.[12]

Anabaptist and Amish disciplines in Europe include no specific reference to paternal responsibility to enforce communal norms, likely because gathered Amish ministers could assume the ubiquitous presence of *Hausvater* practice. The disciplines do mention general parental duties to socialize children. Ministers and elders are usually held responsible for resolving conflict and keeping order in congregations.[13] In North America, however, Amish leaders could no longer assume universal awareness and acceptance of housefather authority, and they found themselves forced to attempt a recreation of housefather rule in their new circumstances. Amish ministers and bishops constructed more and more elaborate cultural distinctives, and they relied on parents, especially fathers, to patrol the borders they constructed.

Crisis and Patriarchal Innovation

The crisis of Amish survival stretched across the late colonial and early national periods of American history. Many immigrant families found themselves isolated and lacking support for Amish group identity. Kinship ties took precedence over responsibility to communal duties within and among these scattered family clusters. Traveling bishops accomplished little more than performing marriages, administering communion, and officiating at baptisms. Amish historian Joseph F. Beiler has maintained that the Revolutionary era nearly destroyed the tiny Amish communities in Pennsylvania:

> For quite a few years we have noticed that most of our initial ancestor families in America have not raised more than one son to remain in the old faith. Some have not kept any sons in the church, some have kept a few, but not one record do we have that kept the whole family within before the revolution. After that there are some. It is evident that many sons who came to this land of freedom were overwhelmed with the air of freedom in America during the revolution period.[14]

Similar isolation, combined with harsh persecution and destructive warfare, resulted in the complete extinction of the Amish in Europe by 1937.[15]

According to anthropologist John A. Hostetler's interpretation, church supervision gradually superseded family autonomy in the effort to preserve Amish communal identity in the early nineteenth century. As settlements grew in size, which occurred slowly—the Lancaster County Amish did not divide into two congregations until 1843, about a century after the first Amish arrived in the county—Amish family clusters "ordained resident [to replace itinerant] bishops, and thus church control began to be exercised over family and kinship rule." Church regulation of lifestyle resulted in the gradual emergence of a reconfigured identity "as Amish were distinguished from non-Amish" in the American context. However, with increasing congregational control over families and individuals, "both religious and secular controversies began to plague the Amish people."[16] Communal directives made effective through family authority deposed individualism and family autonomy in Amish practice, thus preserving a unique Amish ethnoreligious identity on the basis of group dominion.

Historian Paton Yoder followed and expanded Hostetler's interpretation. Yoder used several recorded Amish church disciplines, or *Ordnungen,* behavior-oriented versions of the more familiar confessions of faith, to trace the elaboration of communal regulation in antebellum Amish communities. Yoder pointed to the enforcing of community standards through traditional Anabaptist practices of ban (excommunication) and shunning (*Meidung,* or social avoidance) as the means by which "the authority of the church over the Amish community" was strengthened.[17]

Developments in Amish communities during the first half of the nineteenth century can, alternatively, be interpreted as asserting church control *through* the family rather than over it. Or, more accurately, Amish disciplines tightened the connections among individual, family, household, and community by bonding all four elements in a common patriarchal framework to maintain traditional Anabaptist values of separation from, and nonconformity to, the world. Paternal authority was the blessed tie that bound households to community, forged in the imperative linkages of parents, children, and religious community. Regulation of marriage and household formation, especially restrictions on traditional courtship practices, served as the avenue for strengthening paternal household management.

Historian Helena Wall has argued that colonial Americans believed in an essential relationship of family and community, and they "accepted the preeminent right of the community to regulate the lives of its members" in the interests of community order. Family behavior required special attention since a well-ordered family was a microcosm of orderly society. The right of community oversight, expressed in neighborly supervision of marital and child-rearing practices, eroded during the last half of the eighteenth century. Principles of patriarchy and hierarchy were replaced by republicanism in politics, individualism, and contractualism.[18] Wall probably overemphasized the extent to which patriarchalism disappeared and underestimated the continuation of patriarchy in postrevolutionary ideals of republican motherhood. She was hardly the first to place individualism at the center of an American ethos.[19]

If Wall is correct in finding a disconnection of the family-community nexus in the early American republic, then the Amish found they could no longer set their community against a larger community as they had learned in Europe. Maintaining communal distinction against a set of individuals became more difficult, especially since American ideas of society seemed to be moving toward the Anabaptist and Amish practice of voluntarism. Like the society around them, Amish leaders attempted to preserve the patriarchal household as the bulwark against extremist American individualism. But whereas Americans believed in the necessity of a universal social order, the Amish wished to preserve communal order without recourse to a coercive state. The lack of coercion made patriarchal leadership seem even more essential for Amish communities to retain their cohesion.

The Amish in Europe and North America practiced congregational autonomy and local control, traditions developed in response to persecution and scattered households. Distance and decentralized organization made it difficult to impose conformity, and Amish leaders often resorted to ad hoc local or regional ministers' meetings to resolve disputes and to connect distant settlements. Jacob Swartzendruber attended several ministers' meetings during the first half of the nineteenth century, and he gathered an extensive personal library of handwritten disciplines and minister's manuals.[20] While always seeking to preserve traditional Amish religious values, Swartzendruber and his fellow ministers innovated by reemphasizing housefathers as a crucial link in the chain of authority devised for community continuity.

The first recorded gathering of Amish ministers in America occurred on 17 October 1809, most likely in the Berks-Chester-Lancaster settlement. According to Bishop Jacob Frederick Swartzendruber (grandson of Jacob), his great-grandfather Christian Yoder, bishop of the Glades Congregation in Somerset County, Pennsylvania, wrote the discipline agreed upon by the assembled ministers. The nine points regulated the relationship of individual, church, and world. Members who left the Amish must be banned and shunned, with provisions for disciplining those who did not follow the rule of shunning; swearing of oaths and jury service were prohibited; ministers could preach only at funerals of Amish members, not outsiders; and all members could take part in the council (*Abrath*) of the church, that is, participate in setting community standards and maintaining communal harmony in preparation for communion services. Personal grooming and clothing also fell within the purview of Amish maintenance, as article seven of the 1809 discipline prohibited the cutting of hair and beard, and article nine reads, "Proud dresses, proud trousers, hats, and combs in the hair, and similar worldly clothing shall not be tolerated in the church."[21] Both male and female deportment came under scrutiny, but this discipline did not yet appeal specifically for parental exertion on behalf of general Amish standards.

By contrast, the 1837 discipline drawn up by the three congregations in Somerset County, Pennsylvania, on 18 March (at a meeting attended by Preacher Jacob Swartzendruber) did entreat parents to enforce the lengthening list of concerns. The first article of the twelve encouraged use of the ban and shunning, and blamed neglect of the ban for the "decline" that had "set in" among Amish members. Other articles prohibited the holding of political offices, excessive driving of sleighs, and painting vehicles with two colors, and required keeping the Sabbath and avoidance of fashionable clothing in favor of the "old style" among church members.

The ninth article enjoined "bundling," the courtship practice in which a male and female sleep together while fully clothed:

> With regard to the excesses practiced among the youth, namely that the youth take the liberty to sleep or lie together without any fear or shame, such things shall not be tolerated at all. And when it takes place with the knowledge of the parents and something bad happens on account of it [that is, a pregnancy], the parents shall not go unpunished.

By making parents responsible for their children's sexual behavior, the assembled ministers hoped to cement the bond between parental authority and community moral precepts. Control over courtship and marital practices were keynotes of the 1837 discipline that Jacob Swartzendruber signed.

The second and third articles specifically mention mothers and implied that their tendency to adornment must be curbed, both in clothing themselves and their children and in decorating their houses:

> Second: It is noted that there is awful pride in clothing, namely with respect to silken neck-cloths (*Halstuecher*) worn around the neck, so that mothers tie silken neck-cloths on their children, and make high collars on their children's shirts and clothing, and the mothers permit their daughters to wear men's hats and go with them to church or other places, or that even the mothers have them themselves. Decided that such things shall not be among us.

Not only fashionable clothing but also the tendency to confuse gendered clothing received special attention. Parents were given responsibility for socializing their children into Amish values.

> Third: Decided that there shall be no display in houses, namely when houses are built, or painted with various colors, or filled with showy furniture, namely with wooden, porcelain, or glass utensils (dishes), and having cupboards and mirrors hung on the wall, and such things. . . .
> Eleventh: Likewise, the cabinetmakers are not to make such proud kinds of furniture and not decorate them with such loud or gay (*scheckich*) colors.

The second, third, and eleventh articles dealt with the "feminine" domain of raising children, running the kitchen, and guiding domestic activities. Fashion and color were temptations to pride, the opposite value of humility and lowliness prized by Amish tradition. The potential disobedience of mothers and children in dress and household fashion required careful prevention.

The sixth and seventh articles regulated marriage with persons outside the Amish faith, and both advocated more stringent requirements for acceptance of partners into fellowship. Specifically, non-Amish partners were to be brought "into Christian discipline," meaning submission to the Amish *Ordnung,* and they had to "promise before God and the brotherhood to fulfill the obligations of Christian marriage," in effect holding a second wedding in the church. The ad hoc disciplines of 1809 and 1837 used the politics of gender to enhance community discipline and uniformity. Male authority became the conduit for creating communal distinction, and patriarchy remained the preferred communal principle for confronting uncertain social challenges.

These written disciplines with their renewed paternal authority were not mere documents to be ignored. Jacob Swartzendruber, for example, moved first to Maryland and then to Iowa to escape the practice of bundling in Somerset County, Pennsylvania.[22] He wished to become part of a new community where the ideal of housefather leadership, symbolized by eradicating bundling, could be put into effect. He bought 560 acres of land in 1851 in Johnson County, Iowa, and immediately began settling his adult children on farms of their own, enacting the new church discipline in order to protect his children from worldly influences. One indicator of the anxiety he felt about retaining his family in the faith appears in the form of a dream he had a few years after his move to Iowa.

Jacob Swartzendruber stayed with his stepson, Daniel P. Guengerich, the night of 27–28 April 1858. During his sleep, he dreamed an enemy took a position nearby and shot fiery arrows and bullets at him. All flew by and none found its mark, but the patriarch finally perceived his danger and moved away from his attacker. Daniel appeared in front of his stepfather and, as Swartzendruber wrote to him later, "I pushed you before me away from the fire because there was danger, but you were so heavy that I almost could not get you away; you turned your face from me, and I had both my hands square in your back and pushed with all my strength." Then Swartzendruber awoke, perhaps an hour and a half before daylight, and could not find sleep again.[23]

Swartzendruber wished to warn his stepson about the dangers of associating with a member of his congregation he considered dangerous and unproductive. Earlier in the letter, he admonished Guengerich not to help Levi Miller in any way.[24] He was willing to expend great effort to keep his kin out of harm's way. It appears he perceived his stepson as uncooperative and unappreciative of this warning. But the aging bishop was following a prescription for housefather leadership and responsibility that he himself had helped to develop and that he argued for repeatedly among his fellow Amish ministers.

Another indicator of Swartzendruber's firm commitment to family life was his emotional farewell to his first wife and his subsequent remarriage. Barbara, his first wife, died on 24 January 1856, an event that distressed him greatly. He wrote a moving tribute to his departed wife in October, noting that her commitment to the Amish church was so strong she had insisted he attend a communion service in 1853 at William Wertz's house, some eight miles from home, even though she was seriously ill. Swartzendruber was ordained bishop that same Sunday in 1853. He remarried in 1860 during a trip to visit churches in the East, to Mary Miller, widow of Daniel Miller, a full deacon in Indiana.[25] During this trip, he continued to gather copies of older disciplines and minister's manuals, and he returned even more prepared to institute the new discipline of housefather administration.

Swartzendruber was willing to act the parental role for other communities, albeit not always successfully. Amish settlers in Davis County, Iowa, decided to organize a church in 1861, about seven years after their arrival. They were partly motivated by the Civil War and the impending dangers of coerced military service. They called for Jacob Swartzendruber to visit them, found his teachings pleasing, and asked him to organize a church. He "utterly refused" unless they conformed to Amish clothing practices, shaved their mustaches, and cut their hair in the Amish style. The Davis County Amish demurred and called instead on two change-minded bishops from Indiana to establish their church. Under the progressive leadership of Philip Roulet, they eventually joined the General Conference Mennonite Church.[26]

Swartzendruber wrote two impassioned essays in 1863 and 1865 condemning bundling and appealing to parents to stop the traditional courtship practice.[27] In his August 1863 essay on bundling, he recalled the local ministers' meeting in the Glades congregation in Somerset County on 3 October 1830, which condemned bundling and made parents responsible for enforcing the injunction. No printed discipline survives from this meeting, unless Swartzendruber meant 1837 instead of 1830, but he recalled language similar to the 1837 discipline: "[I]f something evil results" from young unmarried people lying together during the night, meaning a pregnancy, "then the parents should not remain unpunished." Therefore, parents should be careful to "keep good order in their households," since "every House-father and House-mother is responsible before God for their children." By addressing both fathers and mothers, Swartzendruber extended the obligation of adult married women to enforce community moral standards. The essay continued with many biblical citations concerning purity and separation of the church from the world, especially in terms of sexual behavior, and asserted that ministers were not warning their children with all prophetic seriousness. "What must an outside honorable man think of us," Swartzendruber continued, when he hears that "our young people lie together at night and perhaps can be seen going home in the gray light of dawn."

He also worried about outsiders gossiping about weddings and frolics. Neighbors were hearing about Amish failings.[28] Young people should not "make secret vows" without consulting parents and sending a minister to ask for a woman's hand in marriage. Swartzendruber considered parental control over marriage decisions part of the Amish confession of faith and Christian practice; loss of control was represented by bundling and fashionable marriage ceremonies. In Swartzendruber's view, weddings should not be conducted with such great excess, where even English songs and rough talk appear, but with spiritual care and consciousness of marriage under God. He called on both parents and ministers to control weddings and courtship practices among Amish congregations.

In fact, marriage and the administration of households was a central issue in the *Diener Versammlungen* (Ministers' Meetings), which met annually from 1862 to 1878, except in 1877. Several progressive leaders called these meetings and invited representatives from every Amish community in North America in an attempt to resolve conflicts in several local Amish communities.[29] At the first Ministers' Meeting in Wayne County, Ohio, in June 1862, the first order of business was "the difficulties between the Elkhart and Lagrange congregations" in northern Indiana. Tradition-minded and change-minded factions had already parted company by 1857, but there was still some hope for reconciliation. The assembled ministers turned the matter over to a committee of six to attempt reconciliation. As the proceedings continued, some ministers pleaded for toleration of individual conscience, while others argued for stricter attention to the traditional principles of separation from the world and nonconformity to the world. Levi Miller, a traditionalist bishop from Holmes County, Ohio, spoke against lightning rods, photographs, lotteries, meetinghouses, insurance, and the innovation of baptism in streams rather than in houses. Then, in response to a plea by John K. Yoder, change-minded bishop from Wayne County, Ohio, for tolerating differences, someone produced a letter from Jacob Swartzendruber.

> The letter said that he was minded to stay with the articles of faith as they are recorded in the prayer booklet; he is against all innovation. He is against recommending the office of full deacon for a [regular] deacon right at the beginning [before he has gone through a probationary period of some years]. [He] speaks strongly against outsiders [unbaptized young people, not yet members] sitting in a [congregational] council meeting, and against the marriage of near relatives, such as grandchildren [first cousins]. He wants to be patient concerning baptism in water if that is what the assembled ministers approve.[30]

Swartzendruber seems to have been particularly concerned with maintaining traditional Amish social values. His special concern with faithful families and marital ethics appears in the brief minute from 1862, when he wrote against consanguineous marriage.

The assembled Amish leaders at this first Ministers' Meeting discussed church discipline. One critical issue was how to handle married couples when a husband or wife was banned; should the partner who remained in the church be forced to "withdraw" from the other, that is, refuse marital relations? Abner Yoder, then representing the Glades congregation in Somerset County, Pennsylvania, and who later moved to Iowa and carried on Swartzendruber's work, spoke frequently at the 1862 meeting and generally offered tradition-minded opinions. He argued against this extreme application of shunning, or avoidance, "unless it is by consent of both."[31]

At the next Ministers' Meeting, held in Mifflin County, Pennsylvania, in May 1863, Abner Yoder served as chair. Again, the first order of business was attempting to reconcile factions in the local Amish community. Jonathan Yoder, a change-minded bishop from McLean County, Illinois, raised the question of whether a member who was banned because of marriage outside the church can be taken back "without his spouse joining our church?"[32] A committee recommended discontinuing the ban upon demonstration of repentance, without specifying what would be required.

Jacob Swartzendruber attended the following Ministers' Meeting in Elkhart County, Indiana, in June 1864, the only one he observed in person. Once again, the first order of business was to attempt a reconciliation between the change-minded and traditionalist factions in the local Amish churches. After a report recommending local decisions on whether to ban members who left to join another nonresistant denomination (such as Mennonite), Swartzendruber asked, "Is it not immoral if a person leaves the [Amish] church?" He seemed to express traditionalists' frustration when he asked shortly thereafter, "Shall the other side not be heard?" Later, he said he stood "in favor of shunning without regarding the person," and added his intention "to hold to Holy Writ."[33]

The assembly also dealt with the issue of marriage outside the Amish faith and again recommended great caution in applying the ban, especially if the member married into another nonresistant denomination. Jacob Swartzendruber addressed himself to the report, but his words were not recorded; his son Frederick noted the "bad results which generally come from marrying outside the denomination."[34] Issues involving marriage returned later in the conference, leading John K. Yoder to present a lengthy discourse on marriage and the necessity of not mingling church and world. Yoder stated, "[T]hose who are in the church of God have no permission to marry outside the church with those who stand in unbelief," and advocated punishment with the ban. Yoder also said, "A marriage in the Lord between a believer and an unbeliever is surely impossible." When Yoder finished, according to the minutes, "Jacob Schwarzendruber witnessed forcefully to what Johann K. Joder had presented with respect to marriage."[35]

Marriage is a most difficult locale to enforce separation from the world. How can a congregation ban one partner and keep the other in the church? Powerful issues of sexual ethics, bundling in courtship, household order, discipline of children, and reproduction of community are involved. Marital mores were not the central issue of the Ministers' Meetings, but family life was clearly an important and recalcitrant subject, and one to which Jacob Swartzendruber gave his special attention.

Swartzendruber did not attend the 1865 Ministers' Meeting, held in Wayne County, Ohio, in June, the one that finalized the Great Schism between the tradition-minded and the change-minded.[36] Tradition-minded leaders set forth a manifesto that was virtually ignored by the other faction, and very few tradition-minded leaders attended any Ministers' Meetings after 1865. Jacob's son Frederick attended in 1865, as did future Iowan Abner Yoder, still in Somerset County, Pennsylvania. And Jacob Swartzendruber penned a lengthy letter to the 1865 gathering. He offered his position on whether Amish members who left and joined the Dunkards or Mennonites should be shunned (they should); whether anyone should marry closer than second cousins (they should not); the practice of bundling (no one should); the ongoing issues of fashionable clothing, represented by fancy weddings (in his mind an excessive practice and offensive to Amish simplicity); and the $300 commutation fee as an alternative to Civil War military service (frivolous if done to stay home and live in comfort while others died in battle).

As in his 1863 essay, Swartzendruber wrote passionately against bundling and quoted the same 1837 discipline on parental responsibility if a pregnancy occurred from the courtship practice. "The parents should take care" regarding "the young people lying together, pre-marital intercourse," and if "something bad" results, "the parents should not remain unpunished." He lamented occurrences when "the boys go into the beds with the girls when they perhaps have drunk too much and evil consequences follow," as evidenced by illegitimate children and acts of church discipline. "Oh what a great sin it is if ministers and parents and all members do not take enough care for the youth, or the mother of a house perhaps herself helps to prepare the beds." He considered bundling a hindrance to "right knowledge" among Amish youth, an "evil which has rooted itself in all the congregations" that prevented young people from submitting to the truth. He wrote sternly, "[H]ow sad it is that old people say, I cannot forbid this because I myself did it."[37]

Swartzendruber also wrote at length against what he called "the abuse" of holding weddings, expanding his 1863 call for spiritual weddings without revelry. He again advocated that young people should take counsel from their parents when they want to marry and then send a minister to carry a proposal of marriage from young man to young woman, "and not make promises in advance whereby the young people play the hypocrite." Excessive meals and secular music should be condemned, and all members should be responsible to "pay sufficient attention to order," especially ministers, "the watchmen who are to warn the people."[38]

Jacob Swartzendruber's vigorous opposition to bundling brought a response from the 1865 Ministers' Meeting. According to the minutes,

> A letter from an old and experienced minister from Iowa was handed in. But since it was noted that the main thrust of the letter is encompassed in the first ruling [of the 1865 session, on not conforming to the world], it was considered superfluous to vote on the total contents of the letter. But it was considered highly important to lay the following [proposed] ruling before the assembly, which was unanimously adopted:
>
> Ruled [*beschlossen*] that we fully agree with Brother Schwarzendruber's views concerning the vulgarities [bundling] of single people of opposite sexes and we herewith give full support, and admonish all Christian house-fathers to prevent all improprieties of the youth in their houses.[39]

Legislating against the traditional courtship practice did not stop bundling, of course, but the issue makes the connection between household authority and communal norms more explicit.

Another question answered during the 1865 Ministers' Meeting spoke even more directly to the situation in Johnson County, Iowa. Someone asked how to deal in a "scripturally appropriate" way with a member who refuses to take communion for several years. The assembly responded that the Lord's Supper is not to be neglected. If a member does not respond after being "admonished in love with God's Word," that person may not continue as a member of the congregation. In nineteenth-century Amish theology and practice, communion was the central symbol and embodiment of congregational accord. Nothing less than unanimous agreement with the *Ordnung,* tested the week before communion in congregational council meeting (*Abrath*), would suffice as adequate preparation to hold communion. Indeed, the term of choice for communion was *Die Einigkeit,* 'the Union' or 'Unity.'[40] To stay away from communion meant extreme disagreement with the *Ordnung,* and according to the logic of congregational discipline, if the abstinence continued, it could be treated as equivalent to voluntary withdrawal from fellowship.

Should Fathers Rule?

The question of participation in communion existed in Johnson County, Iowa, because of a conflict focused on Preacher Joseph Keim and Deacon John Mishler. Indications are that the issues focused on household management, since Keim complained of colored or decorated dishes, and on male household leadership.[41] Due to the lack of community consensus, no communion could be held from 1863 to 1865; and when Jacob Swartzendruber finally did conduct a communion service, it served more as an occasion to express disunity than harmony. The dissension challenged Jacob Swartzendruber's religious leadership in the Amish community, his personal authority within his own extended family, and the principle of paternal household administration.

On Easter Sunday, 16 April 1865, some six weeks before he wrote to the 1865 Ministers' Meeting, Jacob Swartzendruber held communion in the Sharon Township congregation for the first time in three years. The service took place at the home of John Kempf in section 33, at the south edge of the township. According to a list recorded by Swartzendruber, sixty-six members took communion and sixty refused. The following Sunday in the Deer Creek congregation, Washington Township, thirty-eight participated in communion at the Peter Brenneman residence, again at the southern end of the township, while forty-eight did not. The nearly even division between those who considered themselves in harmony with the Amish church and those who did not reveals a community at odds with itself. Only one week after General Lee surrendered to General Grant at Appomattox Court House in Virginia on April 9, and only two days after John Wilkes Booth shot President Abraham Lincoln on April 14, the Amish of Johnson County, Iowa, continued their own internecine struggle over the meaning of union.

Swartzendruber's cryptic list presents problems in identifying who took communion and who refused. He often used nicknames or first names, and he seldom wrote any female names. Two generations later his grandson, Elmer G. Swartzendruber, identified most persons on Jacob Swartzendruber's list in response to a query from historian Melvin Gingerich.[42] About 70 percent of the names mentioned can be identified from the 1860 and 1870 federal censuses for Sharon and Washington townships. The rest lived in Washington or Iowa counties, arrived after 1860 and left before 1870, or may have been missed by census takers.

Most of the persons listed by Jacob Swartzendruber are married couples. Only adult children appear, in keeping with the Amish practice of considering only baptized adults full members. A number of names appear alone, mostly older widows and widowers. More females chose to refuse the symbol of community unity than males. In the Sharon Amish church, besides married couples, eleven men and three women broke bread, while five men and twelve women refused. The next weekend, besides married couples, ten men and five women partook, while one man and six women refused. Twenty-one men and eight women participated, while eighteen women and six men refused, about a 75 percent majority in either direction based on gender. In addition, at least twelve married couples parted company for these communion services, and in no case did the wife participate. While most women demonstrated their consent to Jacob Swartzendruber's program, a significant number refused their support, and a disparity appeared between the backing of men and the discomfort of women. These refusals to participate are all the more remarkable, given the expectation that husbands and wives be unified in the congregation, and the sanctions against those who married outside the faith or the ambiguities created when one partner was banned and shunned.[43]

Three of the married women who refused to follow their husbands to the communion table were Jacob Swartzendruber's own daughters-in-law: Barbara, married to Jacob's eldest son Joseph; Elizabeth, married to Christian; and Mary, wife of George. Jacob's nephew, Peter Swartzendruber, saw his wife, Barbara, refuse communion; and Jacob's daughter, Lena, wife of Joseph Bender, also stayed away. Mary Shetler Swartzendruber gave birth to twins, Amelia and Lovina, on April 8; and Elizabeth Eash Swartzendruber gave birth to Simon on March 12. Since both families lived near the northwest corner of Washington Township, while the service at Peter Brenneman's took place toward the southeast corner, this may explain why neither attended. Joseph Swartzendruber attended both communion services, and his wife, Barbara Brenneman Swartzendruber, attended neither. Her youngest child, Noah, had been born the previous August. Given the importance of the biennial communion ceremony in Amish theology and practice and the fact that no communion had been held for three years, severe extenuating circumstances would have been required to allow members to miss the service. Twins eight days old would likely excuse the mother but not the rest of the kin network. It appears that the struggle to define household authority reached to the patriarch's own extended family.

Henry Hostetler, the only household head older than age 45 whose wife refused communion, was accompanied to the communion service by three of his sons. His wife, Susannah, stayed home. One of Henry's sons, Emmanuel, had served in the Union Army and met his death at Vicksburg; another son, Christian, had also served in the military but had survived the war.[44] Hostetler was one of the wealthiest farmers in southwestern Johnson County in 1860 and could have paid the $300 commutation fee several times over, but for some reason his sons joined the great national conflict. Perhaps Susannah avoided the symbol of community union because of her grief and the uncertain status the mother of a veteran would carry within a nonresistant ethnoreligious group.

Three couples from Sharon Township went separate ways in their communion service: John J. and Sarah Plank, Samuel and Ann Hostetler, and John and Sarah Petersheim. With the exception of Henry Hostetler, age 60 in 1865, all the male household heads were between 26 and 45 years old. Three of Henry Hostetler's adult male children attended communion, and other cases in which children did not follow parents appear in the record. Three children of John and Magdalene Rhodes took communion even though both their parents refused; and three children, one a daughter, of Joseph P. and Sarah Miller did not attend even though both their parents participated in communion. Both gender and generation divided partakers and nonpartakers.

There are few extant materials written by nineteenth-century Amish women. No document has yet been discovered, for example, in which the women who stayed away from communion explained what they were doing. Silence is a traditional Amish demeanor, especially in church conflicts. A first-person letter or article in which an Amish woman explains her nonparticipation in communion is virtually unthinkable.[45]

A young Amish woman in McLean County, Illinois, kept a diary from 1871 to 1876.[46] Mahala Yoder found time to write because, as an invalid, she could not participate in most household work. Yoder recorded many astute observations of her Amish-Mennonite family and their busy farm, and described the activities of her father, stepmother, and siblings. On 12 May 1871, her stepmother, Catherine Stuckey Fry Yoder, took butter and eggs to market and

Table 3.1. Comparison of 1865 Amish Communion Partakers, Nonpartakers, and Divided Couples in the 1860 Population and Agricultural Censuses

1865 Communion	*Partakers*	*Nonpartakers*	*Divided*	*All Amish*
Number of households	8	14	10	40
Number of farms	7	11	7	29
Age of household head	41.5	42.2	44.8	41.0
Value of real estate	$4,100	$2,154	$2,207	$2,458
Value of personal wealth	$621	$704	$439	$527
Number of children	5.6	4.6	3.8	4.3
Total acres	225.7	144.8	202.9	172.9
Value of farm	$3,357	$2,094	$3,071	$2,567
Value of implements	$101	$96	$73	$88
Value of livestock	$510	$449	$549	$468
Hay (tons)	25.7	27.4	28.6	25.5
Number of heads of cattle	8.4	6.6	11.0	7.8
Butter (lbs.)	393	270	293	296
Number of swine	40.6	31.1	32.1	31.7
Corn (bu.)	1,186	1,068	957	1,005
Wheat (bu.)	127.3	140.5	185.0	146.6
Value of total farm production	$1,825	$1,635	$1,661	$1,593

promised to buy the girls new hats with the money. Mahala's father, Elias, did the field work, and Catherine and the girls took care of the house and garden. Mahala noted several conflicts between her father and her brother Isaac over dancing. Isaac thought dancing should be allowed if properly conducted, but "Father thinks it never is indulged in properly" (15 January 1873). Mahala recalled "cross words with Pa" on 17 June 1871, but seldom mentions him directly in her diary. Elias Yoder enforced Amish-Mennonite rules as a housefather, but from a relatively distant position in the family.

Nothing similar to Mahala Yoder's diary has come to light among the Amish in Johnson County, Iowa. Indirect access through quantitative methods must suffice to examine why some members refused communion in 1865. Tables 3.1 and 3.2 depict household social characteristics of communion partakers, nonpartakers, and divided couples identified in the 1860 and 1870 federal population and agricultural censuses. The tables reveal several interesting points of difference and similarity among the three kinds of household response to the question of whether to participate in the 1865 communion services.

Table 3.2. Comparison of 1865 Amish Communion Partakers, Nonpartakers, and Divided Couples in the 1870 Population and Agricultural Censuses

1865 Communion	*Partakers*	*Nonpartakers*	*Divided*	*All Amish*
Number of households	26	22	12	85
Number of farms	22	20	10	75
Age of household head	42.9	40.1	44.3	40.5
Value of real estate	$5,612	$6,255	$6,508	$5,652
Value of personal wealth	$1,285	$1,332	$1,667	$1,301
Number of children	2.9	4.5	4.9	3.8
Total acres	167.1	191.2	208.5	169.0
Value of farm	$5,859	$5,290	$5,530	$5,249
Value of implements	$402	$300	$335	$320
Value of livestock	$1,075	$1,095	$1,235	$1,051
Hay (tons)	27.1	29.5	26.9	25.4
Number of heads of cattle	11.6	11.6	12.9	10.4
Butter (lbs.)	452	470	500	425
Number of swine	30.9	22.4	36.7	31.2
Corn (bu.)	1,277	1,395	1,480	1,322
Wheat (bu.)	306	308	293	281
Value of total farm production	$2,420	$2,599	$2,657	$2,384

Eight households where both spouses took communion, fourteen where both refused, and ten where husbands participated and wives refused have been identified in the 1860 census (Table 3.1). The mean ages of participants, nonparticipants, and divided households are roughly similar, although household heads in divided families were slightly older. Partakers had the most children, 5.6 per household, while divided households show only 3.8 children. Value of real estate owned shows a difference of $4,100 for participants and $2,154 for nonparticipants, and divided households are closer to the nonparticipants at $2,207. Acres of land owned and value of farm show a similar pattern of great difference between participant and nonparticipant households, with divided households being similar to participant. Partakers owned more implements than nonpartakers, $101 versus $96, similar to the relative size of farms. Partakers may have been somewhat more open to use of new agricultural technology, although the divided households owned even fewer implements, only $73. Divided households show larger figures for value of livestock and tons of hay produced, more in line with traditional Amish agricultural practices emphasizing animal husbandry and manure fertilizer. The greater wheat crops grown by divided and nonparticipant households may show a slightly greater orientation to production for the marketplace.

Production of butter shows an interesting trend, a difference of 393 pounds for partakers, 270 pounds for nonpartakers, and 293 pounds for divided households. The smaller figures may reveal some questioning by Amish farm women of their place in agricultural production, corroborating the existence of contested gender roles in the refusal of more women than men to take communion.[47] In addition, nonpartaker households owned more personal wealth, but the value of real estate owned was smaller, perhaps revealing greater personal consumption and the purchase of more items for the farm house. Household decoration and personal consumption were high on the list of proscribed luxuries in Amish church disciplines, so the higher figure for personal wealth may well indicate a component of female resistance to lifestyle restrictions.

Nonpartakers of communion in 1865 in comparison with partakers were younger, more oriented to new technology and agricultural production for cash markets, but owned less land and spent more on personal consumption. Other differences are visible but do not seem as significant, and there are many similarities. The lower production of butter and the disparity between participation by men and women, especially the ten divided husbands and wives found in the 1860 census, suggest a gender fault line within the Amish community.

The fundamental issue may have been transmitting Amish household structures to the next generation. In 1860 nonpartakers owned less landed wealth and more personal wealth; household heads were slightly older, produced more hay and wheat, owned less value in agricultural implements, and produced less butter. They were more oriented to personal consumption, new technology, and less involvement by women in agricultural production. The younger households of nonpartakers were not in as secure an economic position in 1860 as the older and wealthier partaker farm households. Principles of personal frugality, balancing production for home and marketplace, cautious adoption of new technology, and paternal household leadership were imperfectly transferred. The prescriptions of Amish leaders for ethnoreligious recreation in new settlements that Jacob Swartzendruber helped to formulate and defend, such as careful control over household formation and paternal administration of family and church, came into question in the 1865 refusals to take communion.

By contrast, data from the 1870 census (Table 3.2) reveal a more successful transfer of values from older to younger generation. By 1870 those who refused communion in 1865 actually owned more value in real estate and nearly as much farm land. Those households that were divided in 1865 owned the most real estate and the largest farms in 1870, and women in those households produced by far the most children and even the most butter. The greater wealth of all three groups compared with all Amish households in 1870 likely indicates a large number of new households since 1865 because of migration from eastern Amish communities. The most significant variable in an analysis of the 1870 census is number of children, with nonpartakers producing almost two more children per household than partakers, despite being more similar in age than the 1860 census figures. Partakers continue to own more implements in 1870. Nonpartakers owned more implements, which may indicate greater orientation to new technology and cash production within the mainstream Amish community rather than using the kin network for paid farm labor. Value of farm is higher for partakers, likely due to more developed buildings and fields. Partaker households produced less butter, but the disparity was growing smaller.

Other disparities revealed in the 1860 census had been equalized by 1870. Personal wealth was virtually identical in 1870 between partakers and nonpartakers, $1,285 and $1,332; while divided couples owned $1,667, perhaps a vestige of female resistance to limitations on consumption and domestic embellishment. Nonpartakers actually owned a smaller value of agricultural implements in 1870, $300 versus $402, with divided households falling between at $335. Those who had been in harmony with the Amish community in 1865 were investing in new equipment and paying more for agricultural wage labor in 1870, indicating a mainstream communal shift toward capitalist production. Nonpartaker households produced more butter than partaker households, a reversal of 1860; and divided households produced the most butter, revealing a recovery of traditional patterns of female labor.

Comparison of the 1860 and 1870 censuses substantiates the impression of an Amish community that succeeded in resolving conflicts capable of destroying it. Transfer of wealth and the recreation of the Amish farming and household system by a new generation had been accomplished. The generational and domestic crises of 1865 seem to have dissipated by 1870, producing a community in greater harmony with itself.

But this harmony was not without personal and communal costs. Many Amish families who could not reconcile themselves to the directions the Johnson County Amish had taken chose to move to other Amish communities, and Melvin Gingerich reported faint echoes of hostility resulting from the bitter disputes of the 1860s among families as late as the 1930s. Preacher Joseph Keim and Deacon John Mishler moved to other Amish communities. Mishler was "silenced" (he could no longer serve as deacon) on 6 March 1864 and moved to Polk County, Iowa, in 1868. Keim moved to Douglas County, Illinois, where he became the first Amish bishop in that state.[48]

Abner Yoder, ally of Jacob Swartzendruber, moved to Iowa in the spring of 1866 from Somerset County, Pennsylvania. A communion service in 1868 showed more harmony, at least in the Deer Creek congregation, where eighty-eight observed the ceremony and only nine refrained, although the Sharon Township congregation saw sixty-four communicants and fifty-seven who refused.[49] Jacob Swartzendruber died on 5 June 1868, completing the transition to a new set of community leaders.

There may have been an emphasis in the Iowa Amish community, led in its early years by Bishop Jacob Swartzendruber, toward founding as many strong households as possible, with an accent on male household heads safeguarding the Amish way of life. Raising believing, obedient children, after all, was considered a prerequisite to holding the office of bishop; and "keeping house" was a central metaphor for maintaining congregational discipline.[50] Swartzendruber did put pressure on his family to help "keep house" in the congregation, a peculiarly feminine idiom in English, but a phrase that implies "rule the household" in German.[51]

The effort to suppress bundling may have been an especially sensitive issue. Courtship practices such as bundling and night courting likely offered mothers and daughters greater control over the process of mate selection in eighteenth- and nineteenth-century America.[52] Young women determined access to the bundling bed. An anti-bundling song recorded by Henry Reed Stiles makes the complicity of mothers and daughters quite explicit:

> Some maidens say, if through the nation,
> Bundling should quite go out of fashion,
> Courtship would lose its sweets; and they
> Could have no fun till wedding day.
> It shant be so, they rage and storm,
> And country girls in clusters swarm,
> And fly and buz [*sic*], like angry bees,
> And vow they'll bundle when they please.
> Some mothers too, will plead their cause,

And give their daughters great applause,
And tell them, 'tis no sin nor shame,
For we, your mothers, did the same.[53]

When Jacob Swartzendruber attempted to strengthen household authority and create a structure of preservationist patriarchy—a stable standard of female subordination to male household heads on behalf of the community—it seems logical to conclude that renewed paternal authority threatened female autonomy. Gendered authority models faced resistance during the nineteenth century, but were also strongly defended as an essential levée to restrain the rising flood tide of American individualism.

Clarifying lines of household authority before and during the Civil War prepared the Amish community in Johnson County to survive the conflict and to expand spatially and numerically. However, wartime conditions also challenged the traditional Amish separation from human government.

How does it become us that we do not want to enter into war where thousands of men are slaughtered who died for our freedom, and we want to stay at home and live well and carry on unnecessary weddings[?] Do we think that God will let this go unpunished?

—Jacob Swartzendruber, 1865

Chapter 4

Struggles for Territory

Wars change societies and economies. How much and in what direction are matters of debate when it comes to the American Civil War. Interpretations range from an earth-shattering triumph of capitalism and the centralized American state, to hardly any change at all, since the larger trends of world history would have occurred anyway. Charles and Mary Beard, followed by Louis Hacker, argued the revolutionary case in their 1927 and 1940 interpretations of American history. In the Beard-Hacker view, the Civil War resulted in wartime demand for supplies that American manufacturers could not meet without mechanizing production, leading to an American industrial revolution; wartime inflation provided capitalization for industrialists; and the federal government's deficit financing of the war effort further enhanced industrialization. Revisionists, summarized by Patrick O'Brien in his 1988 book, *The Economic Effects of the American Civil War*, denied any industrial surge resulting from the war. If anything, the war retarded American industrial growth because of extensive destruction in the South and wasteful wartime production in the

North. At the least, the Civil War had only a minimal effect on the nineteenth-century American economy when viewed as a whole.[1]

One area of agreement is the increasing dominance of the federal government in the American capitalist state as a result of both North and South mobilizing for war. Washington extended its power and authority during and after the war.[2] The social impact of the war on gender and race relations, demographics, and even on sexuality, was just as extensive.[3] What impact might the war have had on a small, isolated Amish community in Iowa, far distant from battlefields and the sound of cannon?

Northern farmers adopted new agricultural implements and machinery as a result of labor shortages and found ready markets for their commodities. Machinery and markets likely encouraged specialization and reliance on the market economy. Farmers often used wartime profits to pay debts and improve farms with fences and buildings. Improvements and market demand for foodstuffs doubled land values in Iowa during the Civil War decade, from $12 in 1860 to $25 in 1870.[4] However, the benefits of wartime agricultural prosperity did not fall equally on all Iowa farmers. The Amish in Iowa used the decade to strengthen their separation from the American state through incorporation into the American economy. Land was the key.

Amish leaders were keenly aware of the American sectional conflict and its potential impact on their community. War became part of Amish consciousness, while conflicts within the Amish community sometimes took on the appearance of warfare. During the night of 4 June 1858, three years before the war came, Bishop Jacob Swartzendruber dreamed of two enemy forces mobilizing against one another, preparing for a gruesome war. He was supposed to be on one side, and indeed wanted to be, but felt much anxiety and distress. He surveyed the other side about a quarter-mile away and felt they were all strangers to him, and yet someone appeared to be from his church. Swartzendruber retreated from danger but heard an incredible noise, and people started shooting and swinging weapons and killing each other. He observed the battle from farther and farther away until finally an entire army fell to earth simultaneously and stood up again very slowly. It still seemed as though he knew some of the men, and he thought he recognized David Miller and his own son, Frederick, not far from him, but he could not identify other acquaintances. Then he awoke and could not sleep again that night.[5]

After scribbling his dream on a scrap of paper, Swartzendruber reflected further that he had dreamed of enemies in years past, and each time he had confronted cases of sin in the congregation. For the aging bishop to conceptualize intracommunity conflict in terms of warfare went against the most strongly held beliefs in Amish tradition. He associated internal disagreement with problems beyond his community's direct control.

Three strands of strife during the 1860s plaited together and separated the Amish from the other ethnic communities of Washington and Sharon townships. First, struggles within the Amish community disrupted communal harmony and brought a reconfiguration of the group's repertoire of community. The dislocations of the Civil War intensified the struggles of the Amish community with itself and with surrounding cultures. Second, the American Civil War disrupted rural life directly and indirectly, as a number of families saw sons serve in the Union Army. Some never returned; many moved elsewhere after the war. Finally, as agricultural markets shifted to accommodate the Union war effort, the Amish and neighboring ethnic groups competed for land to establish different systems of agricultural production and for social space to build family and community systems. Civil War military service, relative economic position before and after the war, and continuity of land ownership all reveal the social stress faced by the rural ethnic communities of Washington and Sharon townships. However, by the end of the decade, the Amish community in Johnson County had placed itself in a stronger position in relation to civil society and had resolved, or at least muted, its internal conflicts.

The Amish Nonstatist Repertoire

The Amish relationship to the American Civil War was mediated by the Anabaptist conception of the state.[6] The fundamental stance was one of alienation and suspicion, rooted in the German Peasants' War and the failure of Reformation leaders to dissociate themselves from civil government. The Anabaptists who agreed upon the Schleitheim Confession of Faith (1527) asserted that "the sword is an ordering of God outside the perfection of Christ." Within "the perfection of Christ"—that is, within the church—excommunication provided the only means of dealing with an offender. Christians could take no part in the violence of state-sanctioned punishment or warfare (article 6). The Dordrecht Confession of Faith (1632) taught against the use of violence for defense and again advocated only excommunication (the ban) and avoidance (shunning) without reference to punishment meted out by civil government (articles 13–17). Anabaptists managed to keep some distance from the early modern state even though they were not economically dissimilar from their neighbors.[7] The ability to engage societies economically while dissociating politically is part of the Amish repertoire of community. However, wars challenge the Amish passion for autonomy from civil society. The nation-state makes demands on its citizens for soldiers, finances, and personal sacrifice. The Amish are seldom certain that they want to be citizens whenever citizenship requires military service, a development associated with so-called democratic revolutions in North America and France. They prefer personal loyalty to individual rulers rather than patriotic attachment to a government.

The relatively clear strategy of nonengagement by Anabaptists and their descendants in Europe was tested first in the more tolerant political climate of William Penn's English colony in the New World. Mennonites and Amish were expert farmers and prospered in Pennsylvania, helping to make it the granary of the American colonies. They were exempt from oaths and military service, experienced wide-ranging religious fellowship with the various denominations of provincial Pennsylvania, and were active in politics while supporting the Quaker party.[8] Mennonite and Amish votes helped the Quakers maintain a minority government. Richard MacMaster estimated a Mennonite population of 10,000 to 15,000 during the American Revolution; the peace sects together made up about one quarter of the total population in Pennsylvania. The proportion was much smaller in other colonies.[9]

The French and Indian War of 1754 to 1763 began to fray the idyllic Amish and Mennonite existence in America. Along with other frontier farmers, Mennonites suffered attack and destruction from Indian war parties. Benjamin Franklin visited Lancaster County in April of 1755 and printed a bilingual handbill calling for horses and wagons for General Braddock's expedition in Western Pennsylvania. Mennonites provided as many as one-fifth of the wagons in Braddock's supply train, although they refused to carry guns or ammunition.[10] Mennonites also responded with extensive relief for frontier refugees and offered substantial financial support to the Quaker effort to mediate the conflict, the "Friendly Association for Regaining and Preserving Peace with the Indians by Pacific Measures."[11] Perhaps more to the point, Mennonites prepared for hard times and suffering by reprinting the Anabaptist martyr hymnal, the *Ausbund,* in 1742, 1751, and 1767; and by printing in 1748 a German translation of the 1660 Anabaptist martyrology, *Martyrs Mirror,* reputedly the largest book printed in colonial America.[12]

After Lexington and Concord in April 1775, patriots in each colony agreed to form voluntary military companies, or "Associations," and papers were printed for men of military age to sign. Mennonites and Amish generally refused to sign, since it involved military service. Pressure built on the civil authorities to force non-Associators to contribute to the cause. The Lancaster County Committee proposed a voluntary contribution of 3 pounds 10 shillings, and representatives of the peace churches agreed to "contribute towards the Support of the Rights & Liberties of their Country." In the only Lancaster township represented by extant records, fully five-sixths of peace church members contributed, and the county committee interpreted their support as the equivalent of mustering. Other Pennsylvania counties and other colonies repeated this course of action, but still pressure built for more direct penalties on conscientious objectors.[13]

Mennonites and Dunkards together sent "a short and sincere Declaration" to the Pennsylvania Assembly in November 1775, stating their position as pacifist Christians. The petition read, in part:

> The Advice to those who do not find Freedom of Conscience to take up arms, that they ought to be helpfull to those who are in Need and distressed Circumstances, we receive with Chearfulness towards all Men of what Station they may be—it being our Principle to feed the Hungry and give the Thirsty Drink;—we have dedicated ourselves to serve all Men in every Thing that can be helpful to the Preservation of Men's Lives, but we find no Freedom in giving, or doing, or assisting in any Thing by which Men's Lives are destroyed or hurt. . . . We are not at Liberty in Conscience to take up Arms to conquer our Enemies.[14]

On 13 June 1777, the Pennsylvania Assembly acted to require an Oath of Allegiance from all white males over age 18. The act declared that allegiance and protection are reciprocal and that "those who will not bear the former are not (nor ought not) to be entitled to the benefits of the latter."[15] Nonjurors, those who refused to swear the oath and renounce the king, were barred from voting, holding office, serving on juries, suing for debt, or transferring real estate by deed. Even more rights were denied nonjurors when the Assembly voted on 1 April 1778 to strengthen the penalties for refusing to swear the oath. Almost all rights of citizenship were lost, with double taxation besides, and the law was vigorously enforced in some localities as Mennonites were imprisoned and had their property confiscated and sold. Still, most Mennonites refused the oath. As historian Richard MacMaster summarized the story, "After 1777, Mennonites no longer participated in the political life of Pennsylvania."[16]

The Amish historian Christian Z. Mast recorded a tradition of Amish imprisonment at Reading, Pennsylvania, during the conflict, as well as the story of one "Strong" Jacob Yoder, who consulted with two American officers sent by General Washington during the Valley Forge winter concerning British projects.[17] Historian James O. Lehman has found that Mennonites in Maryland tended to be more willing to pay military taxes and support the patriots. Along with the Dunkards, they presented a petition requesting the privilege of "giving Produce instead of Cash for their fines." Lehman also discussed the case of Mennonite Henry Newcomer, who became involved in a Loyalist plot to release British prisoners from several colonial prisons. Newcomer was sentenced to death, but the judgment was later commuted.[18]

The Test Acts were modified on 5 December 1778, when provision was made for restoration of rights if nonjurors took the oath, and penalties were limited to double taxes and the loss of voting and office-holding rights. However, the Test Acts were not completely repealed until 1789, when civil rights were restored to the peace churches in Pennsylvania. Many Mennonites migrated to Virginia and Canada during the 1780s.[19]

Mennonite and Amish experience during the American Civil War was similarly traumatic.[20] Maintaining social separation from the American government and from Iowa neighbors, and maintaining internal discipline on an essentially voluntary basis, proved extremely difficult during the 1860s, when civil conflict was the order of the day throughout the young American state. At times the lines between church and state blurred in the Civil War years. Ironically, Amish and Mennonite votes in Lancaster County, Pennsylvania, helped keep radical Republican firebrand Thaddeus Stevens in the House of Representatives.[21]

Amish leaders fought a desperate battle to keep the state at bay. The 1863 Amish Ministers' Meeting ruled against enrolling in the militia or serving as a teamster. The ministers also forbade office holding, jury duty, and generally any function that involved coercion in military or criminal adjudication.[22] The Somerset County, Pennsylvania, settlement broke up because so many Amish youths joined the military forces. The last resident Amish bishop, Abner Yoder, moved to Johnson County, Iowa, in 1866.[23] Yoder signed the 1865 discipline drawn up by conservatives in Holmes County, Ohio, as a representative of the Glades Congregation in Somerset County. A Mennonite congregation in Fairfield County, Ohio, disappeared because most members supported the war and were willing to perform military service.[24]

Mennonites and Amish in Virginia faced pressure to join Confederate armies. Peter Hartman recalled that most Mennonites favored the Union instead of secession. Several congregations helped drafted young men pay the $500 Confederate commutation fee.[25] Some Mennonite youths entered the ranks, then tried to escape and landed in a Richmond prison. Others remained in the army but refused to fire their weapons in battle. Christian Good and a few comrades in the 146th Virginia Militia became known as "the boys whose guns are out of order." When Good and his brother Daniel deserted, their $500 fines in return for discharge were paid by their congregation, and they worked for two years to repay their debts. A few young men escaped to the North and found work among relatives. Samuel A. Rhodes kept a diary of his adventures while first hiding in Harrisonburg, Virginia, and then escaping to the North in 1862. His movements ranged from Pennsylvania to Iowa, until he died of consumption in 1864.[26]

Several young unmarried Amish men from Wayne County, Ohio, volunteered for the Union army so that the married men could stay home with their wives and families. They were also opposed to slavery and "wanted to help extinguish this cruelty."[27] On the other hand, an article in the Holmes County *Farmer* in 1862, signed only "S.," took a more traditional Amish stance toward the war. S. cited articles 13 and 14 of the 1632 Dordrecht Confession of Faith on government and warfare. He explained that his people regarded it their religious duty to obey the government except when contrary to the Gospel, and killing met this criterion. He justified the presence of very few volunteers from the two townships where Amish and Mennonites were in the majority because they could not violate their consciences. However, anything the government required for fines or financial penalties because of conscientious objection "will be carefully and honestly paid."[28]

John M. Brenneman, writing in 1863, argued in favor of paying the $300 Union commutation fee. In Brenneman's opinion, Mennonites ought to be thankful to God and the government that provisions exist for Defenseless Christians, "that they have always been permitted to pay an equivalent in money; and in reason we could ask no more."[29] But above all, Mennonites should be separate from the unclean world. Brenneman drafted a petition to President Lincoln in 1862 in which he specifically requested that Mennonites be allowed to "pay a fine when drafted" instead of serving in the military. He allowed the possibility of an extra tax as well, and expressed the traditional Mennonite willingness to suffer at the hand of the state, if necessary, rather than violate their consciences.[30]

Reformed Mennonite Daniel Musser used the distinction between Old and New Testaments to argue against any involvement in worldly governments by true Christians. Regarding the Civil War draft, he argued against inducing volunteers and buying substitutes, but in favor of paying the commutation fee and war taxes. About substitutes, he argued, "If it is wrong for me to go, it is wrong to pay another to go for me."[31] Paying the commutation fee and war taxes is covered by the biblical injunction to pay tribute, meaning the coercive power of the state; however, paying for substitutes is voluntary. Musser continued, "They that vote for officers in the government, and use its power and authority to protect their rights and property, or appeal to law for justice, and yet refuse to defend the government in time of need, are neither faithful to the kingdom of Christ or that of this world."[32]

Musser argued for a version of Christian anarchy:

> God had given man no government before the fall. He needed none. Because he gave it to him after the fall is no proof that God had changed. Man had changed, but God had not. No more is it any proof that He changed, because He gave man a new law, in his new relation under the Gospel. That which made government necessary was taken away, and a self-governing principle reinstated, and they needed no government more.[33]

Amish and Mennonite leaders traditionally experienced war as a time to reaffirm social distance and alternative values.

Leo Tolstoy quoted Daniel Musser in his statement of nonresistant ethics, *The Kingdom of God Is Within You,* completed in 1893. Although Tolstoy did not accept the extreme sectarian separatism inherent in Musser's call for refusing participation in any institution of government, he did summon all Christians to confront the dilemma of faith and violence.[34] The Amish in Iowa found it necessary to face this same issue of Christian pacifism during the era of universal liability to military service. A county history listed several Amish draftees and alternates in the October 1864 draft. One of the alternates was J. Swartzendruber, perhaps Jacob J., son of Joseph J. Swartzendruber and grandson of Jacob.[35] The Amish draftees must have paid commutation fees, judging by the agony expressed by their community leader.

Jacob Swartzendruber wrote to the 1865 *Diener Versammlung* meeting in Wayne County, Ohio, and reflected with anguish on his people's part in the recently concluded American Civil War. Viewing the carnage of many battlefields in his mind's eye, the aging Amish bishop wondered whether his congregation could still consider itself nonresistant, since many members had willingly paid the $300 commutation fee to avoid being drafted and had even persuaded other members to pay this "protection money." At least one former and future member of his congregation, Samuel D. Guengerich, cheerfully paid the $300 in Pennsylvania in 1865.[36] Swartzendruber argued that the Amish "voluntarily paid to seek the friendship of the world because of fear that we might suffer loss of our temporal goods." Going even further, Swartzendruber wrote:

> How does it become us that we do not want to enter into war where thousands of men are slaughtered who died for our freedom, and we want to stay at home and live well and carry on unnecessary weddings[?] Do we think that God will let this go unpunished? Let us just take a view over the battlefields where the crippled men lie and cry or the dead lie in various ways, bodies broken. I believe that this dreadful thing is not to be described, but we want to stay at home and have a vain and easy life.[37]

The dilemma of possessing wealth and letting others protect it arose in Lancaster County newspapers early in the war. Local writers criticized the pacifist sects in their midst and advocated heavy taxes and fines on the "rich but close-fisted farmers" to ensure they "pay their share to the support of sustaining this righteous war."[38]

Swartzendruber explicitly rejected the buying of substitutes for military service. He traced the problem to political involvement and asked, "Who will be responsible for the much blood which has been shed in the war and finally the President's blood?" Instead of voting and participating in partisan politics, Swartzendruber advocated the more traditional Amish stance of separation, writing, "Our people should all keep themselves apart from all party matters in political things." He concluded, "We should be strangers in the world . . . and let the world rule itself."[39] Swartzendruber dreamed of a peaceful Amish society in Iowa, away from the more compromised communities of western Pennsylvania and Maryland. Most Amish young men in Iowa did not serve in the Union military, and their experiences of the Civil War period differed drastically from that of their neighbors.

Table 4.1. Civil War and Non–Civil War Households in 1860

	Without Soldier	*With Soldier*	*Not Applicable*[a]
Households	185	31	17
Farms	109	23	4

Source: History of Johnson County, Iowa . . . (Iowa City, Iowa: 1883); U.S. Population Census, 1860.
[a]No male between ages 18–45 in household.

Table 4.2. Civil War and Non–Civil War Households in 1870

	Without Soldier	*With Soldier*
Households	322	27
Farms	253	23

Source: History of Johnson County, Iowa . . . (Iowa City, Iowa: 1883); U.S. Population Census, 1870.

Amish Soldiers Fight the Rule

Civil War military service affected a large number of families in Washington and Sharon townships. Fifty-two young men who served in the Union Army during the Civil War have been identified in the 1860 and 1870 federal population censuses. Tables 4.1 and 4.2 show the total number of households that sent at least one soldier to military service. Thirty-eight individual soldiers in thirty-one households appear in the 1860 census, and twenty-seven soldiers in twenty-three households in 1870. Table 4.3 names twelve soldiers who appear in both the 1860 and 1870 manuscript censuses, while twenty-five appear in 1860 and not in 1870, and fourteen in 1870 but not 1860. Table 4.4 identifies the twenty-six soldiers who served in one regiment formed in Iowa City, the Twenty-second Iowa Voluntary Infantry. Another twenty-six soldiers served in other infantry and cavalry units.[40]

The 22nd Iowa organized during the summer of 1862 and mustered at Camp Pope just southeast of Iowa City on September 9. The regiment consisted of seven companies from Johnson County (A, B, F, G, H, I, K), and one

Table 4.3. Civil War Soldiers in the 1860 and 1870 Federal Population Censuses from Washington and Sharon Townships, Johnson County, Iowa

Name	*Regiment and Company*	*1860*	*1870*
Andrew Armstrong	47th Iowa Infantry, Co G	X	
Patrick Bevins	6th Iowa Cavalry, Co M	X	
Isaiah F. Bair	22nd Iowa Infantry, Co K		X
James L. Beck	13th Iowa Infantry, Co K	X	X
James Bonham	22nd Iowa Infantry, Co I		X
Leander Bonham	22nd Iowa Infantry, Co I	X	
Patrick Burns	6th Iowa Cavalry, Co M	X	
Thomas Chandler	24th Iowa Infantry, Co D		X
Elliott Cross	10th Iowa Infantry, Co H	X	X
George T. Davis	127th Illinois Infantry, Co H	X	
Thomas D. Davis	22nd Iowa Infantry, Co I	X	
Amos Fry	22nd Iowa Infantry, Co F	X	X
Jacob A. Fry	22nd Iowa Infantry, Co K	X	X
Lysander Fry	22nd Iowa Infantry, Co F	X	
Marshall Fry	22nd Iowa Infantry, Co I	X	
Theodore Fry	47th Iowa Infantry, Co G	X	X
Loren E. Grout	24th Iowa Infantry, Co D		X
John C. Guffin	22nd Iowa Infantry, Co I	X	X
Ernest Haberstroh	22nd Iowa Infantry, Co B		X
William Haines	22nd Iowa Infantry, Co K	X	X
William C. Haynes	22nd Iowa Infantry, Co I	X	
Brodas Haynes	47th Iowa Infantry, Co G	X	
Edward Harris	22nd Iowa Infantry, Co K		X
Pleasanton Harris	14th Iowa Infantry, Co F		X
Marshall J. Hartman	2nd Iowa Cavalry, Co H	X	X
Stewart Hartman	13th Iowa Infantry, Co K	X	X
Christian Hochstetler	19th US Infantry, Co G	X	
Emanuel Hochstetler	22nd Iowa Infantry, Co G	X	
Joshua Hughes	22nd Iowa Infantry, Co A	X	
Sampson Hughes	7th Iowa Cavalry, Co L; and 41st Iowa Infantry, Co B	X	
John T. Jones	8th Iowa Cavalry, Co K	X	
William W. Jones	41st Iowa Infantry, Co A	X	
Hanry Montgomery	22nd Iowa Infantry, Co F	X	
James Montgomery	22nd Iowa Infantry, Co F	X	
Thomas Morgan	1st Iowa Cavalry, Co F	X	

Table 4.3. Continued

Name	*Regiment and Company*	*1860*	*1870*
John Myers	15th Illinois Cavalry, Co G		X
John Oldaker	22nd Iowa Infantry, Co K	X	
William Oldaker	22nd Iowa Infantry, Co K	X	
Thomas Prall	22nd Iowa Infantry, Co G		X
John Roberts	10th Iowa Infantry, Music		X
John Selby	22nd Iowa Infantry, Co K	X	X
James F. Shaff	22nd Iowa Infantry, Co G		X
Phillip E. Shaver	1st Iowa Cavalry, Co F	X	X
Owen Slater	6th Iowa Cavalry, Co M	X	X
John Spencer	24th Iowa Infantry, Co D	X	
Garrett Stephens	22nd Iowa Infantry, Co G		X
Conrad Strickler	22nd Iowa Infantry, Co F		X
Simon Taylor	22nd Iowa Infantry, Co K	X	X
William H. Warner	6th Iowa Cavalry, Co M		X
George Williamson	30th Iowa Infantry, Co K	X	
Thomas A. Williamson	1st Iowa Cavalry, Co F	X	
Michael Yoakam	22nd Iowa Infantry, Co K	X	

Source: History of Johnson County, Iowa . . . (Iowa City, Iowa: 1883); U.S. Population Censuses, 1860, 1870.

each from Jasper, Monroe, and Wapello counties. The unit fought in the battles of Vicksburg, Port Gibson, Jackson, Black River Bridge, Cedar Creek, Fisher's Hill, Winchester, and Champion Hill and mustered out at Savannah, Georgia, on 20 July 1865.[41]

A unit forming in Johnson County increased the pressure on all the boys, including Amish youths, to join the regiment with their friends and neighbors. It seems remarkable that only one Amish youth from either township joined the war effort. Emmanuel Hochstetler, age 28, son of Henry and Susannah Livengood Hochstetler, enlisted on August 5 despite his Amish connections. He received a bounty of $25 and a $2 premium for enlisting. His brother, Christian Hochstetler, served in a national unit formed in Pennsylvania, the 19th U.S. Infantry, Company G. Emmanuel was the eldest son of Henry and Susannah Livengood Hochstetler. Why his father, a wealthy farmer, did not find a substitute or pay a bounty is unknown; perhaps five boys between 20 and 26 in 1860 would have depleted even his financial resources. In addition, there was no military draft in Iowa until 1864, and the draft was limited to certain counties. However, the draft often served as a threat and motivation to enlist.

Jacob D. Guengerich wrote to his brother, Samuel D., in Pennsylvania and reported the situation in Washington County. "One hears nothing about the war," he mused, "and Copperheadism [sympathy with the South] is I believe all settled again." However, three months later Noah Yoder wrote to Samuel D. and confirmed that the draft system was in place: "They have enrolled all the people about here and have every thing ready to go to work in the city but then have no call yet." Yoder stated that there were also soldiers in Iowa City "to keep the Copper heads down."[42] With rumors flying and Copperheads cropping up, Emmanuel Hochstetler likely volunteered on his own. Young men from the most prominent families in the two townships joined the 22nd, including James and Leander Bonham, sons of Smiley Bonham, the speaker of the Iowa House of Representatives, and four members of the wealthy Fry kin network.

Regimental histories and memoirs recount the patriotic fervor of enlistment and drill with wooden bayonets at Camp Pope. While the new regiment drew uniforms and real guns, thousands of visitors turned out every day "to witness the glitter and pomp of military maneuvers."[43] When the 22nd Iowa left Iowa City in a variety of boxcars, cattle cars, and open coal cars headed for Davenport, hundreds of people saw them off, although they departed after midnight on September 14. The laborious journey to Rolla, Missouri, alternated between train and riverboat travel until the new soldiers arrived on the 18th at Benton Barracks in St. Louis. On September 22 they traveled by train to Rolla, where the unit guarded trains and commissary stores, and carried out post duties for several months. While in winter quarters, bored with routine duties, Colonel William Stone set up a snowball fight for the troops after a snowstorm. He divided the regiment into two groups, set the regimental flag between them, and let the troops determine who would have the flag. Stone had been captured at Shiloh as colonel of the 3rd Iowa, then moved to the 22nd after his release.

While stationed at Rolla, Emmanuel Hochstetler wrote to his brother-in-law, Peter Swartzendruber, on November 29, with news from his military unit. Emmanuel complained of a sore eye, but he also boasted that Company G of the 22nd Iowa Infantry "will stand up to the mark all the time." He had received a letter from his brother John and one from Peter the previous day. Hochstetler sent news home about a number of non-Amish boys from Washington Township. Jacob Fry and "Prise" [John] Selby both "got the sore eyes" and were

Table 4.4. Civil War Soldiers in the 22nd Iowa Volunteer Infantry from Washington and Sharon Townships, Johnson County, Iowa

Name	*Born*	*1860*	*Civil War*	*1870*	*1887*	*1903*	*1914*
Company A							
Joshua B. Hughes	Pa.	X	Wounded at Cedar Creek and Winchester		Akron, Iowa	Taney, Id.	Roy, Wash.
Company B							
Patrick H. Burns	Ireland	X			Belknap, Iowa	Belknap, Iowa	(dec'd)
Ernest Haberstroh	Germany		Wounded at Vicksburg	X	Denver, Colo.	—	—
Company F							
Amos Fry	Iowa	X		X	Frank Pierce, Iowa	—	—
Lysander Fry	Ohio	X	Died of disease				
James Montgomery	Pa.	X			Tipton, Calif.	—	—
Henry Montgomery	Pa.	X			—	—	—
Conrad Strickler	Pa.		Wounded at Winchester	X	Emerson, Iowa	Emerson, Iowa	(dec'd)
Company G							
Emanuel Hochstetler	Pa.	X	Died of wounds, Vicksburg				
Thomas Prall	Pa.			X	Carlisle, Iowa	—	—
James F. Shaff	Canada			X	Alice, Mo.	Filley, Mo.	El Dorado Springs, Mo.
Garrett Stephens	N.Y.			X	McCook, Neb.	—	(dec'd—Kans.)

Company I							
James M. Bonham	Iowa		Wounded at Cedar Creek	X	Frank Pierce, Iowa	Frank Pierce, Iowa	Kalona, Iowa
Leander L. Bonham	Iowa	X			Goshen, Iowa	Diagonal, Iowa	Creston, Iowa
Thomas D. Davis	Pa.	X			Iowa City	Iowa City	Iowa City
Marshall D. Fry	Iowa	X	Killed at Vicksburg				
John C. Guffin	N.Y.	X	Musician	X	Bon Accord, Iowa	—	—
William Haines	Ohio	X	Wounded at Vicksburg	X	Belvedier, Ill.	Springfield, Ill.	Springfield, Ill.
Company K							
Isaiah F. Bair	Ohio			X	Hancock, Iowa	Bentonville, Ark.	Bentonvle, Ark.
Jacob A. Fry	Iowa	X	Discharged—illness	X	Windham, Iowa	Oxford, Iowa	Oxford, Iowa
Edward Harris	England		Discharged—disabled	X	—	Ortonville, Iowa	Ortonville, Iowa
William C. Haynes	Ohio	X	Wounded at Vicksburg		Sterling, Neb.	W. Liberty, Iowa	W. Liberty, Iowa
John M. Oldaker	Ohio	X			Frank Pierce, Iowa	Green Ctr, Iowa	Green Ctr, Iowa
John W. Selby	Ohio	X	Wounded at Vicksburg	X	—	—	—
Simon Taylor	Pa.	X	Captured at Winchester	X	Amish, Iowa	Kalona, Iowa	Kalona, Iowa
Michael Yoakam	N.Y.	X			N. Platte, Neb.	N. Platte, Neb.	N. Platte, Neb.

Source: History of Johnson County, Iowa . . . (Iowa City, Iowa: 1883); U.S. Population Censuses, 1860, 1870; *Proceedings of the Twenty-Second Regiment Iowa Volunteers at its First Reunion held at Iowa City, Iowa* (Iowa City, Iowa: Republican Publishing Company, 1887); W. J. Bowen, Secretary, *List of Names and Addresses of Surviving Members of the Twenty-Second Iowa Volunteer Infantry, to September 15, 1903* [n.p., n.d.]; S. C. Jones, Secretary, *List of Names and Addresses of Surviving Members of the Twenty-Second Iowa Volunteer Infantry, to December 1, 1914* [n.p., n.d.].

nearly blind; both were under treatment at the hospital in Rolla. Charles Coons died on the 25th, and his friends wrote to George Coons and sent his clothes. Marshall Shaff had been sick and had since recovered; the Grewell boys were fine.[44]

Emmanuel described a brief chase after "rebbles" around their encampment. After hearing shots Tuesday night (he was writing on Saturday), Company F's captain roused his men, ordered them to load their guns, and they struck for the railroad "on the double quick." No officers for Company G were in camp, but the men could not stand being left out, so they loaded their guns and started for the guard line. As the guard halted them, Company F appeared, and one of its officers gave the order for Company G to march for the railroad. They found no Confederate soldiers but lost Company F. They took the road all the way into Rolla, 250 men in all, but saw no enemy soldiers; likely the shots had been fired at railroad cars. Company F searched the brush and cornfields with the same result. Three Confederate soldiers, however, had been captured the day before only twelve miles from Rolla. "Now you may think," Emmanuel wrote, "that Co. G. is not afraid of the rebbles because we had no ofissers along and we had no captain no lieutenant no sergent."

Emmanuel also discussed the situation of his brother Christian. Peter had written that he was in a hospital in Maryland, but Emmanuel thought Pennsylvania, judging from Christian's last letter. He was looking for regular letters from Jacob "gnaey" (Jacob Swartzendruber?). Peter was hoping Christian might be discharged for his illness, but Emmanuel responded that the men had tried to get Charles Coons and Marshall Shaff discharged, but "a man may trie just as well to role the allegany into the ocien as to get a discharge."

Finally, Emmanuel reported that he had quit smoking and chewing tobacco, although he reported the price as 25 cents a plug. He had trouble getting stamps and would have to pay a dollar to get 50 cents in silver.

The letter shows close relations among the men who volunteered from Washington Township. Emmanuel offered reports on several of his comrades. He tried to help two sick soldiers secure discharges, and he helped send a letter and remains to the father of a soldier who died of disease. Although Emmanuel participated in the military culture of comradeship and shared danger, he also continued the neighborly relationships developed in their home community.

On January 27 the 22nd marched to West Plains, Missouri, and joined the 21st and 23rd Iowa Infantry Regiments to form the 1st Brigade, 1st Division, Army of South East Missouri. The Brigade moved to Iron Mountain and received orders on 9 March 1863 to join General Ulysses S. Grant in military operations against Vicksburg, Mississippi. While marching toward the Mississippi River, the soldiers came upon their first dead Confederate soldier, a tall, red-headed "bushwhacker" dressed in butternut clothing. He was lying in the middle of the road, with his wife and children crying over his body. The column marched on either side of the scene, with the mother calling on the Union soldiers to witness that her husband was a brave man who did not flinch from battle. Reflecting back on the carnage and bloodshed of war over forty years later, Jacob Switzer of A company called the sight of this grieving family "the most affecting scene" experienced by the soldiers of the 22nd Iowa during their entire term of service.[45]

The regiment boarded transports at St. Genevieve, where a number of soldiers chose to desert the company before moving any closer to the enemy. They arrived at Milliken's Bend, a few miles north of Vicksburg, on March 27, the first Union regiment to land on Mississippi territory. The 22nd Iowa was assigned to a brigade composed of the 21st, 22nd, and 23rd Iowa and 11th Wisconsin regiments, part of the 14th Division, 13th Corps, of Grant's assembled forces preparing for the assault on Vicksburg. On April 27 the Corps embarked on river transports and landed at Hard Times, opposite the mouth of Black River.

After a brief engagement at Black River, the 22nd Iowa engaged in a more intense battle near Port Gibson on May 2, in which Company H and Hochstetler's Company G were deployed as skirmishers to make first contact with Confederate forces on Thompson's Hill. Union forces won this encounter, with sixteen casualties in the 22nd Iowa. The 22nd Iowa played a supporting role at Champion Hills on May 16, held in reserve for reinforcement where needed. The regiment later engaged in pursuit and captured some two hundred prisoners. On May 17th, the 22nd Iowa approached the railroad bridge at Black River on the Jackson and Vicksburg line. The attack on Confederate fortifications produced heavy casualties in the 23rd Iowa, including Colonel William H. Kinsman, who was killed. Only one man of the 22nd Iowa was wounded. After building a pontoon bridge to replace the destroyed railroad overpass, the Corps continued toward Jackson and Vicksburg.

General Grant ordered a frontal assault on the fortifications at Vicksburg for the morning of 22 May 1863. During the night of May 21, the 22nd Iowa advanced to a position midway between Union and Confederate lines, within twenty yards of the defending pickets. At 9:30 A.M., the brigade formed for battle, with the 22nd Iowa in advance, followed by the 21st Iowa and 11th Wisconsin. At 10 A.M., the regiments charged over the hill, with the cry "Remember Kinsman." As regimental colors appeared, "a thousand bayonets glittered in the sun" over the parapet of Fort Beauregard.[46] The fortification was a formidable obstacle, with walls fifteen feet high, surrounded by a ditch ten feet wide, and a line of rifle pits. Advancing through grape and rifle fire, only fifty men reached the ditch. Under the leadership of Sergeant Joseph B. Griffith, about fifteen soldiers raised each other up the wall and entered the fort, the only Union soldiers to overcome the obstacle. Griffith held the position the rest of the day, under fire and awaiting reinforcements, but had to withdraw under cover of darkness. Griffith was the only survivor of the exploit, and though his commanding officer recommended him for promotion, Grant's frontal assault failed.[47]

The 22nd Iowa suffered 164 casualties—27 killed, 118 wounded, and 19 captured—about half the regiment. Many were still lying on the slope that evening, calling for water.[48] June Lawson, a soldier in G Company, took a bullet in the chest and lay on the field two full days before an armistice allowed Union troops to remove their dead from between the lines for burial. He was taken to the field hospital and died a day later.[49] Sometime during the abortive assault, Emmanuel Hochstetler took a severe leg wound. He died on June 6 at the Jackson U.S. Army General Hospital in Memphis, Tennessee. He left one blanket, one canteen, and $7.10 in his personal effects. His brother Christian survived the war.[50]

When the disastrous attack failed, Grant settled down for a lengthy siege of Vicksburg, and the 22nd Iowa conducted siege operations and guard duty until the fortress city fell on 4 July 1863. After Vicksburg, the 22nd Iowa fought through to the end of the war. They helped chase General Joseph E. Johnston to Jackson, Mississippi, after the fall of Vicksburg. At Jackson, Colonel William Stone, commander of the brigade and war hero wounded at Vicksburg, was nominated by the Republicans for the governorship of Iowa and left the 22nd Iowa. He resigned his commission on 13 August 1863, won the gubernatorial election that fall, and served two terms as governor.

The 22nd Iowa campaigned briefly in Louisiana and Texas, and was ordered to Washington, D.C., in July 1864. On July 11 the Confederate cavalry commander Jubal Early was within sight of the Capitol dome. Unknown to him, only a few militia were on guard. But while Early considered his position, ships arrived with seasoned Union veterans, including the 22nd Iowa.[51]

In August the regiment joined General Sheridan in the Shenandoah Valley. The heaviest fighting occurred near Winchester, Virginia, on 19 September 1864, when the unit suffered 109 casualties. After a small role at Fisher Hill, the regiment endured 79 casualties at Cedar Creek on October 19. The unit then joined General Sherman in North Carolina and finally traveled to Savannah, Georgia, where they were mustered out on 26 July 1865.

The other twenty-six soldiers from Washington and Sharon townships were distributed among twelve infantry and cavalry regiments. Table 4.3 depicts the solders identified from the two townships and shows whether each soldier appeared in the 1860 or 1870 U.S. population census. Most served in the 22nd Iowa; only four joined the next most popular unit, the 24th Iowa Infantry, Company D. Of the fifty-two soldiers, at least five died in action or from disease, and nine were wounded or captured.

Iowa sent a large percentage of its eligible young men into military service during the Civil War, although likely not the most of any state, despite the claim made by Iowans during and after the conflict. Iowa sent 48.8 percent of its military population (men aged 18–45 in 1860) to Union armed forces, ranking fifth among the Northern states after Indiana (57.0 percent), Illinois (56.6 percent), Connecticut (50.1 percent), and Ohio (49.8 percent).[52] According to figures compiled by historian Robert R. Dykstra, Iowa soldiers suffered relatively heavy casualties. Iowa ranked ninth in percentage of soldiers killed in action or died of wounds, 5.2 percent compared to Pennsylvania at 7.1 percent; but first in percentage who died of disease, 12.5 percent. Iowa ranked third in total mortality of soldiers furnished, 19.0 percent, following Vermont (19.8%) and Michigan (19.3%), and second in total mortality of its military population, 9.3 percent, compared to Indiana (10.0%) and Illinois (also 9.3%).[53] The direct casualties and the indirect experience of warfare affected rural communities in Johnson County.

Local Land Conquest

The impact of war and its aftermath resulted in social and economic changes among the twenty-six men from Washington and Sharon townships who served in the 22nd Iowa Volunteer Infantry. Table 4.4 depicts the direct and indirect stresses of wartime. Three soldiers were killed at Vicksburg, and six were wounded at Vicksburg or other battles. The attrition of war is reflected in the indirect attrition of family residence in the home community, since very few of the 22nd Iowa veterans remained in Washington and Sharon townships. Eighteen soldiers appear in rural households in the 1860 census, and fourteen in the 1870 census. However, by the time of the first reunion of the 22nd Iowa in 1886, only four continued to live in one of the two townships.[54] Later regimental survivor lists show only one veteran, James M. Bonham, still living in Washington Township in 1903, and none in 1914.[55]

The experience of Captain Phillip E. Shaver of the First Iowa Cavalry, F Company, exemplifies the stress of wartime on farm households. Shaver served in the Mexican War and the California Indian War, and received a land bounty of 120 acres in Washington Township in 1854, 40 acres in Section 28 and 80 acres in Section 27.[56] Shaver was one of the wealthiest farmers in Washington Township when he enlisted in the First Iowa in June 1861. Nonetheless, in his absence, his farming enterprise suffered. Shaver requested a thirty-day leave of absence on 19 February 1862, stating his need to take care of farm and family in Iowa. The persons entrusted with managing his farm had warned that he faced "serious pecuniary loss" unless he returned immediately. His commanding officer granted Shaver's request.[57]

Shaver resigned his commission on 5 July 1863 to return permanently to his farm. In his letter of resignation, he requested discharge because his business without his personal management was "almost wholly sacrificed" and only his presence could "save me from great loss." Serious family illness had burdened his wife, impaired her health, and endangered her life "unless soon relieved from the pressing anxieties of her situation." His commanding officer, Colonel James O. Gower, also from Johnson County, approved Shaver's request, and he returned to Washington Township. Shaver had the resources to overcome his wartime absence and thus remain one of the wealthiest farmers in Washington township. He was listed in every census between 1860 and 1900, always near the top in wealth. Phillip E. Shaver appeared often in Iowa City newspaper stories and news notes as Captain Shaver, with the status of Civil War hero. He died on 10 October 1904 at Kalona and was buried in the Pleasant Hill Methodist cemetery.

Shaver managed to stay and prosper. For most soldiers from Washington and Sharon townships, military service represented a step on their way out of the county. On the home front, members of ethnic communities in southwestern Johnson County competed directly and indirectly for land, economic position, and social space. Tables 4.5 and 4.6 depict the relative position of households that produced at least one Civil War soldier compared with households

Table 4.5. Comparison of Households in 1860 with Civil War Soldiers and Households with No Soldiers, Washington and Sharon Townships, Johnson County, Iowa

	With Soldier	*No Soldier*
Age of household head	44.3	38.4
Number of children	4.55	3.35
Value of real estate	$2,656	$1,920
Value of personal wealth	$606	$446
Value of farm	$2,859	$2,133
Total acres	215.3	161.0
Value of implements	$90.4	$84.6
Hay (tons)	21.9	19.4
Number of horses	6.1	4.3
Number of milk cows	4.6	4.6
Butter (lbs.)	213	225
Corn (bu.)	1,126	1,106
Wheat (bu.)	159	178
Number of swine	27.4	27.7
Number of heads of cattle	8.2	7.9

Source: U.S. Population and Agricultural Census, 1860.

that sent no members into the military. Soldier households were wealthier in 1860 and less wealthy in 1870, although the differences seldom reach the level of statistical significance. Table 4.5 shows household heads in 1860 in soldier homes as older than in nonsoldier homes, a mean of 44.3 years of age compared with 38.4 years, and soldier households had more children, 4.55 as opposed to 3.35. Soldier households owned more land and personal wealth, and the total value of soldier farms was about 33 percent higher than of nonsoldier farms. Farming practices were not significantly different, since both kinds of farm households conducted similar agricultural operations.

The 1870 census shows the virtual reverse of 1860. In Table 4.6, taken from the 1870 federal population and agricultural censuses, households that produced at least one Civil War soldier were younger and less wealthy than households with no soldiers. Household heads with a soldier in 1870 averaged 36.8 years of age, and nonsoldier household heads averaged 42.9 years of age. Nonsoldier households owned an average of $4,235 in real estate and 151.6 acres of land, while soldier households owned $3,396 and 128 acres. Again, farming

Table 4.6. Comparison of Households in 1870 with Civil War Soldiers and Households with No Soldiers, Washington and Sharon Townships, Johnson County, Iowa

	With Soldier	*No Soldier*
Age of household head	36.8	42.9
Number of children	2.30	3.35
Value of real estate	$3,396	$4,235
Value of personal wealth	$875	$1,067
Value of farm	$3,352	$4,381
Total acres	128.0	151.6
Value of implements	$225	$255
Hay (tons)	19.0	22.6
Number of horses	3.9	5.4
Number of milk cows	3.4	4.7
Butter (lbs.)	365	275
Corn (bu.)	972	1,202
Wheat (bu.)	155	222
Number of swine	18.6	29.2
Number of heads of cattle	6.0	9.1

Source: U.S. Population and Agricultural Census, 1870.

practices and production decisions were similar. Few of the specific variables reached statistical significance in either 1860 or 1870, but the overall reversal of pattern seems clear.

Figure 4.1 shows how ethnic competition for land slowly began to swing in Amish favor during the decade following the Civil War. Amish land acquisitions show a small surge in purchases after the Civil War and relatively stable demand, while purchases by non-Amish buyers declined steeply from 1865 to 1875. The Amish community became firmly established on the land and gained in wealth in relation to its neighbors, showing greater resilience to the disruptions of the Civil War. There was also a surge of immigration to the community from the eastern Amish settlements, especially from areas where many young Amish men chose to volunteer for the Union army. Raw figures for Amish land acquisitions finally surpass the total acres purchased by non-Amish buyers by the end of the century.

Figures 4.2 to 4.4 graphically display the expansion of Amish land holdings between 1855 and 1875. From extremely modest beginnings in the late 1840s and only 2 percent of the land area in 1850, Amish landowners held over one-third of the two townships by 1875. As Table 4.7 shows, much of the growth occurred between 1860 and 1875, during the Civil War and the decade following. The Amish community doubled in geographic area, while neighboring ethnic communities suffered the direct and indirect stresses of war and its aftermath. The increase in Amish land ownership slowed perceptibly after 1875, growing by less than 2 percent between 1875 and 1889.

Amish landowners marched through these two Iowa townships like Sherman marched through Georgia. Despite the conflict surrounding and suffusing the Amish community, the group managed to keep some distance from the worst effects of Civil War. Their mentality of alienation from civil society aided their quest for land and social space in relation to ethnic neighbors in Iowa. However, even the Amish were not averse to noticing the effect of warfare on market prices. Eli L. Yoder, writing in 1861 from Wayne County, Ohio, said there would soon be a regiment quartered in Wooster, "which is expected to raise the market some." The government also called for one thousand "good cavalry horses," and Yoder planned to offer a 7-year-old mare for $85; however, "The government does not buy mares."[58]

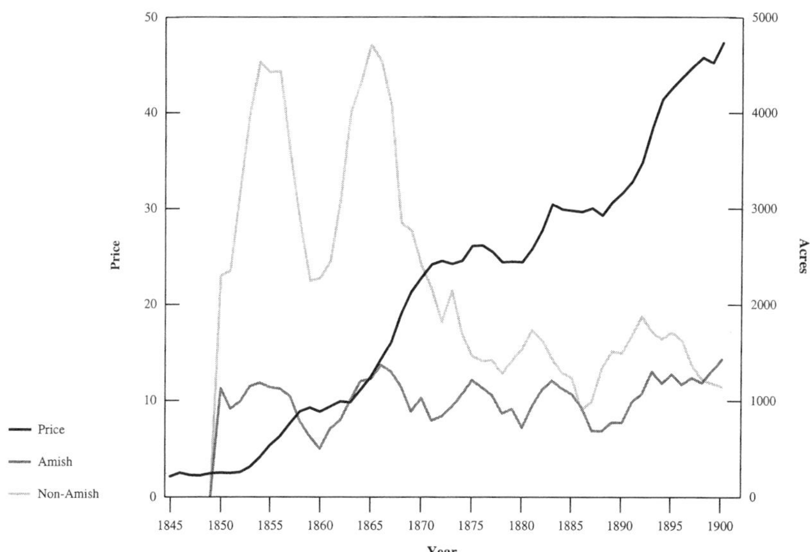

4.1. Land purchases by Amish and Non-Amish buyers in Washington and Sharon Townships, Johnson County, Iowa, 1845–1900.

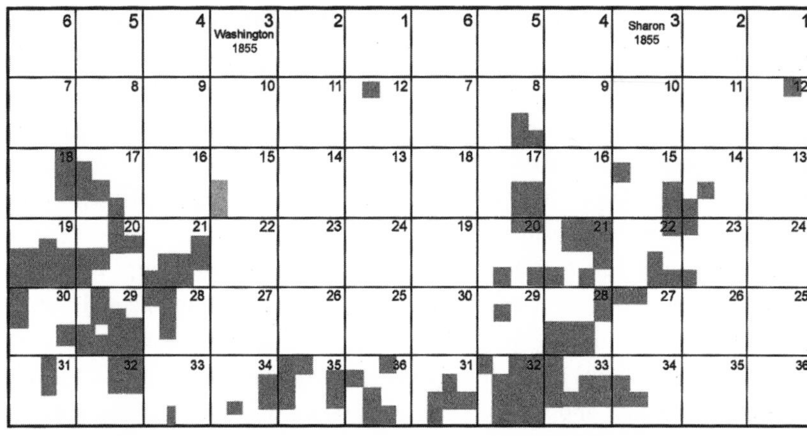

4.2. Land owned by Amish persons in Sharon and Washington Townships, Johnson County, Iowa, 1855.

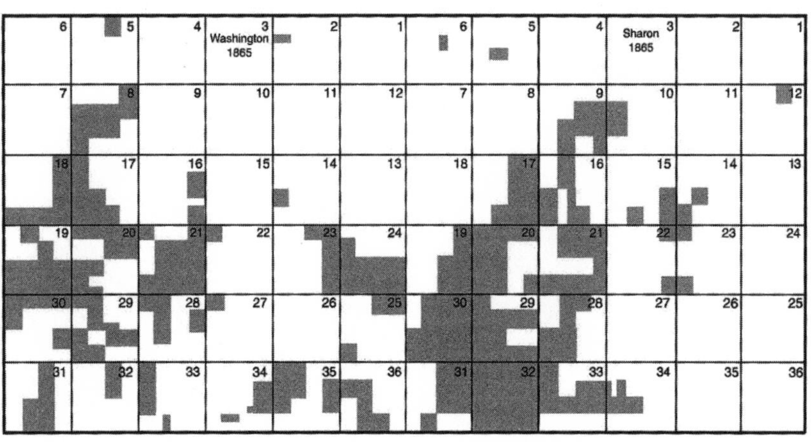

4.3. Land owned by Amish persons in Sharon and Washington Townships, Johnson County, Iowa, 1865.

Amish farmers in Johnson County may have continued acquiring land during and after the Civil War, but their relative success at creating space for communal expansion must be balanced by an awareness of internal Amish debate over participation in the military and the broader relationship with American civil society that military service represented.

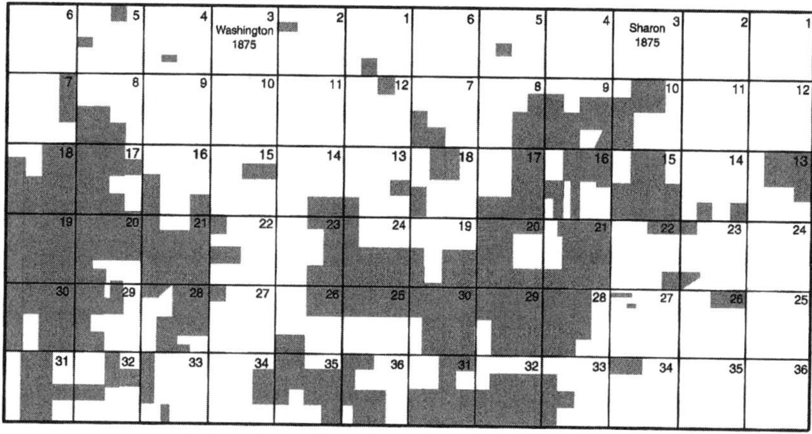

4.4. Land owned by Amish persons in Sharon and Washington Townships, Johnson County, Iowa, 1875.

Table 4.7. Land Owned by Amish Persons in Washington and Sharon Townships, Johnson County, Iowa, 1850–1889

	Acres in Sharon	*Acres in Washington*	*Total Acres*	*Percent of Total Land*[a]
1850	480	400	880	2.15
1855	2,840	2,700	5,540	13.53
1860	4,320	3,460	7,780	18.99
1865	5,160	4,930	10,090	24.63
1870	6,410	6,665	13,075	31.92
1875	7,060	7,825	14,885	36.34
1880	7,595	7,680	15,275	37.29
1889	7,210	8,370	15,580	38.04

Source: Johnson County Land Records.
[a]approximately 40,960 acres in the two townships.

After gaining land during the 1860s, Amish farmers next confronted the question of what to do with all their land. Wealth brought the Amish community face to face with American practices of individual economic autonomy and unlimited private use of property. Unrestrained private property threatened Amish patterns of communal responsibility.

> I remember very distinctly the time when he [John Wagler] was married. She was quite handsome and young with a great deal of vivacity and sprightliness and he was very proud that in his old days divine providence had given to him such a wife. In after days when they should have lived in peace and quietness they led such lives as was not right neither in the sight of man nor that of the God whom they had pretended to adore and worship.
>
> —J. O. Kimmel to Abner Yoder, 1876

Chapter 5

The Limits of Common Property

Easy access to land in Iowa allowed the Amish to take advantage of Civil War economic upheavals to expand their real estate holdings. Their economic good fortune, ironically, strained the Amish moral economy of regulating private property with communal responsibility. Adjusting to success required coming to terms with land holding and inheritance, and their meaning for community reproduction. The Amish traditionally practiced a modified form of community of goods. Rather than renouncing private property, like the Hutterites and utopian socialist societies, the Amish followed Anabaptist practice by stressing the responsibility of each individual and family to use material wealth for community good.[1]

Private property represented both opportunity and danger to nineteenth-century Europeans and Americans. Utopians, socialists, agrarians, and capitalists offered competing visions of the future. The midcentury Republican economic program promised land for farmers and support for industry. Utopians offered protection from rapacious capitalism but seldom challenged patriarchal hegemony.[2] For Amish adherents trying to wend their way through the thicket of early industrial capitalism, there was little guidance from their European experience. To be sure, Anabaptist theology encouraged mutual aid among church members, as illustrated by the famous Amish barn raisings and the many lesser known aid societies and other forms of voluntary economic community. Dealing with the American civil order, oriented to protecting private property, led to an uncomfortable marriage among the Amish of cultivated alienation with aggressive acquisitiveness. The ambiguity of curbed involvement—taking advantage of private property, while fearing the danger inherent in greed and wealth—may have been the source of another of Bishop Jacob Swartzendruber's dreams.

During the night of 29 December 1857, Swartzendruber dreamed he was conducting his milling business in the tiny village of Mengeringhausen in the Waldeck region of north central Germany.[3] Jacob perceived himself going from the *Galgenmühle* (Gallows Mill) at the edge of town to the house of a certain Folmer on business, carrying a large tin bowl with him. Folmer spoke to him, and Swartzendruber had the feeling Folmer intended to mock him; Swartzendruber pulled a curtain back and saw Folmer in person. Folmer told him that Christian Guengerich at the *Galgenmühle* wanted to give him the gold. Jacob thought to himself, "Gold, that would be rather strange to me" (*das war mir etwas sonderbar*). He took the long street downward, and everything was bright and clear before him all the way to the mill; but it was as if he had to seek his friend (Guengerich) "in heaven itself" (*himelmans*) and could not find him.

Then Swartzendruber awoke from his search, found himself back in Iowa, and the clock struck midnight. He could sleep no more until daylight. With a great many thoughts amid tears about the course of his life, he reflected on how God had indeed been gracious to him until that very hour. He ended his note with this comment: "A dream came into my mind that I have dreamed for 10 years; now I wrote it down."[4]

Economic relations often stretched Amish persons between community and world. Swartzendruber perceived a barrier between himself and a resident of the village, a curtain he had to pull aside to converse. Gold, the medium of business exchange, seemed "something strange" to him. And he returned to his mill at the edge of town, away from the center of local community. Most of Swartzendruber's Amish contacts, such as Christian Guengerich, lived on isolated rented farms. From their historical experience, Amish persons carried the conviction that sooner or later they would encounter irreconcilable differences with civil society. Preserving and, at times, creating a consciousness of separation and alienation from the larger social world was a function of the Amish repertoire of community in Iowa.

After the divided Iowa Amish communion in 1865 (Chapter 3), and the reunion of a divided United States the same year, a new divisive conflict began to appear in Bishop Swartzendruber's community. It was an intractable conflict over family inheritance and the responsible use of private property, leading to another sharply divided communion only weeks before his death in 1868.

Moses Kauffman was situated at the center of a family inheritance dispute involving land in Sharon Township. Melvin Gingerich reported an oral tradition some eighty years later that Kauffman had taken too large a share of his father's estate and that for a long time he refused to acknowledge his transgression.[5] His perceived violation of familial responsibility in favor of individual self-assertion and entrepreneurship focused several issues in the Amish community: private property, family obligation, and the critical balance between individual ambition and submission to community purposes.

Access to land is a critical component of Amish community. Land ownership practices, as opposed to renting or leasing as in Europe, had to be developed afresh in North America. From an examination of land transaction records, it appears that priority for ownership transitions favored first the household patriarch, then his immediate and extended family, and finally his church and ethnoreligious community. Ideologies of economic individualism and private use of property, especially land, threatened this principle in the Amish repertoire of community. In addition, property ownership by women imperiled the principle of housefather priority in the household. The inheritance controversies, centered first on Moses Kauffman and his extended family, and second on Eva Wagler, reveal communal concern over the holding and disposition of private property.

Land and Family

Jacob J. Kauffman, Moses's father, bought 200 acres in Sharon Township from Iowa City land speculator Charles H. Berryhill on 14 June 1852. The block lay near the center of Sharon Township in sections 14, 15, 22, and 23; Kauffman paid $500, or $2.50 per acre for it.[6] Kauffman, born on 17 April 1793 in Somerset County, Pennsylvania, had married Rebecca Plank and settled in Holmes County, Ohio, where the twelve children they raised to adulthood were born. He moved to Iowa from Holmes County, Ohio, in 1855. Two sons, Abraham J. and Moses J., bought land in sections 28 and 33 in February of that year. Moses returned to Ohio and married Catherine Beachy. He did not move back to Iowa until 1858.[7]

Jacob J. Kauffman died on 17 January 1859. He wrote and signed a will four days before his death, naming his son-in-law, Joseph C. Swartzendruber ("Ioway Joe"), as heir of the home place. He set the price at $3,500, with a one-third dower portion still belonging to his wife, Rebecca. Swartzendruber and his wife, Lydia, were to make equal payments to cover the other two-thirds, the money to be divided equally among the heirs. He willed to a son, Seth Kauffman, a quarter section of land "the same as the others got theirs," and appointed Jonas Kauffman and Joseph C. Swartzendruber as executors. Finally, he left his wife one horse and buggy and harness, one cow, and several household chairs. Kauffman assigned Swartzendruber the task of caring for his wife and the three younger boys. The will was witnessed by Bishop Jacob Swartzendruber, his son Joseph C. Swartzendruber, Abraham J. Kauffman, David J. Kauffman, and John Rhode. Jacob Kauffman was buried in the Peter Miller cemetery.[8]

During the year before his death, Jacob Kauffman sold parcels of Johnson County land, all in Sharon Township, to a son and two daughters. Jonas Kauffman bought 100 acres on 1 January 1858; and Magdalena Yoder, married to Jacob J. "Red Jake" Yoder, bought 100 acres on 2 January 1858, both at $10 per acre. However, nine days before he died, Jacob sold 100 acres in section 17 to his daughter Lydia, wife of Joseph C. Swartzendruber, for only $3 per acre.[9] This sale at below market price may have caused some of the initial friction. Swartzendruber had sold the same parcel of land to Moses J. Kauffman on 31 October 1859 for $8 per acre, closer to the average market price for land in Washington and Sharon townships of $9.80 per acre in 1859. Moses Kauffman also bought another 140 acres in sections 17 and 20 from Joseph C. Swartzendruber on 31 October 1859 for $30 per acre, and still another 40 acres in section 16 from John Kohler on 10 October 1859 for $12.50 per acre.[10] By the end of 1859, Moses owned 280 acres in Johnson County, more than any of his siblings. Ownership of so much land carried an important responsibility in the

Amish sense of community, namely preserving family and community through land rather than using land for individual aggrandizement. Apparently some members of the community became suspicious about Kauffman's motives in acquiring land.

The 1860 census shows the Kauffman offspring located in six households, although Rebecca Plank Kauffman, Jacob's widow, does not appear in the manuscript schedules. Moses and Seth Kauffman headed households in Sharon township, and their sisters appear in households headed by husbands Jacob Y. Yoder, Joseph C. Swartzendruber, and Christian Shetler. One unmarried son, Elias J., resided in Swartzendruber's home, and another, Joseph J., with Swartzendruber's cousin George, Jacob's son. Of all the six households, Moses Kauffman reported the most wealth to the census taker, a total of $4,500 in real estate and personal assets. And he apparently resided on the "home place" in section 17, willed to Joseph C. Swartzendruber, but sold to Moses Kauffman. The Kauffmans were involved in very few land transactions between 1860 and 1865.

The issue of land ownership within the community began to take center stage in May 1865, only a month after the divided 1865 communion. As if to display the issue within the community, Moses Kauffman sold 160 acres in section 33 of Sharon Township to William Enfield on 3 May 1865 for $15.63 per acre.[11] Sale of land to a non-Amish person, albeit of German parentage, was the best possible means to flout the expectation of keeping land in Amish hands. Enfield's father, Philip, was a veteran of the War of 1812 and a member of the Grout Methodist church. Worse yet, Kauffman sold 80 acres of the land in section 17, acquired in 1859 from his brother-in-law, Joseph C. Swartzendruber, to August Northouse on 24 June 1867 for $30.30 per acre. Kauffman sold the last of his land on 27 February 1868 to his brother-in-law, Christian Shetler, for $74.30 per acre, not including his mother's dower portion. Shetler only acquired free title on 19 September 1873 when Rebecca Plank Kauffman and the rest of the family acknowledged payment of the one-third dower to Jacob J. Kauffman's widow.[12] Suspicion of excess profit-seeking by Kauffman, and discontent with his selling land to an outsider, began to poison relationships in the local Amish community.

Congregational conflict focused on the Kauffman case began to appear in Jacob Swartzendruber's church notes on 29 April 1866, when he wrote, "Talked of getting outside ministers." Outside ministers, or "foreign" ministers, were often invited to help mediate Amish conflicts, since the Amish lacked any centralized coercive mechanism of a typical church hierarchy. The next Sunday the congregation voted, but the proposal to bring in outside arbitrators failed to carry. On May 13, Pentecost, the vote finally carried.[13]

The Annual Ministers' Meeting in Illinois appointed, as "outside ministers," Andrew Ropp, Christian Ropp, Jonathan Yoder, Joseph Stuckey, and Joseph Goldsmith.[14] The visiting ministers met with the Sharon Township congregation on June 12, 13, and 14 at the home of John I. Plank, a nephew of Rebecca Plank Kauffman and first cousin of Moses. According to Bishop Swartzendruber's notes, all the ministers spoke at the first meeting, after a reading of the second and third chapters of the Gospel of John. On the third day, the group held a formal council meeting (*Abrath*) and voted "mostly in favor of communion." Holding communion would have been symbolic of consensus, so it seemed on Thursday that the conflict may have been resolved.

By Sunday, however, consensus was blocked again, and Swartzendruber mentioned Kauffman by name for the first time. The Washington Township congregation met at "Old Schoettler's" (Daniel and Helena Swartzendruber Shetler) on 17 June 1866 and took a vote to see whether the members were ready for communion. Jacob wrote in his minutes that the church members were "mostly in favor of communion but Mose Kauffman spoiled it all." The next Sunday, at the Sharon Township congregation, Kauffman was "willing to submit to the church"; but a week later, in Washington Township, "the Opposers" were "not willing to submit to vote of the church." The Amish concept of communion requires consensus but not necessarily unanimity. One person or a small group of members can deny consent, and the rest of the congregation may or may not proceed. Moses Kauffman came to represent the theme of individual obedience to the group as well as its alternative, individual self-assertion and independence. Moses Kauffman was a symbol of this fundamental dilemma of community life.

On July 15 the ministers talked to the church about the conflict. Swartzendruber wrote, "Jacob [meaning himself?] told Abner [Yoder] to finish it, but he would not." Swartzendruber's notes are missing from 15 July 1866 to the end of that year. On 6 January 1867, the Washington Township congregation again took council regarding a proposal to bring in outside ministers to arbitrate, but most members opposed the move. Jacob Swartzendruber sent a letter to Bishop Joseph Stuckey in Illinois, and Stuckey's reply was read to the Sharon Township congregation on 27 January. At this meeting, Seth and Elizabeth Kempf Kauffman, the former a brother of Moses, were "read out" of the church. Probably they were threatened with banning, or excommunication, for their role in the family conflict. The following Sunday, February 3, the Washington Township congregation discussed calling an outside arbitration committee, but without taking a vote. Seth and Lizzie Kauffman were reinstated to full fellowship in the congregation on March 10, probably after some sort of public confession. On April 7 and 14, Jacob Swartzendruber noted that he was sick and that Abner Yoder had "set forth matters" to both congregations. All the ministers gathered at Daniel Yoder's on May 29 and at Benedict Miller's on May 31.

The community continued to struggle throughout the summer and fall of 1867. On June 16 and 23, a letter from the 1867 *Diener Versammlung* was read before both congregations, but the members could not reach consensus for calling outside ministers to resolve the ongoing conflict. In late July and early August, Jacob twice delayed the announcement of "young converts" in the Sharon Township congregation for baptism because the procedure "was spoiled by Mose Kauffman." By September 22 Daniel P. Guengerich, Jacob Swartzendruber's stepson, "ordered Mose K. not to eat at the table" after the worship service at Guengerich's house in Washington County. Clearly, the situation was disintegrating, and the Old Order Amish versus Amish-Mennonite schism seemed about to arrive in Iowa.

The two divided congregations held council regarding new converts on September 29 and October 6; and on 13 October, Jacob Swartzendruber baptized sixteen young people, while five deferred their final commitment. This was the younger generation's equivalent of refusing to take communion to show the lack of consensus in the community. After further council meetings on the issue of calling outside ministers, on 3 and 10 November both congregations finally voted with a large enough majority to enable the calling of three outside ministers as an ad hoc arbitration committee.

On December 10 and 11, a Tuesday and Wednesday, four ministers spoke to the entire community at Daniel Yoder's farm in Washington Township. The church paid $163 in railroad expenses to the four men who acted as the arbitration committee.[15] The committee decided that Kauffman should make the "highest confession" to the church, "which he finally did," and the ministers left for Illinois on Thursday, December 19. In the "highest confession," the guilty person kneels before the congregation, admits his sins, and then is received back into the church fellowship.

Two months later, on February 16, Kauffman requested his church letter and moved to Illinois. He sold his last 115 acres in Sharon Township to his brother-in-law, Christian Shetler, on 27 February 1868. Moses J. Kauffman was later ordained a minister in Illinois, where he lived until his death in Douglas County in 1898. His brother, Jonas J., was the first Amish minister ordained in the Arthur, Illinois, community. Jonas sold his 140 acre portion of the family inheritance in Sharon Township to Andreas Schauserl on 14 February 1865. Like his brother, he left by selling his land to a non-Amish buyer.[16]

The two congregations finally held communion on 26 April and 3 May 1868, the first communion since the divided service in 1865. This communion service showed more harmony, at least in the Deer Creek congregation of Washington Township, where eighty-eight observed the ceremony and only nine refrained. However, since the family land controversy was centered in the Sharon congregation, it continued to be about evenly divided, with sixty-four communicants and fifty-seven who refused.[17] Jacob Swartzendruber presented the traditional Amish communion sermon on the patriarchs on May 3, the last Sunday for which he wrote notes on the church services in Johnson County, Iowa. Thereafter he became ill, was not able to attend church anymore, and died one month and two days later.

Land and Community

This family conflict over land perturbed the entire Amish community in Iowa for the better part of a decade. Any tendency toward individualism in land ownership could alter the delicate balance of individual and community, of short-term profit and long-term community enhancement. There is strong evidence in Johnson County land records to identify why a small family dispute would affect congregational relationships to such an extent that communion could not be held for several years.

Amish patterns of acquiring, holding, selling, and bequeathing land become visible in comparative analysis of land transaction records. These patterns show the Amish commitment to family and community health and less concern with speculative profit. Once land fell into Amish hands, it seldom escaped. Following initial purchases in the 1850s, most land acquired by Amish farmers was sold to them by their coreligionists. Conversely, when Amish families sold land, it seldom went to persons outside the local community and usually went to persons of German ancestry in Washington and Sharon townships. In addition to keeping land under Amish control, Amish families tended to buy land

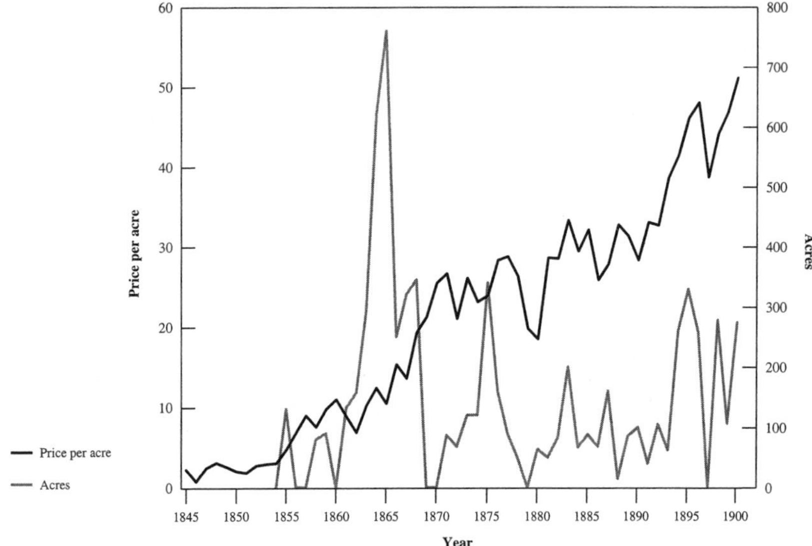

5.1. Land sold by Amish sellers to Non-Amish buyers in Washington and Sharon Townships, Johnson County, Iowa, 1855–1900.

from each other at higher than market prices, but they purchased land from non-Amish owners when the price of land dipped, rather than at inflated price levels.

During most of the years between 1850 and 1900, Amish sales of land to non-Amish buyers amounted to less than 200 acres per year. In many years, fewer than 100 acres left Amish hands. Three peaks in Amish sales to non-Amish buyers appear in Figure 5.1, however, around 1865, 1875, and 1895. Since the purchase, holding, and disposition of land are critical to the continuity of an Amish community, these peaks can be viewed as an index of stress within the community. The largest number of acres sold to non-Amish buyers, over 760 acres, occurred in 1865; external sales hit at least 250 acres in each of the following three years. Amish farmers sold more land to non-Amish buyers than to each other in 1862, 1864, 1865, and 1867, and again in 1875, the only years this occurred. Some families sold out and moved to other communities; some distant Amish landowners, such as Joseph Helmuth of Holmes County, Ohio, sold land to native-born purchasers;[18] but likely some sold to non-Amish purchasers to test or even flout Amish expectations to keep land within the ethno-religious community. They contested Amish priority in the local ethnic land market as the preferred method to organize buying and selling decisions.

The sizable land sales to non-Amish buyers during the Moses Kauffman controversy indicated the nature and severity of community disagreement over the significance of individual land ownership and its relationship to community responsibility. After Bishop Jacob Swartzendruber died in 1868 and Moses Kauffman moved to Illinois, the family land dispute no longer preoccupied the Amish community. Amish landowners in Johnson County sold no land whatsoever to non-Amish buyers in 1869 and 1870. In resolving the conflict, community leaders reasserted Amish sales to Amish buyers as a priority in the land marketplace, reinforcing the repertoire of ethnic land ownership in maintaining rural community.

The surge in Amish sales to non-Amish purchasers from 1874 to 1876 occurred just before Noah Troyer began his spiritualist preaching; there were no sales above 200 acres in the years between 1876 and 1894; and the upswing during the 1890s occurred during the growing schism between Old Order and Amish-Mennonite factions, finally resulting in two separate denominations in Johnson County.

The expectation of keeping land within the Amish community is related to the assumption that land will be passed to the next generation through family inheritance structures. Tables 5.1 and 5.2 depict a series of regressions in the relationship of age to amount of land owned in the 1860 and 1870 federal popu-

Table 5.1. Regression of Farm Size and Age among 1865 and 1868 Amish Communion Partakers, Nonpartakers, and Divided Households in the 1860 Federal Population and Agricultural Censuses

	Intercept	*Slope*	*Beta Coefficient*	*t-Value*	*Sig t*
All Non-Amish	43.9	2.96	.319	3.45	.000 ***
All Amish	161.9	.27	.029	.149	.883
1865 Partakers	134.6	2.18	.188	.428	.686
1865 Nonpartakers	302.6	−3.54	−.695	−2.90	.018 **
1865 Divided	−243.9	4.63	.740	2.46	.057 *
1868 Partakers	135.6	1.22	.113	.411	.688
1868 Nonpartakers	240.8	−2.33	−.555	−1.49	.196

Significance: * = .1 level.
** = .05 level.
*** = .01 level.

Table 5.2. Regression of Farm Size and Age among 1865 and 1868 Amish Communion Partakers, Nonpartakers, and Divided Households in the 1870 Federal Population and Agricultural Censuses

	Intercept	*Slope*	*Beta Coefficient*	*t-Value*	*Sig t*
All Non-Amish	70.8	1.62	.209	3.00	.003 ***
All Amish	8.8	3.99	.496	4.88	.000 ***
1865 Partakers	−45.9	5.14	.593	3.29	.004 ***
1865 Nonpartakers	16.0	4.23	.520	2.58	.019 **
1865 Divided	−24.6	5.64	.409	1.27	.241
1868 Partakers	−74.7	6.76	.707	5.91	.000 ***
1868 Nonpartakers	80.6	2.23	.324	1.33	.205

Significance: * = .1 level.
** = .05 level.
*** = .01 level.

lation and agricultural censuses. If there is a statistically significant relationship with a positive slope and beta coefficient between the two continuous variables, then an older person would tend to own more land than a younger. Conversely, a negative slope and beta coefficient indicate that as a person grew older, he would tend to own less land, which can be taken to mean more commitment and success in transmitting land to the younger generation.

In 1860 the contrast between non-Amish and Amish landowners is quite clear. The non-Amish landowners show a statistically significant relationship between age and acreage, while the Amish show no relationship. By 1870, however, both non-Amish and Amish landowners show a significant relationship, meaning that the Amish in general shifted, during the 1860s, toward older members holding land longer. Within the Amish community, the situation is more complex. Partakers and nonpartakers in the 1865 and 1868 communion lists recorded by Bishop Jacob Swartzendruber exhibit differences in their approaches to bequeathing land to the younger generation.

Partakers and nonpartakers identified in the 1860 censuses from both 1865 and 1868 differed in the relationship of acres of land to age. Table 5.1 shows a positive regression slope for partakers in 1865 and 1868, and a negative slope for both groups of nonpartakers. Only the negative slope for 1865 nonpartakers is statistically significant, at the .05 level, although the opposite direction in both cases seems important. Divided households in 1865 show the strongest positive relationship of age to land ownership, with a slope of 4.63 and statistical significance at the 0.1 level.[19] For every year older, a household in which the husband took communion and the wife refused would tend to own 4.63 more acres of land. At the other extreme, for every one-year increase in age of a nonpartaker household head, that household would tend to own 3.54 fewer acres of land.

In the 1870 censuses, taken closer to the 1868 communion, there are fewer differences among the communion groupings from 1865 and 1868. In Table 5.2, every equation except the 1865 divided households and the 1868 nonpartakers shows a statistically significant positive relationship between age and land ownership. Even the two exceptions show a positive linear relationship, though not as strong. Nonetheless, the mainstream Amish movement seems to be toward older members retaining land, with a minority still mitigating the trend of greater age producing more land ownership.

Taken together, the regression tables for 1865 and 1868 Amish communion groupings in the 1860 and 1870 censuses show a trend in the Amish land ownership system toward associating increased age with increased land holdings. The tables also reveal resistance against that trend, perhaps in a conservative demand to retain the more traditional pattern of passing land on to the next generation as soon as feasible. As seen in the following tables, the issue was not so much age itself as a generational conflict, as it was the timing and approach of including the next generation in the Amish economic community. Perhaps Moses Kauffman considered it his right as a son to inherit as much as possible as soon as possible, and those who refused communion were, in part, protesting against the older generation holding land too long. On the other hand, it may have been that older Amish farmers held their land longer during this decade to preserve the Amish agricultural system and avoid excessive orientation to market crops and specialized farming.

A more direct examination of the 1868 communion list reveals differences from the 1865 list. Only one congregation, Sharon Township, remained evenly split. Moses Kauffman and his family lived mainly in the Sharon community. Almost everyone took communion and expressed communal harmony in the Deer Creek congregation of Washington Township. Two of the nine who re-

Table 5.3. Comparison of 1868 Amish Communion Partakers, Nonpartakers, and Divided Couples in the 1860 Population and Agricultural Censuses

1868 Communion	*Partakers*	*Nonpartakers*	*Divided*	*All Amish*
Number of households	20	8	3	40
Number of farms	15	7	1	29
Age of household head	43.3	40.1	48.3	41.0
Value of real estate	$2,526	$2,557	$2,823	$2,458
Value of personal wealth	$582	$557	$345	$527
Household size	7.1	7.1	7.7	6.9
Number of children	4.5	4.4	4.7	4.3
Total acres	188.5	146.4	160.0	172.9
Value of farm	$2,615	$2,828	$3,200	$2,567
Value of implements	$94	$66	$75	$87
Value of livestock	$510	$381	$800	$468
Hay (tons)	36.4	14.3	25	25.5
Number of horses	5.2	4.4	7	4.7
Number of milk cows	6.1	4.3	6	5.4
Number of heads of cattle	9.4	5.9	12	7.8
Butter (lbs.)	410	168	500	296
Number of swine	36.9	28.1	52	31.7
Corn (bu.)	1,213	864	1,000	1,005
Wheat (bu.)	172	110	180	146
Value of total farm production	$1,952	$1,284	$1,769	$1,593

fused communion were Noah and Magdalena Kauffman, the former a cousin of Moses's, who were residents of Iowa County. Another critical difference was the reduction in the number of divided households, only three in the 1860 census and only five in the 1870 census, all in Sharon Township. There is no discernible pattern in 1868 of single women avoiding communion at a higher rate than unattached men, as in 1865. The central issue had shifted from gender roles to the Amish land ownership system, a component of the Amish repertoire that was still being contested in the American republic.

Tables 5.3 and 5.4 depict family and agricultural characteristics of partaker, nonpartaker, and divided households in the 1860 and 1870 federal population and agricultural censuses. In each case, including the regression tables above, the Sharon Township Amish congregation was isolated for analysis. Swartzendruber listed six households from Washington Township from the 1860 census and eight from the 1870 census in the Sharon congregation, and four from Sharon Township in the Deer Creek congregation. The distinction made little difference, even though there were more nonpartakers in Sharon. In general, the nonpartaker households are wealthier, but their farms are less diverse and less productive, and they rely less on female labor. They seemed to be moving away from the Amish agricultural system. Nonpartakers do not practice as much diversity in their farm operations as partakers, and they may be attempting to reorient their production more toward the marketplace and cash crops. The smaller amount of butter produced indicates less reliance on female labor in nonpartaker households.

Data from the 1870 censuses continue to show differences in wealth and farm diversity between partakers and nonpartakers. Table 5.4 lists variables from both Washington and Sharon townships, but the differences are sometimes greater in Sharon Township alone. There is a greater disparity in average

Table 5.4. Comparison of 1868 Amish Communion Partakers, Nonpartakers, and Divided Couples in the 1870 Population and Agricultural Censuses

1868 Communion	*Partakers*	*Nonpartakers*	*Divided*	*All Amish*
Households	43	19	5	85
Farms	37	17	5	75
Age of household head	40.8	43.6	46.4	40.5
Value of real estate	$6,683	$5,805	$6,600	$5,652
Value of personal wealth	$1,511	$1,295	$1,560	$1,301
Household size	6.9	7.4	6.4	6.5
Number of children	4.0	4.5	4.0	3.8
Total acres	195.8	176.4	158.0	169.0
Value of farm	$5,816	$5,694	$5,480	$5,249
Value of implements	$391	$285	$310	$320
Value of livestock	$1,193	$1,041	$1,250	$1,051
Hay (tons)	32.3	23.3	26	25.4
Horses	6.8	5.8	7.0	6.0
Milk cows	6.5	5.5	4.8	5.5
Cattle	14.4	7.9	9.8	10.4
Butter (lbs.)	545	385	360	425
Swine	32.6	40.2	31	31.2
Corn (bu.)	1,516	1,265	1,440	1,322
Wheat (bu.)	315	280	315	281
Value of total farm production	$2,795	$2,349	$2,370	$2,384

age of household heads in the Sharon congregation (38.8 years for partakers versus 44.8 for nonpartakers), and nonpartakers owned much more land—191 acres compared to only 146.6 for partakers. Data from both townships show partakers owning more personal wealth, but the situation is reversed in Sharon Township, with nonpartakers listing an average of $1,350 and partakers $1,315. Economic inequalities between dissenters and supporters existed for a longer time in Sharon Township, where the Moses Kauffman land dispute took place.

In the Amish community as a whole, by 1870 nonpartaker households had recovered some of the diversity missing in 1860, perhaps because a number of dissenters moved away during the late 1860s. However, butter production stayed lower for nonpartakers, perhaps revealing some continuing resistance to full participation in farm production by women.

One household that illustrates some of these trends is the Isaac and Magdalena Schrock Eash family. Isaac was widowed in 1859 and remarried in 1861. He participated in the 1865 communion service but refused in 1868. One of Eash's daughters married Noah A. Kauffman, a nephew of Moses Kauffman; another married Christian C. Swartzendruber, a brother of Joseph C., who lost the Jacob Kauffman home place to Moses.

Eash bought 160 acres in Section 32 of Sharon Township in 1852 from a military service government land grantee and passed 139 acres on to his son-in-law, John I. Plank, in May 1860, a year after his first wife died. He sold another 40 acres in 1863 to his nephew, Paul Miller, son of Peter B. Miller, a brother of Eash's first wife. Later in 1860, Eash bought 170 acres in Sections 6 and 9 from George Davis.[20] After Eash died intestate in 1877, Gideon Marner, his nephew, was named administrator and sold 63 acres to James C. Schrader to meet the estate's debts. Eash's widow, Magdalena, sold 40 acres to Samuel J. Plank, her grandson, in 1885.[21] At age 50, Eash sold about half the total amount of land he owned in Sharon Township to close relatives; the rest was sold by an estate administrator and his widow after his death.

In the 1860 population census, Isaac Eash lived with his son-in-law, John I. Plank, in Sharon Township. Plank is listed on the agricultural census as owner of 120 acres of land. The farm follows the pattern of 1868 communion nonpartakers in the 1860 census (Table 5.3). It was valued at $4,400, a high figure, and Plank owned $75 in farm implements. The farm focused on corn, wheat, oats, and hogs; there were only two milk cows and three horses, and no rye, potatoes, barley, hay, or molasses were produced. The farm listed no butter production. In 1870, with Isaac Eash again living on his own farm, he owned 170 acres in the agricultural census listing, with 100 acres under tillage. He raised no rye or barley, but his wife churned 500 pounds of butter. Eash listed $300 worth of farm implements and paid the very high figure of $300 in wages for farm labor.

Isaac and Magdalena Schrock Eash illustrate the nonpartaker pattern in the 1868 communion ceremony. They had kinship ties to the Kauffman family, bequeathed land to sons and relatives fairly early in life, engaged in less diverse agriculture in 1860 but somewhat more according to the Amish system in 1870. In sum, kinship ties, land inheritance patterns, and commercial and subsistence farming systems interacted in complex ways to prevent a number of Amish households in Sharon Township in 1868 from expressing spiritual harmony with themselves and their Amish neighbors.

Dangerous Property

Abner Yoder imported another property dispute into the Johnson County Amish community. Yoder, a tradition-minded bishop from Somerset County, Pennsylvania, moved to Iowa in April 1866. He attended the Ministers' Meeting the next month in McLean County, Illinois, and immediately became involved in adjudicating the dispute in Johnson County. Yoder knew Jacob Swartzendruber from the Glades congregation, where Swartzendruber had served as a minister before moving to Iowa. Yoder chaired the 1863 Amish Ministers' Meeting and participated actively in four of the first five annual meetings, but he accepted the tradition-minded position and attended no more after 1866.

A member of Yoder's congregation in Pennsylvania, John Wagler, married a certain Eva Keck. Some years later, a friend described the marriage in less than discreet language: "I remember very distinctly the time when he [John Wagler] was married. She was quite handsome and young with a great deal of vivacity and sprightliness and he was very proud that in his old days divine providence had given to him such a wife. In after days when they should have lived in peace and quietness they led such lives as was not right neither in the sight of man nor that of the God whom they had pretended to adore and worship."[22] Such harsh attitudes toward the young wife continued for many years after her husband's death.

John Wagler died on 11 April 1851. He had filed a will on March 20, leaving his possessions to his wife and to the Amish church for poor relief after her death. He named Abner Yoder one of his executors.[23] The court inventory of his assets and real estate came to $2,287.[24] In August 1866, the 133 acres in Stony Creek Township that her deceased husband bequeathed to Eva sold at auction for $2,500. By agreement of the Glades Amish congregation, proceeds of the sale were paid to Abner Yoder as trustee "for the maintenance and support of Eva Wagler, widow of John Wagler dec., during her lifetime, and whatever balance remains at her death to be paid by him to the Amish church for the benefit of the poor of said church." Two Amish ministers from the Glades congregation affirmed the agreement before the judges of the Orphans' Court of Somerset County.[25]

Why the Glades church put Abner Yoder in charge of Eva Wagler's finances is unclear. It may have had something to do with discomfort over a widow owning property.[26] In any case, when Yoder moved to Iowa in April 1866, Eva moved with the Yoder family and lived with them in Sharon Township. Yoder built a small house for Wagler on his property at a cost of $525, in effect a "grossdoddy house" for the widow. On 3 March 1870, she and Yoder signed an agreement, witnessed by Yoder's wife, Veronica Schrock Yoder, in which Wagler "promised me that during her lifetime she will not ask me again for a dram or any other alcoholic drinks."[27] On 15 May 1870, the Sharon Township Amish congregation required the highest confession from Eva Wagler.[28] Perhaps the agreement and confession offer clues for why the Glades church appointed Yoder to take charge of Wagler's financial assets.

Eva Wagler's confession did not end her conflict with Abner Yoder, however. Yoder found himself called to account by the other ministers in his community regarding his treatment of Wagler, according to a notebook of church affairs he kept. The disputes appeared on the Sharon congregation's council agenda on 14 September 1869 as a conflict between Yoder and Jonathan Marner. By the summer of 1876, drastic measures became necessary. Yoder sent to Somerset County for a copy of John Wagler's will, apparently to document his status as executor and his later appointment as trustee of Eva Wagler's assets.[29] The ministers gathered on 16 May 1876 at Wagler's home to examine complaints pressed by Marner "on account of the ill treatment of Eva Wagler." The congregation discussed the matter on 28 May, but they found nothing against Yoder, and required a confession from Marner and a promise "that he will leave Abner Yoder more in peace from now on." Marner consented to make peace, but he refused to shake hands and exchange the holy kiss of peace, a traditional Amish symbol of unity, because he wanted to keep a clear conscience and said "it would be a Judas kiss."[30]

More ministerial gatherings to investigate the conflict took place on 24 and 29 June, and again on 9 and 16 July. On 23 July the Sharon congregation discussed the matter "concerning Eva Wagler and her possessions" and agreed that Wagler and all her possessions should be moved to Jonathan Marner's. Her assets were divided into three equal parts, with one part going to Marner, for her maintenance, and the other two parts to ministers John Petersheim and Jacob J. Marner. The three designated trustees, Yoder's replacements in taking responsibility for the widow, met on 25 July and agreed to move the house on 12 August, but they absolutely refused to pay the cost. Yoder finally picked up the $40 tab for two house movers from Iowa City. Workers started preparing the house on 7 August, and by Saturday noon, 12 August, the house was standing at Jonathan Marner's residence.[31]

Even moving the house did not settle the issue, however. Yoder made another entry on 4 December 1877, in which Jonathan Marner charged Yoder for withholding interest on Eva Wagler's assets.[32] It appears that Wagler was resisting the suffocating supervision of both her religious and economic affairs by one man. Communal concern for the disposition of the widow's property appears in the constant church discussions and arbitration. Whether because of a specific case of alcohol abuse or because of a general principle of male administration of property, Amish congregations in Somerset County, Pennsylvania, and Johnson County, Iowa, placed men in charge of the Widow Wagler's property. Eva Wagler died on 3 June 1888; the bitter feelings aroused during her life by her relationship to Abner Yoder were palpable.

The bitterness surrounding the property relations cases of Moses Kauffman and Eva Wagler reverberated for many years. On 8 April 1877, Abner Yoder excommunicated Christian D. Shetler, son-in-law of Jacob Kauffman and brother-in-law of Moses Kauffman. On 3 July 1877, Shetler deeded 210 acres in Sharon Township to creditors Moses P. Miller, S. G. Luke, and J. N. Coldran. By 25 September 1879, his land went through a debt sale,[33] and Shetler moved to Clay County, Nebraska.

Shetler sent a letter to Samuel D. Guengerich on 6 April 1879, complaining about his treatment by the Sharon Township Amish congregation. They had shunned him, and he found Nebraska more congenial because "people are not so stuck up or high toned here as they are back there. This country is mostly settled up by people that have ben broke up in the east like my self & they feel for each other & accommodate each other where they can." Shetler boasted of preaching twice every Sunday to congregations from four or five different denominations. Guengerich had written to him that one should remain in the faith one first confessed, and Shetler replied, "I have no faith whatever in the ways & doings of the Johnson Co. Amish for the last 6 or 7 yrs." Still, Shetler claimed he harbored no hard feelings toward anyone.[34] Working out the principles of communal responsibility within the American regime of private property and economic independence strained the mutuality of the Amish in Iowa.

Bishop Jacob Swartzendruber had dreamed of forming a renewed and purified Amish community in Iowa that would leave behind the conflicts and problems associated with Amish settlements in Europe and in the eastern United States. His dreamy retrospective reflections on his life in Europe, Pennsylvania, and Iowa express the personal cost of carrying responsibility for both church community and family. In a letter dated 18 October 1866 to three of the ministers assigned to investigate Johnson County conflicts by the 1866 Ministers' Meeting—Jonathan Yoder, Andrew Ropp, and Christian Ropp—Swartzendruber wrote an emotional assessment of his life experience:

> God knows everything. I have often stood before the church in fear and in a troubled spirit and in tears have warned the congregation, in recognition of the importance of my office to stand between God and humanity, according to Ezekiel's teaching. And what is my reward for these 15 years in Iowa? The dear God knows that often I did not feel myself worthy to stand before the church, but my calling compelled it.[35]

After recounting his forty years of ministry, thirty-three in America (seven in Pennsylvania, eleven in Maryland, and fifteen in Iowa), Swartzendruber noted how often the worthy leaders he knew had been opposed by impatient congregations. "It does not surprise me that the same thing happens to me in my weakness." He took special exception to Levi Miller's waiting several years before lodging a complaint against him. He had earlier warned his stepson to have nothing to do with Miller, and he claimed that Miller had even taken communion while cloaking anger at his bishop! With an almost audible sigh, Swartzendruber concluded his letter thus:

> Once more a hearty greeting to you, John, Andrew, and Christian, written by me, a distressed and depressed human being, Jacob Swartzendruber. Write an answer to me when it is convenient for you.
>
> It seems I must live my short life with nothing but cross and sorrow, and if I were not in the ministry I could be in peace with almost all people, according to the teachings of Paul.

5.2. Grave marker of Preacher Jacob Swartzendruber, d. 1868, in the Peter Miller Cemetery in Johnson County.

Toward the end of his life, Swartzendruber seems to have felt his dream of living in harmony with all beginning to slip away. Clearly, the 1860s were a difficult decade for the aging Amish bishop. He had helped recreate a sustainable agricultural system, established a strong patriarchal household structure, and shepherded his flock through the Civil War era. Yet, even a few weeks before his death, Swartzendruber found himself in the midst of yet another dangerous conflict over community values, one that tormented his successor as lead bishop in the community (figure 5.2).

The recalcitrant division in Sharon Township served up the conditions for gradually increasing the distance between the households that eventually joined the change-minded Amish-Mennonite path and those that retained the Old Order Amish traditions. Social conflict and separation broke through to shocking visibility in one Amish farmer's personal dissociation during the 1870s and 1880s.

I must talk to the people, and as soon as they and the ministers see how they are letting the church go down, the Lord will release me. I am not ordained by man, and I do not want to be. There are ministers who are chosen by men, only ordained by men. They have nothing to say.

—Noah Troyer, 1878

Chapter 6

Sleeping Preacher Strains

One Wednesday evening in August 1878, a preacher stood in Sharon Township before about fifty persons and drove home a message that challenged several components of the Amish configuration of community. He told his listeners: "[T]here are rules in the church instituted by man. They stand against the rules of Jesus Christ. Christ says, Let all come unto me. We have some ministers in the church chosen of men, but not ordained of God. These are the ones who make the rules, and make the trouble."[1] In a few sentences, Noah Troyer questioned the central Amish concepts of *Ordnung,* ordination by lot, and even the vision of religious community as a select few separated from secular society.

Traditionalists, in favor of upholding the "old order," found it difficult to confront Troyer's harsh words, even though a preacher so out of step with Amish values would normally be silenced or at least disciplined by the community. For Troyer was preaching in his sleep. Not a preacher himself, he claimed direct ordination by God Himself; his message seemed unassailable, offering a vision of community that veered wildly away from Bishop Jacob Swartzendruber's dreams of a stable and ordered Amish community in Iowa. Troyer's alternative visions called into question the critical balance of individual initiative and communal allegiance in the Amish repertoire of community.

Sleeping preachers were a familiar feature of nineteenth-century Spiritualism. In turn, Spiritualism lent itself to many manifestations of radical individualism in opposition to established authority. In many cases, trance speakers were women finding a voice apart from social and religious limitations on their speech. Spiritualism reinforced a number of radical reform movements, including woman's rights, abolitionism, free love, and other challenges to nineteenth-century American society. In an exquisite coincidence, both Spiritualism and the movement for women's equality began in 1848 in the "Burned-Over District" of upstate New York—the former with the spirit rapping of the Fox Sisters in Hydesville, the latter at Seneca Falls.[2]

The phenomenon of trance speaking was not limited to North America. Aarni Voipio, for example, described six female sleeping preachers in Finland. Banned from Lutheran pulpits, these "peasant ecstatics" nonetheless followed the form of Lutheran sermon collections and preached orthodox doctrine. In one Finnish parish in the 1770s, eighty-seven sleeping preachers appeared. Clergy called it the "preaching-disease" and worked at suppressing the movement by having the preachers arrested and compelled to accept medical treatment, and by fining the listeners.[3]

Not all the trance preachers were women, either in Finland or the United States. A Presbyterian sleeping preacher in Alabama, Constantine Blackmon Sanders, known as "X + Y = Z," wrote and preached while in trance states lasting several weeks. His eloquence moved many audiences to tears.[4] A number of other somnambulist or trance preachers, both male and female, made appearances in every corner of America.[5] Two of the most active somnambulists, Noah Troyer and John D. Kauffman, preached in Amish communities in Iowa and Indiana.

Apart from interpreting trance speaking as outright fraud, genuine contact with souls of the deceased, or the direct voice of God, observers and scholars have understood sleeping preachers from a bewildering variety of perspectives. Medical opinions include severe mold allergy or yeast infection, temporal lobe seizures accompanied by a phenomenon called epileptic automatisms, or other types of neurological disorders.[6] Others have suggested schizophrenia as a psychiatric diagnosis because of hearing voices and disorientation to reality. Hysteria, paranoia, projection, narcissism, catatonia, and even "historical group-fantasy" have appeared in the literature on Spiritualist altered states of consciousness. Self-hypnosis is one of the more promising proposals.[7]

Hypnosis and self-hypnosis fit well with neodissociation theory. Dissociation as a psychological term was first used by the French neurologist and mesmerist Pierre Janet in 1889. Revived more recently as "neodissociation" by Ernest Hilgard at Stanford, this theory holds that consciousness is not unitary and that the various centers of control are coordinated by an overall "hidden observer." Hypnosis and trance states allow access to subordinate voluntary and involuntary control systems.[8] In the most recent diagnostic manual published by the American Psychiatric Association, the dissociative disorders category includes Dissociative Amnesia, Dissociative Fugue, Dissociative Identity Disorder, Depersonalization Disorder, and Dissociative Disorder Not Otherwise Specified. The last diagnosis incorporates trance states, or altered states of consciousness, with "disturbances in the state of consciousness, identity, or memory." Dissociative disorders may be entered by a form of self-hypnosis.[9] According to dissociation theorists, hypnotic behavior can be purposeful *and* nonvolitional, in the sense that actions represent a genuine part of the personality without initiative or ongoing effort on the part of the controlling consciousness. Many religions have institutionalized trance states as prophets, mystics, shamans, or other social forms of religious leadership. In one survey of 488 societies, some 90 percent displayed naturally occurring trance and/or possession states.[10]

In the case of Noah Troyer, it seems plausible that his personal experience of dissociation reflected the social dissociation of his Amish community. He lived as a perfectly acceptable Old Order Amish farmer during the day and spoke as a change-minded Amish-Mennonite in the evening. Troyer thus gave expression to alternate strategies of community that could not be reconciled in one consciousness. Like a person trying to keep one foot on both boat and dock while the boat drifts to sea, he experienced the breach in his own personality. At first, he entered a trance state involuntarily, but later he learned to control the process to some extent and began to induce his trances via self-hypnosis. Like a poet, his inspired artistic idiom took place just outside the arena of communal accountability, in the liminal area between alternate communities.[11]

As a cultural phenomenon, trance speaking may be understood as giving voice to opinions beyond the reach of communal mechanisms of accountability and control. Female trance speakers circumvented nineteenth-century limitations on their public voices, although without challenging fundamental stereotypes of women's essential passivity (as channels for spirit voices) or nurturing natures (as medium healers).[12] Perhaps more important, trance speaking gave radical American individualism a point of entrée into many corporate structures of American society. As Ann Braude pointed out, "Spirit communication carried its own authority. If one accepted the message, one had little choice but to accept the medium." Spiritualism, abolition, and women's rights movements shared an element of anarchic individualism, since they "sought to liberate the individual from physical and spiritual domination by others and from the oppressive power of the state." The principle of individual sovereignty tended to undermine all received patterns of authority.[13]

Noah Troyer validated a more individualistic strand of religious experience among the Iowa Amish. Individualism had offered little challenge to the Amish in Europe, where the issue was to which corporate entity one should belong. Radical American individualism presented one of the most dangerous alternatives to Amish corporatism. There was no precedent in Amish history, no repertorial niche on which to depend, no commonsense response to religious individuality. The unpredictable Troyer unveiled the tension and incipient division of Old Order Amish and Amish-Mennonites in Iowa.

Noah Troyer, Trance Speaker

Noah Troyer was born on 10 January 1831 in Holmes County, Ohio, to John and Elizabeth Yoder Troyer. Both parents had been born in Pennsylvania, and the family lived in Holmes, Knox, and Champaign counties in Ohio and Lagrange County, Indiana. John and Elizabeth were finally buried in the Pete Miller Amish cemetery in Johnson County, Iowa. Noah J. was their second child and first son. At age 26, he returned to Holmes County from Indiana and married Veronica Mast on 19 March 1857. Veronica, known as "Fannie," was born in Lancaster County, Pennsylvania, the youngest child of Christian and Susanna Kurtz Mast. Noah and Fannie produced six children, although only four survived infancy. According to the 1880 population census, the four children were born in four different states: Ohio (John N. in 1860), Michigan (Daniel N. in 1866), Indiana (Lydia in 1871), and Iowa (Fanny in 1875). After living five years in Holmes County, Noah and Fannie moved in 1862 to Lagrange County, Indiana, then to St. Joseph County, Michigan, one year later. They lived in Michigan four and a half years, then returned to Lagrange County, and finally settled permanently in Iowa in 1875.

Troyer bought 180 acres in section 32 of Sharon Township on 15 April 1874 from his maternal uncle, David D. Yoder, a younger brother of his mother. He paid the hefty price of $8,850, just over $49 per acre. Another maternal uncle, Stephen D. Yoder, had bought 160 acres in Section 21 of Sharon Township on 25 March 1870.[14] Troyer's letter of transfer from the church in Indiana noted that he had not been attending services there because of "dissatisfaction." The letter was signed by Troyer's brother-in-law, Preacher Christian Warey, husband of his younger sister, Mary. Despite the note of discontent, Noah and Fannie Troyer were accepted as full members of the Sharon Township Amish congregation on 22 November 1874.[15] This extended family would bring permanent change to the Johnson County Amish community.

Noah Troyer had experienced severe headaches and abdominal cramps two or three times a week since his childhood, sometimes painful to the point of losing consciousness. In March 1876, only a year after moving to Iowa, he became ill for several days. One evening he became very nervous, and that night he talked at some length in his sleep. His wife, Fannie, called in several neighbors for help, but they decided to keep the mystifying matter quiet. When Fannie told Noah Troyer about his nocturnal speech and what he had said, he refused to believe the story. A few weeks later, he had a second less severe attack in which he talked a few minutes. All was quiet for nearly a year. Then the odd ailment returned, and he began to talk again while asleep. At first the attacks were light and irregular, but they continued to grow more severe and more frequent until by April 1878, the convulsions were occurring every evening. The spasms and speaking occurred only rarely during daylight hours. The family and a few neighbors who knew of Troyer's torment remained quiet.[16]

One Sunday morning shortly after April, however, Troyer entered a trance during an Amish worship meeting and spoke at some length. The secret of his unconscious preaching remained secret no longer, and curious local residents began flocking to see this improbable event. The *Iowa City Daily Republican* sent a reporter to rural Johnson County on June 13 and published an account on 15 June 1878. Gideon Marner sent the newspaper clipping to the *Herald of Truth* in Elkhart, Indiana, and editor John F. Funk printed the story in the July issue. Both Amish and Mennonite households, including a number of Amish families in Iowa, subscribed to the periodical. The article caused a sensation in Johnson County and among Funk's Mennonite and Amish constituency.[17]

The Iowa City reporter took with him S. T. Yoder and W. D. Lichty, both living in Iowa City, met Bishop Abner Yoder and David J. Miller in Sharon Township, and continued to Noah Troyer's house. They arrived at 8:00 on a Thursday evening, and the Troyer family welcomed the curious entourage. Troyer himself was still awake, but he soon felt the customary attack coming on and retired to a bed prepared on the floor in a large room. The family allowed the visitors to enter the appointed room and observe the proceedings. Troyer's stomach and bowels were "badly bloated," and he was shifting restlessly, "striking his breast with his fists, gnashing his teeth, as if suffering great bodily pain." At times his breathing seemed to stop altogether, and he muttered in a strange language. His attendants had to prevent him from doing harm to himself. These convulsions lasted an hour, and the empiricist reporter noted that his pulse was normal, head hot, feet cold, and eyes set.[18]

Troyer began speaking at about 9:00 P.M. and continued until 10:10 P.M. He spoke with his eyes closed but with appropriate gestures, in good English, forcefully and distinctly. Every ten or twenty minutes he seemed to lose his breath, but when attendants applied cold water to his face, he revived, took up his line of thought, and proceeded. When finished, he again went into convulsions, but soon he quieted and slept until morning without regaining full consciousness.[19]

The *Daily Republican* reporter transcribed only one long paragraph of Troyer's sermon and justified the terse treatment by asserting that "it contains nothing remarkable and nothing but the orthodox teachings of the Bible." Troyer spoke of the star over Bethlehem, Creation, separation of good from evil, preparing a heavenly mansion, the narrow and broad roads, and the creation of woman as a companion for man.[20]

Fannie Troyer, described by the reporter as "an intelligent and pleasant Amish woman," consented to an interview while the company waited for Troyer to begin speaking, and she narrated much of his personal history. She told of his beginning to speak in an unconscious state and how he would not believe her when she told him what he was doing; in fact, her husband "seemed ashamed of himself" and strongly denied knowing anything about it. Since he had no control over the phenomenon, he asked his family not to mention it to strangers. He refused medical attention, since he believed a physician would not help him. During the ten weeks before the reporter's visit, beginning in April, the attacks came every night except two, and four times during the day. His stomach began to bloat every day at about 3 o'clock in the afternoon, sometimes so badly that it would "burst the buttons off his pantaloons."[21] But Troyer never remembered much pain and always awakened the next morning feeling relaxed and refreshed. His nocturnal speeches lasted from one hour to just over two.

After the reporter's interview with Fannie Troyer, and after Troyer finished preaching, the Iowa City visitors retired. They arose very early the next morning, only to find the sleeping preacher already awake and feeling well, albeit a bit sore. After breakfast, Mrs. Troyer asked the reporter to read his article to her husband and family and several others who were present the night before. She seemed "very anxious" for him to hear a full account of the previous night's events, since he had continued to doubt what he had been told about his talks. The reporter ended by vouching for Troyer's good reputation and promised to say more about the "remarkable case" in the future.[22]

In July 1879, the *Iowa City Daily Republican* published transcriptions of six Noah Troyer sermons, along with a brief biography.[23] The forty-page booklet contains five sermons from August 1878 and one dated 17 April 1879. Six of Troyer's Amish neighbors signed a statement authenticating the sermons; however, despite Bishop Abner Yoder's assistance to the reporter on his initial visit, no Amish minister or bishop signed the witness statement. The declaration is dated 1 July 1879 and appears at the beginning of the booklet:

> We, the undersigned citizens of Johnson County, State of Iowa, do hereby affirm that we are acquainted with Noah Troyer and have known him since he settled in this State, and we assert that we have seen him and heard him talk when in an unconscious state, and we believe the biography and report of his sermons herein published are substantially correct. We further state that up to the present time nothing has occurred to cause us to believe that Mr. Troyer is in any way conscious during these strange attacks.

Benedict Miller, Joseph P. Miller, Joseph S. Yoder, David Miller, Jacob Boller, and E. P. Hershberger all signed the brief deposition. The first four were members of the Sharon Township Amish congregation, while Boller and Hershberger attended the Washington Township church. The biography repeated most of the original newspaper story of 19 June 1878 and asserted that as a result of the story, "hundreds of persons came from a distance to hear him talk." The biography did make a new claim, however, that would appear repeatedly in later accounts. A skeptical German doctor who wished to test for fraud approached the sleeping preacher while he was praying and "run [sic] a silver pin into his leg an inch and a half, but he did not flinch." Later accounts usually added that Troyer merely complained of some puzzling soreness in his leg the following day.[24]

John F. Funk reprinted the *Daily Republican* pamphlet verbatim at his Mennonite Publishing Company office in Elkhart, Indiana, and also published a German translation.[25] Funk sold out his first printing by February 1880 and promised a second edition in a few weeks.[26] Several distant relatives wrote to Bishop Abner Yoder and requested information about the sleeping preacher or copies of the pamphlet. One writer to Yoder lamented the fact that Troyer probably would not come to Illinois so she could hear him. She noted that she felt sorry for him and his family, but "if it pleases the Lord they should bear it patiently. It is a mistry to me." Yoder's nephew, John M. Schrock, wrote from Stony Creek in Somerset County, Pennsylvania, and requested a copy of the pamphlet Yoder sent to Schrock's father, preferably in English.[27]

The second book, rushed to press by March 1880, printed six new sermons, two from August 1878 not previously published, and four from February 1880. The new book also included a lengthy defense by Troyer's brother-in-law, Preacher John P. King of West Liberty, Logan County, Ohio. King's article contained brief notes from thirteen sermons preached in November and December, 1879, while Troyer visited relatives in Indiana. The new booklet also published a table showing dates and lengths of Troyer's sermons in 1879, with 249 sermons listed for the 365 days; a brief account of Troyer's sermon on 9 November 1879 at Wayland, Iowa, written by Jacob Naffziger of Archbold, Fulton County, Ohio; and a 20 November 1879 article published in the *Cincinnati Times,* Vistula, Indiana. Due to the extensive new material, Funk apologetically raised the price to 25 cents, or $2.40 per dozen.[28]

John P. King's article runs twenty-five pages. King concerned himself with careful documentation and proofs of authenticity. He wrote a long description of the stages Troyer experienced during his trance preaching. When combined with the first description penned by the Iowa City *Daily Republican* reporter and compared with several shorter eyewitness accounts, a detailed portrayal of the sleeping preacher can be constructed.

Troyer usually began feeling sick and going into convulsions late in the afternoon, and after a short time would lie on his bed or a couch and enter an unconscious state. His arms and legs were rigid, "as hard as a pole of wood" in one account, and attempts to startle him or awaken him with noise or touching were unsuccessful.[29] After about 30 minutes, he would sit up in bed, stretch his hands upward as if in supplication, and pray aloud very intensely for 10 to 15 minutes. Then he knelt by his bed another 15 to 20 minutes, continuing to pray fervently. His assistants helped him to his feet and steadied him until he could stand alone, and thereafter guarded against his walking into a hot stove or otherwise injuring himself. When first standing, his arms remained raised, then dropped slowly; and while speaking, he used appropriate gestures and walked about the room in a natural way. His eyes were closed, and he was oblivious to touch or noise, although skeptical observers put their hands on him, tried to startle him with sudden noises, and even pulled his eyelids open. (King repeated the story of the doctor in Iowa who had inserted a needle in Troyer's leg with no response.) Troyer then began speaking in a loud voice, in English or German, depending on the composition of his audience. His sermons lasted from one to three and a half hours, but his voice never faltered, and he showed no fatigue or even perspiration. He indicated a precise knowledge of how long he had been speaking by using the phrase "two times" or "two times and half a time," indicating two hours or two and a half hours respectively.

After his sermon, he asked the ministers present to testify to the truthfulness of his words, in German or English, and he usually requested a hymn or two in either language. He announced whether he would speak the next evening and knelt in prayer for about 30 minutes, almost always including the Lord's Prayer. Upon saying "Amen," he immediately folded his hands over his chest and fell backwards into the arms of his attendants, who carried him back to his bed. He lay completely still on the bed, "rigid as a stick," for 5 to 30 minutes; his respiration and pulse seemed to cease altogether. Then he straightened his arms and legs, his breathing and pulse returned, and he slept soundly until 4 A.M. During his night's rest, he could not be awakened by any amount of effort. The next morning he retained no memory of the previous night, and he put in a normal day's work on his farm.[30]

Themes in Troyer's Trance Sermons

In addition to the sensational circumstances of Noah Troyer's sermonizing, the content of his sermons raised direct and indirect questions about the validity of Amish traditions. An individual questioning the community so powerfully and in a way that could not be disciplined or controlled shifted the balance of power between individual self-assertion and communal responsibility, at least temporarily. The extant sermons by Troyer exhibit at least five crucial motifs that diverged from traditional Amish communalism: a repetitive set of Bible quotations that emphasized urgent individual conversion; a critique of ministers and the traditional methods of ordination; a call for ecumenical unity and an end to church divisions; spiritualist comments and manifestations; and questioning of religious traditions as human creations, not sparing Mennonite and Amish founders like Menno Simons and Jacob Ammann.

The twelve more or less complete sermons and numerous sermon fragments recorded from Noah Troyer return repeatedly, almost monotonously and hypnotically, to the same biblical passages. He usually chose a sermon text and returned to it often, but used the same set of biblical themes in almost every sermon. He inevitably spoke of Noah and of God's judgment, and of how sinners were left outside the ark after the opportunity for repentance had passed. He used the Gospel of John's physical description of communion as "eating my flesh and drinking my blood," an implicit critique of traditional Anabaptist views of the communion elements as symbolic rather than actual, following the Swiss Reformation leader Ulrich Zwingli. Communion, he said, should be held much more often than the twice yearly Amish practice, perhaps even daily.[31] He spoke of Jesus as the True Vine, and used that verse as his sermon text several times, making a great divide between those attached and nourished by the Vine and those who stayed apart. He seemed fascinated by light, and used Jesus' saying, "I am the light of the world," as a sermon text and reference point. He returned repeatedly to Saul and the bright light on the road to Damascus, resulting in sudden conversion and great power as Saul changed to Paul the missionary. He constantly referred to the Creation in Genesis and the rebellious angel who was expelled from heaven and became Satan, the opponent of God. He attributed human conflict to the devil and presented a stark choice of following the broad road to hell or the narrow road to heaven, with absolutely no other possibility. Troyer returned often to King Herod and his attempt, prompted by Satan, to kill the baby Jesus in Bethlehem. He seemed fascinated by the noncanonical idea that, as the Holy Family fled to Egypt, Satan spat a stream of water after them, but the desert swallowed it up and protected the family. He focused on the rich man and Lazarus in Jesus' parable and emphasized how there was no more time for the rich man to repent after death came upon him suddenly. Troyer quoted the saying "As the tree falls, so it lies" to show the permanence of death and the passing of any possibility for changing one's mind. Lot's wife and the destruction of Sodom and Gomorrah, and her disobedience in looking back and punishment as a pillar of salt, reminded Troyer of certain judgment and the need for believers never to revert to the sinful world.

Taken together, Troyer emphasized, in this potpourri of biblical texts, a number of themes usually associated with Protestant Revivalism: sudden conversion, constant preparation for inevitable death and judgment, emotional warnings of hell, and the absolute choice between good and evil. By contrast, Amish theology focuses on a semi-Pelagian view of the human will and the need to shape the will to obedience over the course of a lifetime. It requires constant effort and communal vigilance, in the Amish worldview, to maintain faithfulness to the end.[32]

In addition to a standard Bible miscellany, Noah Troyer almost always mentioned Amish ministers in his sermons, ranging from including ministers in his prayers to indicting church leaders for weakness and divisiveness. Regarding his own authority to preach as an unordained man, he usually said something like, "Dear friends, do not think hard of me, I speak only as power is given me from God." By contrast, Troyer said, many properly ordained ministers fail to teach the people with power, seeking earthly riches instead. He went so far as to say, "I stand between God and you, come down to the foot of the cross," at the same time blaming the ministers for not admonishing the poor works of their people—"The ministers let the people go back into sin."[33] One of Troyer's indictments of ministers became especially harsh:

> There are good and bad in all churches. There are good and bad in our church. The ministers do not preach with power. They are not ordained of God but of man. When they get up before the people they have nothing to say. They are striving too much for this world's good—they are empty vessels. The whole heart is taken up with worldly affairs. They can talk of earthly things but not of heavenly things. . . . The ministers do not admonish their people with power.[34]

Yet he also often included in sermons disclaimers about his preaching and his role, such as the ending of a sermon in April 1879:

> Dear friends I shall stand before you until my Saviour the Lord gives it to me to stop. I see no stopping place. I must stop off now, dear friends for a time. God does the work through me. My prayer to God is that you will not make a Jesus Christ out of me—leave me as I am. The day is coming when those who are standing against me will be sorry for not doing as I and Christ have told them.[35]

The problem of ordination and authority to preach loomed large for Troyer's hearers. Rumors swirled among the Amish communities about Troyer refusing ordination and, consequently, his being forced by God to preach. A promise to accept ordination should the lot fall is part of the Amish baptismal liturgy. Sanford C. Yoder reported hearing a story from Troyer's son (John?) in 1915 that Troyer had received votes for the ministry in an Amish church before moving to Iowa. Since he was unhappy with some of the regulations in that particular church district, he had declined to let his name go through the lot, a serious breach of his baptismal commitment. Some time later his two sons, who had joined the instruction class in preparation for baptism, withdrew a few weeks before the baptismal service, also because of disagreement with the *Ordnung* in their church.[36]

Preacher John P. King, Troyer's brother-in-law, attempted to allay some of the rumors in his article for the second book of Troyer's sermons. King asserted that Troyer had united with the church in Indiana and received a certificate in good standing on 15 November 1874, "although for sometime they did not attend public worship, on account of a disturbance among the members." King specified that the church letter was read at a meeting in the house of Jacob B. Miller and signed by Preacher Christian Warey (Figure 6.1), the latter another brother-in-law of Troyer.[37] Second, King said Troyer did take his place in a lot for choosing a minister, but the lot simply did not fall on him. Third, there was a persistent report that Troyer disobeyed the church and refused to participate in a lot at the house of Frederick Swartzendruber on 20 March 1878, just before his trance preaching became public. However, the congregation excused him due to "bodily infirmities," and King cited several names of persons who attended that particular meeting. If Troyer began preaching just after being excused from the heavy responsibilities of the Amish minister, it must have seemed logical to conclude that trance preaching was some sort of divinely imposed penance or an alternate route for God's will to be revealed. However, later accounts emphasized that Troyer actually began preaching in 1876, nearly two years before his preaching became public. King invited doubters to write for confirmation to Bishop Abner Yoder in Iowa or Preacher Christian Warey of Lima, Lagrange County, Indiana.[38]

The third component of Troyer's preaching consisted of pronouncements on church unity and the evils of division. According to Troyer, there were only two churches, Christ's church and the devil's church. All other distinc-

6.1. Christian and Mary Warey, sister and brother-in-law of Noah Troyer. Christian Warey became the first minister of the Union Church.

tions and denominational differences were distractions when compared with the sharp contrast of good and evil. "I do not speak for one church, but for all the churches," Troyer claimed. "All churches are good except one, and that is the Devil's church. There are good and bad in all churches." Far from attacking other denominations and upholding Amish uniqueness, Troyer often intoned, "It is the Saviour's wish that all the human family shall come to Him."

Troyer made statements that may have sounded like universalism to his hearers, such as, "There is only one true church on this earth. . . . It makes no difference what church you belong to—one church is as good as another, so the soul is right. We ought to worship together."[39] He deplored divisions and conflict within the church, and he asked, "Dear friends, why are there so many divisions? We are all striving to enter one heavenly home, and yet we are standing apart. It is my wish and Christ's will that we be all of one mind and one soul." He called on his hearers to "lay aside all quarreling, all partings" and "let us be united and of one mind."[40] This talk of unity and only one true denomination went directly against Amish traditions of separation from the world and nonconformity to the world, often expressed as suspicion of "worldly" churches that simply followed the wide way to destruction. The notion that Christians who persecuted the Amish and their ancestors were members of legitimate churches was a wrenching shift from traditional Amish understandings of the nature of the church.

Fourth, Troyer exhibited visionary spiritualism. He seemed to speak in tongues, although the evidence is sketchy due to the unfamiliarity of observers with the phenomenon of glossolalia. The Iowa City reporter who first heard Troyer in 1878 noted that "his mutterings were in a strange language" as he experienced convulsions before beginning the sermon itself. Sometimes the sermon notes included words that resembled glossolalia, emphasizing the consonants l, s, m, and w: "Walla sea, Walla sea, Trellama; Mattralama, Walla sea, Mattralama."[41] Troyer also described visions of the future, hidden knowledge, and heavenly places. He perceived "light streaks" and "dark streaks" in his audience, seeming to imply that the former were among the saved, while the latter were unsaved. He saw a bright streak extending directly from his mouth to Christ's mouth in heaven, while dark light streaked down to hell.[42] He prayed that his hearers would become "bright, shining lights" in the world and said again, "Let us, dear friends, be bright, glowing lights unto the Lord."[43] Troyer spoke repeatedly of blasphemy against the Holy Spirit, the unforgivable sin, and made it seem the equivalent of opposing its spiritual manifestations.

Fifth, much of Troyer's preaching questioned Amish-Mennonite tradition, implicitly or explicitly. He discounted as an issue mode of baptism, one of the critical controversies in the Amish Great Schism as Amish leaders argued over stream or house baptism. He resisted the concept of church rules, calling them "man made" and sometimes "against the rules of Christ." This blow against the *Ordnung* struck at the heart of Amish concepts of community membership and obedience. Troyer found rules especially offensive when they kept young people from joining the church, and he admonished his hearers at one point: "If any young people come and want into the church do not keep them out on account of little rules of man's own make."[44] He insisted that it was not God's will that one soul be lost, not only a rejection of Calvinist predestination but also an implicit critique of the Amish trust in banning and shunning. He even discounted Mennonite and Amish founding leaders Menno Simons and Jacob Ammann, stating that Menno caused a division over irrelevant modes of baptism, and that both "took man's way."[45] At other times, Troyer identified with the core of Amish tradition. He encouraged persistence to the end and expounded the necessity for obedience and faithfulness in life beyond mere belief as intellectual assent to theological doctrines.

Noah Troyer used the Bible to delineate a stark choice between good and evil and promoted conversion. He taught that many ministers were not truly ordained, emphasized church unity and the irrelevance of denominations, spoke in tongues, revealed spiritualist visions and manifestations, and disparaged Amish tradition. As a result, members of Amish and Mennonite communities questioned their traditional customs of authority and ordination, traditional gender roles, and the very need to preserve Amishness as a separate community. The repertoire of Amish community, the "old order" developed in Europe and preserved in America, seemed of little importance compared to the unmediated voice of God. In Iowa these questions made leaving the traditional community possible and made a parting of ways thinkable, resulting in a hardening of tradition-minded and change-minded positions.

Making Meaning from Celebrity Sleeping Preachers

Troyer's impact reached far beyond Sharon Township. After publishing its initial report of the sleeping preacher in June 1878, the *Iowa City Daily Republican* accorded Troyer the status of local celebrity by relating with regularity his activities and whereabouts. On June 27 the paper reported that Mr. Noah

Troyer, "the gentleman who talks while unconscious," was in Iowa City the previous day. Troyer, the editor reported, "is feeling about as well as usual" and still speaking every night. Mr. Rodgers from the *Daily Republican* visited Troyer for a week in August and transcribed eight sermons for the first booklet of sermons, although only six appeared in the final product. Between twenty and one hundred fifty people heard Troyer speak that week, some from great distances.

On Sunday evening 18 August, with 150 people present, Troyer failed to swoon as usual after his hour and twenty minute discourse, but rather opened his eyes and was "very much astonished" to see so many people. He informed his hearers that the Lord had "released him from his labor," and that henceforth he would be "a natural man again." Troyer made an appearance on his front porch to allow everyone to see and talk with him, and the crowd dispersed. Rodgers reported that Troyer was "good company" during the day, "as fond of fun as any man." The editor regretted that more people were not able to hear Troyer preach, but promised the pamphlet of sermons would soon be published.[46]

Believing it necessary to wrap up the story because of Troyer's release from further preaching, the *Daily Republican* ran a long story about the local trance preacher on August 22. Many readers had been asking for more details since the first report in June, and the paper repeated its description of Troyer's nightly routine, observing, "The Spiritualists believe he is a medium under control of a deceased Amish minister." However, other observers claimed fraud. Several times after completing his sermons, he rose from his prone position and left the house, "bounding along as if a rubber ball." Twice he tried to run away, and his watchers caught and brought him back inside "with great difficulty."

On Saturday 17 August, during Rodgers' visit, Troyer left the house, went back in, then went out on the porch, sat down, and "took a chew of tobacco and would spit as a child blows water from its mouth." His wife finally brought him back inside, and he rested quietly the remainder of the night. Despite not having an English Bible in his house and reading very little, he preached fluently in English and quoted extensively from the Bible; the next day, when asked about passages of Scripture he used in his sermons, he could not say whether or not they were even in the Bible. Rodgers stated that there were many false rumors making the rounds, but so far as he could tell, the Amish "endorse him and believe he spoke only as the Lord directed him."

The article reported again that Troyer had opened his eyes after preaching

Sunday evening and said, "It has been revealed to me that this will be the last time I shall speak to you. My work has been done and I am released." His wife was so thrilled at the news that she could not sleep that night. Up to three hundred people had been coming to their house every night to hear her husband speak, and the crowds kept them up late at night and made a great deal of extra work. The article closed with the observation that the former sleeping preacher had not spoken since Sunday evening, and Troyer "is confident he will not be troubled any more."[47]

Troyer's wife must have been disappointed shortly thereafter, because her husband began preaching again on the third night after his Sunday evening release. Troyer visited the Eicher settlement just north of Wayland the very next weekend, preaching every evening "with renewed vigor."[48] A brief note in the September 7 issue of the *Daily Republican* reported that Troyer was preaching every evening again, and some Iowa Citians were making travel plans to see him, perhaps thinking he might soon stop permanently. Other brief notices in September show Troyer visiting Henry County again, along with his wife and parents, and picking up a younger brother from Indiana at the train station in Iowa City, accompanied by his father.[49]

In January 1879 Troyer paid a visit to the *Daily Republican* office in Iowa City and told the editor that he continued to preach, but not every night; he had talked for two hours and twenty minutes the previous night, Monday, January 6.[50] No further news about Troyer appears in the paper until July, when the pamphlet with his sermons became available. The *Daily Republican* claimed advance orders for hundreds of copies, though the paper planned to sell the pamphlet at cost, or 20 cents each, to avoid the appearance of profiting from the event. In addition to heavy local demand, orders arrived from "nearly all parts of the United States." Troyer at that time preached an average of twice a week, but the "spells still continue to come on every evening." The story continued, "What the result of the phenomenon will be is not known and the case may continue to be enveloped in mystery for several years."[51]

In November the *Daily Republican* reprinted the article from the *Cincinnati Times* (Vistula, Indiana) that John F. Funk also picked up for the second book of Troyer's sermons. The account called Troyer "one of the strangest exhibitions of spirit control of modern times" and said the trance preaching created an extraordinary stir throughout the community of Vistula, Indiana, near Troyer's former residence. "No one can hear him and remain unmoved, and whoever hears him once is eager to hear him again," the report concluded.[52] This was the last mention of Noah Troyer in the *Daily Republican* until his death in 1886.

Just as Troyer disappeared from the pages of an important Iowa City newspaper, a flurry of articles about the sleeping preacher surfaced in the *Herald of Truth.* After the initial reprint of the *Iowa City Daily Republican* story in June 1878, the *Herald* had failed to mention Noah Troyer even once in 1879. But in 1880 editor John F. Funk carried many accounts and news stories about the Iowa sleeping preacher, including an increasing number of references to opposition to Troyer and to the controversy he aroused. Troyer himself often referred to his opponents. In one sermon he said, "There are men today who are talking all the evil they can against me. I feel good over it. . . . You must prepare your own souls. I cannot do it for you."[53]

In January Funk clarified two quotes attributed to Troyer by the Iowa City reporter in the first sermon booklet and cited a letter from Benedict Miller modifying the statement he and the other five Amish men had signed for the booklet. The first quote seemed to assert that Jesus cast out devils through Beelzebub, the prince of devils, whereas Troyer likely said that Jesus was thus accused by his enemies; and the second quote seemed to say Paul healed the sick and lame rather than Jesus. Funk attributed both misstatements to Troyer's abrupt speaking style or, more likely, errors by the reporter due to Troyer's rapid speech. Or, one might add, the reporter's lack of theological sophistication may have contributed to the seemingly heretical statements. As for Benedict Miller's revised statement, the changes tended to soften any witness to the truth of Troyer's sermons in favor of the less threatening assertions of unconscious condition and personal acquaintance. Rather than attesting "We believe the biography and report of his sermons herein published are substantially correct," Miller changed the wording to "We believe that the biography and present condition of Noah Troyer as given in the pamphlet to be substantially correct." The undersigned preferred "leaving the sermons to the judgment of the reader."[54]

On the same page as Miller's cautious corrections, a news note regarding a four-week trip by Troyer appeared. The "well known 'Trance Preacher' " was to visit parents and relatives in Indiana and Michigan. He spoke every night during the trip, even though the purpose of the trip was visiting relatives rather than conducting an itinerant preaching tour. An audience of one thousand persons at an Amish-Mennonite meetinghouse in Indiana highlighted the excursion. His final sermon before returning to Iowa occurred at a schoolhouse near Bristol, Indiana, and he prayed that he be spared any speaking burdens while traveling home by train.

When Troyer visited influential editor John F. Funk in Elkhart on the way home, Funk remarked, "Bro. Troyer is certainly one of the wonders of the age" due to his unconscious preaching while retaining the ability to switch between English and German according to his audience. Funk, a progressive Mennonite leader, also implicitly recognized Troyer as an authentic preacher by calling him "Brother" in print, usually a signal of formal ordination. He did not have as much trouble affirming Troyer's legitimacy as did those defending a traditional Amish position. Funk also commented, "In his remarks he spares none, and has awakened a great interest in all who have heard him."[55]

On the very next page, Joseph Yoder of Bristol, Elkhart County, Indiana, reported on a trip he took to Nebraska and Iowa. Joseph P. Miller met Yoder and his companions, Gideon Yoder, Joseph's brother, and David Kurtz, a brother-in-law, in Iowa City and hosted the travelers in his home. They visited the Deer Creek Church on 2 November 1879 at Christian Swartzendruber's house, and nine "precious souls" were baptized. Yoder's use of such individualistic and revivalistic terminology indicates his progressive orientation. The group also visited Noah Troyer and heard him ten evenings. "His preaching is one of the wonders spoken of in the Scriptures," Yoder wrote; and he compared the experience with that of the Queen of the South who came to hear the wisdom of Solomon, for despite reading Troyer's sermons and hearing so much about the phenomenon, "the half had not been told me."[56]

Yet one more article appeared in the same issue of the *Herald of Truth,* this one by Jacob Ramseyer of Ligonier, Indiana. Ramseyer attended on the last evening that Troyer spoke in his father's house in Lagrange County during his trip to Indiana in late 1879. He praised Troyer with equal enthusiasm, claiming that his preaching brought many hearers to tears and that such power was manifested that some persons standing close before him began to be afraid and stepped back "as though God was personally before them warning them to be baptized and united with His Church." More importantly, for the first time in print, Ramseyer made unflattering comparisons between the power of Troyer and the powerless ministers who he said were selfish, proud, and obsessed with mode of baptism rather than meaning. Ramseyer asked why God had to appear in this way and then answered his own question: "Probably because the ministers have not sufficient power to persuade all persons to come to Christ."[57]

Troyer's spiritualist preaching raised questions about the traditional structure of authority in both Amish and Mennonite denominations, and ministers ordained by lot usually came out second best.

In the February 1880 issue of *Herald of Truth* and in the second book of Troyer's sermons, Preacher John P. King, husband of Noah Troyer's oldest sibling, Rebecca, wrote at great length about Troyer's sermons. King's approving articles represent a new departure in Troyeriana. After the initial burst of interest, curiosity, and amazement, attitudes hardened into those who opposed the trance preacher versus those who defended Troyer to further their own agenda of breaking apart the "backward" old order. King (*Kinig* in the German versions) offered the most thorough descriptions and thoughtful interpretations of Troyer's preaching, but his observations still exceeded the bounds of what traditionalists could accept. In effect, King depicted Troyer approvingly as a radical spiritualist, speaking in unknown languages (glossolalia), aware of information in his trance state that he could not know while conscious, and even able to see into the future. In the religious periodical, and as a minister himself, King emphasized, above all, that Troyer preached against church divisions, blaming contentious ministers; emphasized the need for ministers to preach with greater power; and advocated unity in the church, even including other denominations.

In July John P. King also reported on a May 1880 visit to Iowa, when he had accompanied Noah Troyer on a visit to the Amish community near Wayland. Since Bishop Sebastian Gerig was ill, Troyer spoke in a trance four evenings, and King reported that "his sermons gave me great satisfaction and produced deep emotions."[58] Troyer visited Indiana, Ohio, and Pennsylvania in August and September 1880 and spoke in the Mennonite meetinghouse in Elkhart on August 25. John F. Funk heard Troyer for the first time at this meeting, along with a large audience, "who listened with attention to the strange phenomenon" of Troyer's unconscious preaching. After hearing Troyer's two-hour sermon, Funk confirmed the facts he had published in papers and pamphlets. Troyer was carried to the minister's house after his sermon, and the next day he traveled on to visit his father in Lagrange County. Troyer did normal farm work during the day and was in good health and appetite, but he succumbed to the strange attacks every day at about five or six o'clock. Funk concluded, "This is indeed a most remarkable case."[59]

Troyer's trip to the East generated reports to *Herald of Truth* along the way. John S. Coffman, the Mennonite evangelist, published a dispassionate article in the October issue. Coffman reported in great detail on Troyer's sermon in Elkhart, Indiana, on August 25. His account generally agrees with that of John P. King and with other descriptions. As Troyer was first entering his trance state, Coffman tried to bend his arm at the elbow, using all his strength, but could not bend the joint. He also reported unintelligible language at the very beginning of Troyer's speech. Coffman recounted a standard set of biblical allusions made by Troyer: the rich man and Lazarus, mode of baptism, the woman caught in adultery, and so forth. The lesson gleaned by Coffman from the experience of hearing Troyer was that "people should not be so ready to accuse others when they have faults themselves." Coffman found Troyer's subjects and practical applications compelling. After the sermon, a number of people surrounded him on the bed in the Mennonite meetinghouse, touching him and handling his legs and arms, "but nothing seems sufficient to rouse him." Although there was room for doubt about Troyer, Coffman asserted, "It is the opinion of the writer that no one would fail to be convinced of his honesty, if he were present and would carefully watch him from the beginning of the strange phenomena." Finally, Coffman marveled at Troyer's good health and stamina, given the labor of preaching 133 nights in succession in one stretch.[60]

Troyer visited relatives in Mifflin County, Pennsylvania, where his deceased grandfather, Andrew Troyer, had been a member of the Amish community. An article in the local newspaper stated Troyer held large evening audiences "spell-bound" in the three Amish congregations.[61] Troyer also spoke during this same trip East on October 13 in the Amish Mennonite meetinghouse in Wayne County, Ohio. C. P. Steiner stated cautiously, "Since so much has been said and written of him I will merely state that he preached the word of God so far as I understood him."[62]

After this cluster of reports, nothing of Troyer appeared in the pages of *Herald of Truth* for a year, until Funk published a note in December 1881 in response to a query, "What has become of Noah Troyer?" Funk reported that Troyer had been relieved of his labors (the lapse again proved temporary), and he noted that John D. Kauffman, from just east of Goshen, Indiana, had turned up as a sleeping preacher and had been speaking every Wednesday evening. Funk also wrote that Christian Zook of Lancaster County, Pennsylvania, spoke in his sleep every evening. Funk interpreted the other two trance preachers as a fulfillment of Troyer's predictions that two others would follow him "and would have to do as he did." And Funk advertised his edition of Troyer's sermons, as he had been doing in every issue.[63]

Funk and his readers found themselves forced into a growing awareness of other sleeping preachers, which precluded treating Troyer as an isolated event. In the 15 January 1882 issue of *Herald of Truth,* a report from Holmes County, Ohio, told of yet another trance preacher in the Amish community. John Opliger, 27, working as a hired man for Samuel Mast, began preaching in August 1881 while unconscious. At first he preached lying down, but later while standing. He emphasized moral issues, such as swearing, drunkenness, gambling, quarreling, and fighting; and he warned his hearers to repent and be baptized. Like Troyer, he referred to God's warning before the Flood, and cautioned that similar punishment might occur now. Doctors could not cure him, and when Opliger entered his trance state, one doctor remarked, "One of his limbs could be amputated without disturbing him." The correspondent from Ohio closed with the comment, "Truly strange things are transpiring in our midst."[64]

Funk himself visited the home of sleeping preacher John D. Kauffman on 2 March 1882, some four miles east of Goshen, Indiana, and wrote a long account of the experience. Many of the specific themes and phrases used by Kauffman are identical to Troyer's preaching, and even many of the behaviors, such as speaking unintelligible language when he wanted a drink of water while preaching. He also criticized the self-righteousness and false teachings of ministers and implied that persons who opposed him were in danger of blaspheming the Holy Ghost.[65] Noah Troyer visited Elkhart on 5 May 1882, and spent an evening with Kauffman. Each trance preacher spoke about two hours, but Kauffman did not begin until Troyer closed. "Neither seemed conscious of the other's presence," and neither had any memory of the experience the next morning.[66] Kauffman continued speaking to large crowds, such as at Yellow Creek Mennonite Church on Sunday evening, 7 October 1883. Kauffman spoke every Wednesday and Sunday evening. Troyer visited Elkhart again in April 1883 and spoke over an hour at the home of Preacher Joseph Summers.[67]

After 1883 there are few mentions of Troyer or Kauffman. The *Herald of Truth* followed a pattern similar to that of the *Iowa City Daily Republican:* after an initial frenzy of curiosity, there was a period of reporting and reflection, and finally silence because of the unacceptable implications of full belief in sleeping preachers as divine prophets. There was no direct condemnation of Troyer or Kauffman. What if they were legitimate? However, silence about the trance preachers did not free Amish and Mennonite communities from confronting their activities.

Mennonites reacted to the sleeping preacher phenomenon with brief, though intense discussions in *Herald of Truth* on ordination and gender roles. In response to the apparent divine ordination of Troyer and Kauffman, Mennonite writers found it necessary to defend traditional methods of selecting preachers (by lot) and traditional sermon presentations (unemotional calls for obedience, not impassioned pleas for conversion).[68] Such questions about religious authority necessarily provoked doubts about proper behavior for men and women, because patriarchal gender roles are closely tied to traditional authority in Amish and Mennonite communities. Mennonite writers found it advisable to reemphasize the subjection of a wife to her husband and the special responsibilities of mothers in raising children and making the home a place of rest and refuge. One writer in 1883 even addressed the question, "Has a Woman the Right to Preach?" Of course not, he concluded—but raising the question at all indicates some uncertainty.[69]

Those Amish leaders in Iowa who disapproved of Troyer's nocturnal sermonizing tended to respond with public silence, in accord with their tradition-minded approach. Three episodes offer clues that traditional authority and gender roles needed mending. First, Full Deacon Frederick Swartzendruber and Bishop Abner Yoder found themselves in constant conflict from Troyer's advent to Yoder's death in 1883. Yoder wrote in his notebook on 6 February 1879 about a gathering of the ministers to hear complaints brought by Swartzendruber about Yoder's involvements with the Henry County change-minded ministers and about Christian Warey from Pretty Prairie, Indiana. Yoder probably allowed the ministers to speak in his congregation, while Swartzendruber considered them too progressive for this indication of agreement. The ministers evidently could not achieve complete peace with each other, for they gathered with the same agenda on May 6. This time Swartzendruber assented to confess a mistake in front of his congregation. Again on May 16 the ministers agreed to make peace, with the understanding that "each [minister] shall serve in his own congregation except when requested by the ministers in the other congregation."[70]

The strife grew more serious on 28 October 1879. Apparently Abner Yoder instructed baptismal candidates from Frederick Swartzendruber's congregation, infringing on the latter's turf. Swartzendruber actually silenced or "set back" Yoder and appointed another minister to perform the baptisms. The following year on 27 May, the ministers gathered yet again to negotiate ministerial duties, but Swartzendruber pointed toward further agenda: the church-house ministers (those from change-minded communities who had constructed church buildings) and "listening to Noah Troyer." Yoder quoted Swartzendruber as saying, "Whoever engages again [with Troyer?] after these proceedings shall not remain unpunished." The 18 November 1880 communion service at Samuel D. Guengerich's house had to be postponed when Abner Yoder refused to attend.[71] The difficult negotiations between change-minded and tradition-minded factions came to focus on Noah Troyer and the issue of ministerial cooperation.

Second, Preacher Jacob F. Swartzendruber, grandson of Bishop Jacob Swartzendruber and son of Frederick, found it necessary to study proper behavior for Christian women. He wrote across the top of a page of notes for a sermon or article, "How the Sisters Shall Conduct Themselves." Swartzendruber copied a number of verses having to do with women keeping silence in the church and remaining subordinate to their husbands. He quoted 1 Corinthians 11 on wearing a head covering to show submission, a traditional Amish and Mennonite accent. Most symbolic for an Amish preacher, he cited 1 Corinthians 14:33, "For God is not a God of disorder [*unordnung*], but of harmony." And an important aspect of the Amish *Ordnung* was patriarchal authority.[72] Swartzendruber's careful study of the issue indicates some anxiety about traditional patriarchal authority.

Third, Frederick Swartzendruber completed a marriage contract in 1883 with his wife, Barbara, to keep all their personal and real estate property separate. At the settlement of Frederick's estate in 1895, the heirs agreed that the couple "did always keep their property separate and distinct from each other."[73] No similar contracts have surfaced in the Johnson County Recorder's Office before 1900. Even the relationship of women to property holding may have been under some consideration. However, the task of working out the full implications of Troyer's preaching came to a sudden halt in 1886.

Noah Troyer was killed in a bizarre accident on Tuesday, 2 March 1886. He went to shoot a chicken to provide a dinner for the carpenters who were building a house for one of his sons. His son loaded the gun, but not feeling well, he asked his father to shoot. The gun barrel exploded, driving the 1.75 inch breech pin through Troyer's left eye, with such force as to fracture the skull at the back of his head. He lived only three hours. After Troyer's death at age 55, Dr. Allen of Kalona extracted the pin. Troyer was buried March 4 in the Peter Miller cemetery after funeral services conducted by his brother-in-law, Christian Warey, and Stephen T. Miller from Wayland (Figure 6.2). Sanford C. Yoder recalled walking three-quarters of a mile across a field of new snow with

6.2. Peter Miller Cemetery in Johnson County, burial place of Noah Troyer, Jacob Swartzendruber, and other early Amish leaders.

his twin brother, Samuel, to view the body lying in a homemade coffin. A white cloth covered Troyer's left eye to hide the wound.[74] John F. Funk reflected on the news, "Wonderful indeed are the ways of God, and we have in this life the assurance only of the present moment." The following week, Funk offered the booklets with Troyer's sermons at 10 cents post paid. Some twenty-four years later, Funk was still promoting his publication of Troyer's sermons in *The Budget,* still at 10 cents, shipped to any address.[75]

John D. Kauffman continued preaching until 1913. Kauffman moved to Shelby County, Illinois, in 1907 and formed a congregation composed of his followers. "Sleeping preacher Amish" congregations were organized in Illinois, Kansas, Oklahoma, South Carolina, and Oregon by his followers. Several of these congregations continue to meet today, although there have been no more sleeping preachers.[76]

The two sleeping preachers reflected and catalyzed shifts in religious consciousness among the Amish. In Iowa, Troyer encouraged a shift among the more disaffected elements of the community away from unspoken shared community values and toward a more individualistic authority figure. In a sense, he threatened both functions of the repertoire of community—to mediate between Amish individuals and larger social structures, and to guide individual behavior on the basis of consensual values. Instead, Troyer appealed to individual conscience as the direct voice of God. As a consequence, those holding to the older repertoire of community and those who chose to follow Troyer's message no longer shared the same worldview.

As Old Order Amish and Amish-Mennonites dissociated from one another, however, both religious groups retained selected components of ethnic Amish identity. Household formation and agricultural systems were among the most tenacious.

Dear friends, where do you stand? Why will you not work out your soul's salvation while it is called today? We have not the promise of tomorrow. We are as a vapor. We may be blooming in the morning, but be cut down in the evening. You ought to know where you stand.

—Noah Troyer, 1878

Chapter 7

Unaccustomed Choices

In the late 1890s, Bishop Jacob Frederick Swartzendruber copied into his own notebook many of the Amish documents collected by his grandfather, Bishop Jacob Swartzendruber. Old disciplines, letters, sermon notes, records of church events—all he carefully preserved. Furthermore, the third-generation Swartzendruber leader added his own commentary. He expressed dismay at three immoral practices that had crept into the Amish world: bundling, fancy weddings, and tobacco. Each had become "*ein alter Gebrauch,*" an established custom, and as such almost impossible to eradicate, given the core Amish value of respecting old ways. Swartzendruber lamented the Amish attachment to anything that could be called "*alter Gebrauch,*" even practices that later turned out to be useless or even sinful. But he felt unable to challenge these behaviors because such action would lead immediately to religious tensions. He noted, with more than a tinge of bitterness, that even ministers were known to claim they could not preach without a chaw of tobacco in their cheeks![1]

Swartzendruber confronted a consistent fragment of the Amish repertoire of community: an instinctive preference for anything old, combined with suspicion of self-conscious religious activism. In Swartzendruber's ruminations, change in Amish communities had occurred while Amish leaders were looking the other way. An individual or two would do something new, such as smoke cigars or promote Sunday schools, and if leaders failed to marshal communal consensus against it, the new thing would gradually become an Old Thing.[2]

Swartzendruber perceived a persistent pattern in Amish history. Individual assertion functions like an acid in Amish community, eating away at communal obedience. As a result, leaders seeking strategies to do away with offensive customs sometimes accept new religious methods and carefully planned change as positive values. Aggression against new customs, ironically, opens the door for acceptance of American cultural, social, and economic values. Innovation, even in the conservative service of resisting assimilation, is dangerous for Amish identity. Those seeking change find themselves outside the Amish way of life and discover for themselves the Trojan Horse of planned modification. When Old Order Amish religion becomes self-conscious, it is no longer Old Order.[3]

Amish-Mennonite (formerly Amish) and Mennonite denominations chose to pursue a general increase in their pace of religious activity during the last third of the nineteenth century. Mennonite historian Theron Schlabach has termed this period *The Quickening:* it was called *The Awakening* by an earlier generation of progressive Mennonite historians who were critical of the quietist withdrawal of Amish and Mennonites in America. The period was characterized by increased mission activity, aggressive institution building, and individualistic religious experience with a focus on conversion. By contrast, traditional Amish and Mennonites eschewed proselytizing, distrusted institutions, and focused on communal obedience. Schlabach detected more openness to North American cultures among Mennonites, encouraged by contact with revivalistic Protestantism. The borrowing of religious structures "gave the acculturation process an aura of religious vitality and sanction."[4]

Mennonite sociologist Beulah Stauffer Hostetler depicted the late nineteenth century in the eastern Pennsylvania Franconia Mennonite Conference as "defensive structuring," a concept borrowed from sociologist Bernard Siegel.[5] Mennonites responded to the increasing pulls of assimilation and acculturation with more authoritarian control over members, consciously choosing symbols of identity and creating associations designed to keep social activities internally focused. Chosen symbols included the head covering, or "prayer veiling," for women and the "plain coat" (a coat without lapels) for ordained men, once again linking patriarchy with ethnic preservation. Franconia Conference Mennonites sought to limit contact with the wider world by selectively appropriating aspects of that world, such as bureaucratic organization and artificial identity mechanisms. But selective interaction proved difficult to contain.

Many societies have attempted to limit interaction with a dominant culture in order to preserve their separate identity. However, these "strategies of adaptation" may actually contribute to the process of change they were designed to limit. Paradoxically, in Kirsten Hastrup's study of Iceland, "social reactions to disruptive development themselves contributed to disruption."[6] Anthropologist Marshall Sahlins made a similar point in his study of Hawaiian contact with Captain Cook in 1779. Hawaiian culture "changed radically and decisively" even as islanders assimilated Captain Cook's landing into their own worldview and acted accordingly. Sahlins noted that every conscious attempt to prevent change or even to adapt to it brought other changes in its train; he concluded that all cultural reproduction involves alteration.[7]

The key phrase in understanding assimilation is "conscious attempt." Scholars have often sought explanations for cultural persistence or change. Students of African cultures have stated most clearly that highly integrated cultures tend to be closed and hence resistant to change, while less integrated cultures tend to be more open to external influences and therefore more likely to assimilate.[8] While it is true the Amish display a highly integrated culture, this does not suffice to explain their remarkable cultural persistence. As an alternative explanation, one might consider their historical mistrust of civil society and consequent renunciation of coercive force. Like the proverbial willow tree that bends with the wind and survives, members of Amish culture persist by refusing to use political or coercive power to take control of their own destiny. Amish conscious refusals produce a less self-conscious interaction with dominant social structures and fewer avenues for external influences to gain access to their lived experience of community.

The increasing pace of Amish-Mennonite activity and assimilating tendencies during the late nineteenth century reveals, by its absence among the Old Order Amish, the traditional Amish caution about self-chosen schemes to manage cultural contact. This reticence is a very important part of the Amish repertoire of community. After the Sleeping Preacher appeared in Iowa, an event somewhat analogous to Captain Cook landing in Hawaii, the change-minded group increased its religious exertions in order to preserve its Amish identity. New activities such as Sunday school, publications, and interaction with civil government produced a variation in essential consciousness, or *mentalité*. Amish-Mennonites shifted their repertoire of community away from unselfconscious communal household continuity to consciously seeking salvation for individuals in the next generation, imitating the larger Protestant revivalist agenda. Thus, Old Order Amish and Amish-Mennonite communities became increasingly distinct from one another during the last quarter of the nineteenth century in Johnson County.

The period between 1880 and 1910 brought the nineteenth-century Amish Great Schism to Iowa. Tradition-minded Old Order Amish and change-minded Amish-Mennonite groups chose different paths of religious development. Across several decades, a slow process of "sorting out"—like fractional distillation settling a complex liquid at various levels—agitated all the Amish settlements in nineteenth-century America. The issues separating Old Order Amish from Amish-Mennonites varied in each community, but the overall outcome placed Amish communities along a continuum of greater and lesser acculturation. Defining a relationship to American society and the American nation-state produced most of the troubles.

The schism occurred first in Indiana, where a temporary split took place in 1845. A permanent parting of change-minded and tradition-minded factions ensued in 1854, with four explicit issues: clothing, serving in worldly occupations, toleration of business enterprises, and schooling.[9] Similar splits occurred a few years later in Mifflin County, Pennsylvania, and Holmes and Wayne counties, Ohio. The structural problem was the same—change-minded persons expressing more openness to American society—but the specific issues varied. The innovation of conducting baptismal services in streams, when the traditional practice took place only in private homes, troubled several communities. More issues emerged: defining the exact duties of the various ministerial offices, building meetinghouses, dealing with a multitude of lifestyle and clothing questions, and holding local civil offices.[10] The Amish in Illinois avoided schism by shifting as a group toward the change-minded position; the Amish in Lancaster County, Pennsylvania, generally chose a conservative stance. In Iowa, the Amish flirted with schism several times, but avoided a permanent split until the 1880s.

Amish Bishop David Beiler (1786–1871) of Lancaster County, Pennsylvania, blamed the later Amish immigrants from Europe for corrupting the church with "strange manners and customs." Beiler looked backward with longing for the days when "Christian simplicity was practiced much more, and much more submission was shown toward the ministers, especially toward the old bishops."[11] In 1870 David A. Treyer (1827–1906), an Amish bishop of Holmes County, Ohio, compared the *Ordnung* to a "spiritual fence" (*ein geistlicher Zaun*) that protects the church from the world. Without such sanctuary, he asserted, "a church cannot long survive."[12] Attempting to draw boundaries against American culture during the nineteenth century was the Amish version of inventing ethnicity.[13] An uncontrollable individual could damage this justification of limits on individuality and spoil the scheme of counteracting poisonous American individualism.

Just such an individual, Noah Troyer, accelerated the changes in Amish-Mennonite religious consciousness in Iowa. He transformed the binary configuration of Amish community, church versus world, to a revivalist and individualist version of binary antagonism, heaven versus hell. He transmuted horizontal binary citizenship to vertical binary spirituality, making it simpler for the change-minded Amish to modify their religious beliefs. Thus, the change-minded Amish-Mennonites began to accept carefully limited interaction with American culture. Troyer's personal dissociation served as a catalyst for the socioreligious dissociation of Old Order Amish and Amish-Mennonite visions of the Amish configuration of community.

Noah Troyer spoke extensively of heaven and hell, and he saw "bright streaks" and "black streaks" in his audiences. For example, on 10 February 1880, he told his listeners: "Dear friends, I am glad that there are so many bright streaks this evening. What a sorrowful time for me, when I stood before more than a thousand people, when two-thirds of that large number were black streaks, and were streaking down to hell, and only one-third were bright streaks, streaking up to the light of heaven."[14] Troyer's troubling vision of duality affected the religious consciousness of his Amish hearers, especially those already inclined to accept change.

Traumatized by unpredictable and uncontrollable sleeping preachers in Iowa and Indiana, the Amish ability to balance individual, family, and community interests was challenged and nearly destroyed during the 1870s and 1880s. The tendency toward individual self-determination in the economic realm, narrowly averted during the 1860s, reappeared in so many aspects that it could not be controlled all at once. Amish progressives began using some of the language and techniques of American revivalistic Protestantism. Church members who no longer wished to live with the restrictions of the traditional Amish lifestyle sometimes migrated to other communities, sought closer ties with more progressive settlements, or simply refused to attend church meetings.

Noah Troyer focused and animated the search for an alternative to the old order through his sudden appearance in Sharon Township in 1878. He stretched the dialectic of individual freedom and communal responsibility, a critical component of the Amish repertoire of community, to the breaking point, and sometimes beyond. However, the most deeply rooted aspects of the Amish repertoire of community, their household formation and farming systems, persisted among the splintered Amish groups long after the religious divisions. Religious consciousness shifted at an accelerating rate, but the social and economic repertoire continued, and the economic base of the Amish community in Iowa remained remarkably stable until at least 1910.

Religious Consciousness

A number of conflicts appeared in the Johnson County Amish community during the 1870s, predating the beginning of Noah Troyer's trance preaching. Shortly after 1870, Amish families who did not wish to follow the Old Order Amish way of life began moving into the Sharon districts from eastern Amish communities. Other families who had been living there for years were also discontented.[15] Noah Troyer associated with this group when he moved to Iowa in 1875. Preachers from Amish-Mennonite churches were not allowed to preach in the Sharon church because they were not in harmony with the Old Order lifestyle. Bishop Frederick Swartzendruber refused permission for Bishop Joseph Schlegel of Sugar Creek in Wayland to preach and considered Johnson County ministers out of fellowship with Henry County ministers.

On the advice of Bishop John K. Yoder of Wayne County, Ohio, several families transferred their membership to Sugar Creek in Henry County in 1878 or 1879. Their identification with the more progressive congregation to the south occurred as Noah Troyer began his trance preaching. Sebastian Gerig from Sugar Creek traveled to Johnson County and held services in the homes of change-minded families, and they sometimes traveled to Wayland for church meetings.

A committee of arbitration, composed of preachers from Sharon and Sugar Creek, met in 1882. The committee decided that the Henry County preachers could hold one more communion service for the discontented, and no more services thereafter. The separate group was to return to the Old Order church, and the Old Order preachers were to cooperate with the Sugar Creek ministers. Bishop Frederick Swartzendruber would not give his unqualified promise to fellowship with the Henry County preachers and soon refused completely, so the incipient Amish-Mennonites continued their separate meetings.[16] They began meeting in Prairie Dale schoolhouse north of Kalona, and they organized their first Sunday school in 1883.

In 1884 Preacher Christian Warey moved from Elkhart County, Indiana, to Johnson County with the intention of joining the Old Order church. He attended a service his first Sunday in the community, but he was not asked to preach because he had a top buggy and a raincoat, two conveniences outside the *Ordnung* at the time. When confronted, he replied that he was unwilling to give up anything that protected his health. The separated members then invited him to preach for them, and he became the first minister of the Union Church, later East Union. Warey was ordained to the office of bishop by Bishop Joseph Birky of Tiskilwa, Illinois, in 1885. The group continued to hold services at Prairie Dale schoolhouse until building a church in 1889 (Figure 7.1).

With his preaching on unity and on the satanic origin of divisions and quarrels, Troyer made the Union Church thinkable and may have influenced the new congregation's name. Troyer often stated there were only two churches, God's and Satan's, and human denominations counted for nothing. After the Union Church, also known as the "Warey Church," came into existence, the distinction among Old Order Amish, Amish-Mennonite, and former Amish in Iowa became clearer.

One way to trace the long-term changes in religious consciousness is to follow the experiences of Samuel D. Guengerich (1836–1929).[17] Guengerich attempted to bridge Old Order Amish and Amish-Mennonite communities and sought to preserve the Old Order by self-conscious and intentional strategies in his several areas of concern: education and youth socialization, government relations, business success, and relief work. His emphasis on individual action and involvement with the larger culture reveal a person caught in the transition between Old Order Amish and Amish-Mennonite repertoires of community. Guengerich was never ordained but was quite influential as a layperson. He did everything possible to preserve the Old Order, but he ended his life in a Conservative Amish-Mennonite congregation. His journey illustrates the paradox of activism in the Old Order Amish repertoire of community.

7.1. The first Union church building, constructed in 1889.

Guengerich came to Iowa with his parents in 1846 at age 10. He attended school in rural Johnson County about two months a year from age 15 to age 20. At age 24, he applied for a teaching certificate in the Johnson County public school system and received a certificate for the winter term, dated 10 November 1860. Guengerich worked as a carpenter and helped raise many Amish barns in 1861. He noted in his diary a "thrilling sermon" preached by Jacob Swartzendruber at Joseph Keim's on 21 September 1861.[18]

Guengerich moved to Somerset County, Pennsylvania, in 1862 and transferred his membership to the Casselman River Amish Church. The bishop at Casselman River was Joel Beachy, his future father-in-law. He attended six weeks of Normal School in the borough of Salisbury and gained his teacher's certificate on 12 September 1864 at Millersville, Pennsylvania.[19]

While in Pennsylvania, Guengerich courted Barbara Beachy, his second cousin and daughter of bishop Joel Beachy. He wrote a letter to her in 1864 in which he said he planned to go back to Iowa and asked if she would like to go along. She replied with some reservation because he had not yet proposed formally:

> I saw in your letter you are going to Iowa and would like to have me along. I took it to be a question to me, but I am not planning to take such a trip at this time, although it might happen after all if it is the Lord's will—and I do not want anything but the Lord's will. I was very happy to hear from you again and to hear that you are in good health. . . . For this time I will close now and greet you very sincerely, my dearest friend. Please don't be offended; my intentions are sincere, and better than my writing. And please write to me soon again if it is worth your while.

Guengerich wrote to Barbara's father on 11 February 1865 and asked his permission to marry Barbara "and let her come to my home soon if she consents."[20] They were married on 19 March 1865. A family tradition records that a Union army officer stopped the newlyweds on their way home from the wedding service and presented Guengerich with his draft papers.[21]

Guengerich submitted a personal petition stating his conscientious opposition to bearing arms for military purposes: "I am forbidden so to do by articles of faith and rules which govern the Menonite *[sic]* Amish Church of which I am a member for ten years of good and regular standing." The Casselman River congregation affirmed his membership and "deportment . . . consistent with his above declaration." Guengerich obtained a financial receipt for $300 from the Office of Receiver of Commutation Money for the 16th District of Pennsylvania and a Certificate of Non-Liability from the Board of Enrollment at Chambersburg, dated 5 April 1865.[22] Apparently his congregation in Pennsylvania paid for part of his commutation fee, since he recorded in his diary a letter from Joel Beachy "in which he sent $72 ½ of my draft money."[23]

Shortly after their marriage and Guengerich's escape from the Civil War draft, the young couple moved to Iowa. Guengerich taught school during the winter months, worked as a carpenter during the summers, and operated his farm in Washington Township. He bought 92 acres from his father, Daniel P. Guengerich, in 1859, and another 30 acres in 1868, at market rates of $7 and $16 per acre respectively.[24] Samuel and Barbara lived in the Deer Creek Amish district; when the district divided in 1877, they became part of the Upper Deer Creek congregation.

Guengerich's interest in education is one of the strongest themes in his life. He ordered both the German and English versions of *Herald of Truth* in 1865, just one year after John F. Funk began publication of the unofficial Mennonite denominational newspaper in Chicago.[25] He supported the founding of a union (interdenominational) Sunday school in Washington Township in 1870, organized by Amish bishop Joseph J. Swartzendruber and David Jackson, a member of the Campbellite church. About fifty Amish children attended on Sunday afternoons from May through July, along with children from other churches. The following spring, April 1871, a similar Union Sunday School was organized in Sharon Township. A list of 151 students shows that about 51 were Amish children, and several of the teachers were Amish.[26] Deer Creek organized a separate Amish Sunday school in 1871, with Guengerich as superintendent. Sharon district followed suit in 1873. The Amish Sunday school met every other Sunday afternoon and held classes in both German and English. A major concern was preserving the German language. Guengerich published an article in the July 1877 issue of *Herold der Wahrheit* on the necessity of religious instruction for children.[27] A notice in the *Herald of Truth* of 1 July 1882 reported three Sunday schools in the two Deer Creek districts with 180 scholars and noted optimistically that parents were taking more interest. However, the 15 October 1883 issue contains a report that parents and older people "take very little interest in the work," despite a "large and successful Sunday School" in Johnson County.[28]

In order to promote Sunday schools, Guengerich founded a new youth newspaper, *Christlicher Jugendfreund,* in 1878. The initial issues included a series of articles on the history of Sunday schools. Each issue published Sunday school lessons and songs to encourage Bible study and German language skills. John F. Funk promoted Guengerich's periodical as "the first attempt at publishing a paper by our Amish brethren." The subscription price was 25 cents a year.[29] The monthly magazine did not find wide circulation among the Amish, and Guengerich edited the *Jugendfreund* only through the December 1880 issue. John F. Funk and his Mennonite Publishing Company in Elkhart, Indiana, took over publication with the January 1881 issue. The *Mennonite Encyclopedia* called it "the first youth periodical published anywhere in the Mennonite world."[30]

Guengerich included a regular column in *Christlicher Jugendfreund* called *Fragen und Antworten* (Questions and Answers). He published a catechism in 1888 with the help of local ministers and his brother Jacob.[31]

Guengerich helped incorporate the German School Association in 1890. In 1889, the Sharon district had started a weekday German school during the winter. In Washington Township, eight Old Order men—the brothers Jacob D. and Samuel D. Guengerich; George, Peter, Christian C., and Jacob F. Swartzendruber; and Jacob A. and William K. Miller—incorporated the "German School Association of the old order of Amish Mennonites" on 15 November 1890. They gave the nonprofit purpose as educational: "to teach and promulgate the German language and the religious Principles and Discipline of the Amish Church." Membership was limited to members of the Old Order church and required payment of $25 to an endowment fund. S. D. Guengerich often served as teacher, and he had twenty-seven pupils in March 1897.[32] Guengerich published a booklet in 1897 on the need for German schools to preserve German language and culture.[33] The school met until 1916, probably closing because of anti-German sentiment during World War I.

In addition to encouraging education, S. D. Guengerich aided Russian Mennonites resettling in the United States and Canada. In 1874 Guengerich and his wife loaned $100 to the Russian Relief Fund. He asked for the money to be paid off in labor instead of cash, commenting, "I think thereby I could accommodate the destitute to greater satisfaction." Guengerich, who needed both male and female hired help the year around, also offered to house a family in return for their labor.[34] A year later, Guengerich and several other Iowans questioned whether the "Executive Aid Committee in Pennsylvania" should settle any more Russian Mennonites in Kansas, where employment and provision were scarce. Preachers Peter Brenneman and Joseph J. Swartzendruber, and members Peter and J. C. Swartzendruber, Daniel P. and Samuel Guengerich, and Michael Bender signed the letter. After an investigative trip by several persons to Kansas, they asked for the destitute refugees to be settled among existing Amish and Mennonite communities in the East and Midwest, but no farther west than Iowa.[35]

Guengerich had little to do with Sleeping Preacher Noah Troyer and was sharply critical of the Union Church. Troyer appeared in Guengerich's diary on 12 September 1878, when he visited Guengerich's home on that Thursday evening and "preached about 2 hours."[36] Guengerich named Troyer as the leader of "the Seceders from the old order," those who "did not feel like coming under subjection of the church ordinance" and "endeavored to establish a church to suit their taste."[37] According to Guengerich, Troyer spoke only once or twice a week during the last several years of his life, and "the throng of listeners dwindled away to only a few."[38]

When writing to Barbara's parents in Pennsylvania, Joel and Elizabeth Beachy, Samuel D. and Barbara referred to the Union Church as a "side church" (*neben Gemeinde*) and expressed fear that it would simply offer a refuge for disobedient church members.[39] In 1888, S.D. reported that "recently several more lukewarm members joined the side churches. There they can do in some respects whatever they want, and it will be called good." Many Old Order parents found it painful when their children joined the change-minded congregation. Barbara wrote to her parents in 1890, "O it is a very bad thing with this Warey church. It makes some parents much trouble."[40] When Samuel and Barbara attended a funeral at the Union Church, Barbara sniffed, "Their ways were much like the Methodists." The minister, Christian Warey, preached in English. Barbara continued, "Some Warey people said our ministers would have kept [the deceased] out of heaven, if they could have. I thought that was some very hard talk."[41] Guengerich opposed the new Amish-Mennonite congregation even as his own church, Upper Deer Creek, contemplated constructing a church building.

In the late 1880s, Amish members of the Deer Creek districts wanted to hold church services in buildings rather than homes. Tradition-minded leaders were strongly opposed. Bishop Christian Miller blocked meetinghouse construction several times in 1889. Finally, both Deer Creek churches promised in writing to keep the buildings "a model of plainness" and to "cling fast" to the *Ordnung*. Lower Deer Creek members promised to continue putting away whatever went against "the rules and regulations of the church" and pledged not to let the meetinghouse "be a cause to more liberty."[42] The conservatives relented. Bishop Frederick Swartzendruber, conservative on the issue of cooperating with the Henry County Amish ministers, did not oppose building a meetinghouse. He wrote in his notebook, "In the entire Bible there is not a word concerning the kind of house in which Christians should worship," but the important question was what kind of people went into the building to worship. During the bitter dispute, he also wrote, "*Das ist ein Elender Zank*" [This is a pitiful dispute].[43]

In July 1890 Lower Deer Creek completed a building, and on 10 August they held a dedication service with 400 people present (Figures 7.2 and 7.3). Upper Deer Creek built its first building the same summer and held its first service there on 31 August 1890. Samuel D. Guengerich was on the building committee at Upper Deer Creek, contributed $50 to the construction, and was elected one of the first trustees. Both churches moved into plain frame buildings that cost only $1,300 each. Sharon churches continued holding services in their homes, although the two South Sharon districts bought an old schoolhouse in which they held Sunday school every two weeks.

7.2. The first Lower Deer Creek church building, constructed in 1890.

By spring communion in 1900, the Old Order Sharon churches were debating again whether to "continue with" the Amish-Mennonite Deer Creek congregations—that is, whether to remain in fellowship. After several months of debate about calling outside ministers to help bring peace, the two sides agreed in April to call Amish ministers from Indiana and Ohio. The visitors held a series of meetings in early June and secured an agreement from the more progressive churches "to discontinue whatever is a stumbling block for the old churches in order to get along." The Deer Creek ministers also undertook to "clean up pride," but they asked for patience in dealing with the question of church buildings. The visitors led a communion service on June 12, and John D. Hershberger believed that "the churches seemed to be in quite good unity."[44]

This fragile unity would not last, however. The conservatives and progressives continued to disagree, and in April 1902 they discussed "fancy top buggies" and how shunning should be enforced.[45] The Lower Deer Creek telephone controversy in 1911 to 1912 settled the issue of religious unity once and for all. The Amish-Mennonite versus Old Order Amish division was permanent, made clear when Lower Deer Creek divided over the progressives' insistence to allow some use of telephones, a step intolerable to the Old Order. Members who adamantly opposed telephones transferred their membership to the Sharon districts.[46]

In addition to his involvement in religious disputes, Guengerich was very active in new business ventures outside of farming. He helped incorporate the Deer Creek Mills Dairy Association, located near Hickory Grove School on Deer Creek, on 16 March 1895. The creamery ran by water power from the creek. Farmers brought milk to the plant, where it was separated and the cream processed into butter, then took the skim milk home. Jacob D. Guengerich was the first president of the corporation and also ran the mill on steam power nearby. At one time there were seventy customers, and the business processed 733,242 pounds of milk.[47] This activist business and corporate organization represents a step away from the Amish agrarian lifestyle.

Guengerich operated a small print shop by his house in Washington Township. In 1892 he agreed with his brother, Jacob D., to purchase a small press with some of their inheritance. He published booklets and pamphlets, and he started a second church periodical, *Herold der Wahrheit,* in 1912. He named it

7.3. The first Lower Deer Creek church building, in a grove of trees within sight of the first Amish farmsteads along Deer Creek in Washington Township.

after the earlier periodical published by John F. Funk that had ceased in 1901. Guengerich and his brother Jacob published an abridgment of the *Ausbund* in 1892 called the *Unparteiische Liedersammlung*. Guengerich corresponded with state senators C. S. Rank of Iowa City and J. A. Riggen in 1895 and 1896, requesting a state law to exempt people from jury duty because of religious convictions. Such political activism stretched the Amish separation from the world in order to protect that separation. Guengerich argued that the government must use coercion and violence to enforce the law, but that the Amish had renounced violence. Aided by Guengerich's advocacy, Amish men were exempted by an amendment to Iowa law.[48]

Religious, social, and political activism to preserve the Amish repertoire of community also acted as conduits for external influences. Samuel D. Guengerich did not choose to leave the Old Order Amish; however, when his congregation built a meetinghouse and stopped meeting in homes, they effectively became Amish-Mennonite. When Upper Deer Creek joined the Conservative Amish-Mennonite Conference in 1915, Guengerich stayed loyal to the congregation where he was baptized.[49]

Guengerich's fervent efforts to protect the traditional Amish religious consciousness led to greater opportunities for acculturation. However, not without paradox, patterns of household formation (establishing youth on farms) and agricultural system followed the ancient paths among both Old Order Amish and Amish-Mennonites.

Household Formation

Shifts in religious consciousness and the Old Order Amish versus Amish-Mennonite schism did not affect the continuity of household formation and agricultural system in either group.[50] Amish communities survive and even thrive during times of rural distress. American economic cycles often find Amish farmers positioned to expand, acquire new land, and establish new farm households when other farm operations collapse. The Amish community in Johnson County, Iowa, formed a large number of new families during the American agricultural depression of the late nineteenth century. The reproduction and expansion of Amish households became more conspicuous during the period from 1880 to 1895, with the effect of more sharply defining the Amish as an ethnic community distinct from neighboring ethnic groups. The capacity to expand while others contract might be termed countercyclical social reproduction.

Two family stories illustrate the gradual process by which the ethnic Amish, both Old Order Amish and Amish-Mennonite, came to dominate the agricultural landscape of southwestern Johnson County. In 1841 Carr Hartman, a Pennsylvania Quaker, migrated to the prairie of frontier Iowa and settled in southern Johnson County. During the following nine years, four brothers and cousins joined Hartman in Sharon Township, making a total of five households by 1850. In 1850 Carr Hartman owned 288 acres of Iowa land; Thomas J. Hartman owned 320 acres; Lewis held 190 acres; Jonas had 104 acres; and Joseph Hartman, age 22, did not appear on the agricultural census as a landowner.

Only Carr Hartman and his brother Lewis remained in 1860, although Carr owned $10,000 worth of real estate, the highest in the township. Carr and Susan Hartman occupied 320 acres of land and were raising nine children; Lewis and Ruth owned 200 acres and produced four children. Carr Hartman, described as "deeply religious," interested neighboring families in meeting together for prayer. By 1867 they had organized a Methodist church, known informally as the Grout Church from the first name listed on the deed for 85 square rods.

By 1870 Carr Hartman and Lewis Hartman appear as wealthy farmers, each with an elder son married with young children of his own. The sons, however, do not appear on the agricultural census, and by 1880 only Carr Hartman remained in Sharon Township. Between 1880 and 1895, two of Carr's younger sons, Porter and Creton, established households; in 1900 Porter owned a mortgaged farm, and Creton owned a farm free of debt. In 1910 no Hartman families appear in the federal population census.[51]

A second family in Sharon and Washington townships in Johnson County, the Swartzendruber kin, followed a different track. No Swartzendruber households appear in the 1850 census. Amish Preacher Jacob Swartzendruber bought 360 acres in Sharon Township on 21 May 1851 and moved to Iowa from Allegheny County, Maryland. By 1860, six Swartzendruber households appear in the federal census, all sons or relatives of Bishop Jacob Swartzendruber. None held as much land or listed as much personal wealth as Carr Hartman; however, forty-seven persons lived in those six households. The number of Swartzendruber households held constant between 1860 and 1880, with three new families formed during the twenty-year period. However, between 1880 and 1895, eight new Swartzendruber families appear in the state censuses. During this same period, at least fourteen Swartzendruber descendants pioneered a new settlement in Wright County, Iowa.[52] By 1900 twelve Swartzendruber households appear in the federal census. And in 1910, after the Hartmans had disappeared completely, there were ten Swartzendruber households.

These two family stories illustrate opposite processes of assimilation and differentiation between 1850 and 1910. The Hartman family faded into an increasingly homogeneous rural and urban landscape, while the Swartzendruber kin network participated in creating an increasingly separate and well-defined ethnic community.[53]

Appendix Tables 1 and 2 compare households in the several ethnic groups. Table 1 includes native-born and foreign-born Amish household heads; these categories shift in 1885 to Old Order Amish and Amish-Mennonite, since so few are foreign-born after 1880 and the Amish Great Schism had reached Iowa by 1890. The 1885 figures are for Sharon Township only, since the census manuscripts for Washington Township are missing. Irish households nearly disappear after 1880, while Welsh households remain relatively constant in number. The larger numbers appear in Amish, German immigrant and (after 1885) German ancestry, mid-Atlantic, and Welsh categories. Appendix Table 2 combines these categories to simplify the picture. The residents of Washington and Sharon townships are divided into five groups: Amish, German, Native-born, Welsh, and Other, the last category containing mainly Irish households.

Tables 7.1 and 7.2 reveal a consistent pattern of growth in the Amish community during this sixty-year period when compared with other ethnic households in the same townships. Starting with only 2 percent of all households in 1850, Amish represented over 52 percent of the households in 1910. The mean age of Amish household heads remained quite stable and was younger than other ethnic categories. In 1900, for example, Amish household heads averaged 43 years old; while Germans were 47.2, native-born American were 44.9, and Welsh were 52.8. Whether growth occurred from migration among Amish communities or through establishing sons in farming, the Amish formed households at a younger age than their neighbors.

The discontinuity among these ethnic communities becomes more visible in Table 7.2, which depicts the four groupings with the most variation. Between 1880 and 1895, the number of Amish households increased from 115 to 158, a 36.2 percent expansion, while the number of native-born and German households decreased by 4.7 percent and 22.2 percent, respectively. The Amish continued to gain more households after 1895, while the number of

Table 7.1. Number of Households and Farms by Ethnicity in Washington Township, Johnson County, Iowa, 1880–1910

Year	*All*	*Amish*	*Old Order Amish*	*Amish-Mennonite*	*German*	*Native*
1880						
Heads	187	53	9	44	23	103
Farms	156	47	8	39	20	84
Age[a]	46.2	44.7	46.7	44.3	49.7	45.8
1895						
Heads	192	82	9	68	34	76
Farms	157	69	9	57	24	60
Age	45.0	41.5	41.2	41.3	50.2	45.9
1900						
Heads	221	106	11	92	41	69
Farms	187	92	9	80	32	58
Age	43.8	41.6	42.9	41.1	46.1	45.7
1910						
Heads	171	109	15	89	26	32
Farms	154	101	13	85	24	27
Age	44.5	42.0	34.9	43.0	48.5	49.2

Source: U.S. Population Censuses, 1880, 1900, 1910; Iowa State Census, 1895.
[a] Of heads of households.

native-born families continued to decline and German households fluctuated, rising to 92 in 1900 but declining again to 73 in 1910. The transition occurred in the fifteen-year period between 1880 and 1895, a time when the Amish as an ethnic group greatly strengthened their presence, while other ethnic groups weakened theirs. The change occurred not so much because the Amish grew more rapidly, but because the other groups declined in population. The Amish retain a higher rate of growth for every census year after 1870.

What occurred between 1880 and 1895? How were the Amish able to establish more second-generation households while other ethnic communities contracted? These fifteen years represent a period of severe agrarian distress in the American Midwest, due in part to currency deflation that enmeshed farmers in a cycle of falling commodity prices and rising mortgages. The Patrons of Husbandry, the Grange, founded in 1867, reached a membership of 1.5 million by 1874. Farmers' Alliances and the vision of large-scale cooperatives as alternatives to railroads and middlemen began during this period of agricultural

Table 7.2. Percent Change in Number of Households by Ethnicity in Washington and Sharon Townships, Johnson County, Iowa, 1850–1910

Year	*All*	*Amish*	*German*	*Native*
1850				
Total	107	3	12	82
1860				
Total	233	40	37	128
Percent Change	117.8	1233.3	208.3	56.1
1870				
Total	349	85	84	151
Percent Change	49.8	112.5	127.0	18.0
1880				
Total	380	115	84	153
Percent Change	8.9	35.3	0	1.3
1885				
Total[a]	190	70	54	47
Percent Change[b]	−2.6	16.7	−12.9	−11.3
1895				
Total	386	158	81	123
Percent Change[c]	—	36.2	−4.7	−22.2
1900				
Total	423	188	92	119
Percent Change	9.6	19.0	13.6	−3.3
1910				
Total	374	196	73	88
Percent Change	−11.6	4.3	−20.7	−26.1

Source: U.S. Population Censuses, 1850, 1860, 1870, 1880, 1900, 1910; Iowa State Population Censuses, 1885, 1895.

[a] Sharon Township only.

[b] From Sharon Township figures for 1880.

[c] From 1880.

adversity. And, of course, Populism arose during this period. The national depression that started in 1893 only intensified the depression in the rural economy. Throughout this economic disaster, which was in many ways more severe than the Great Depression of the 1930s, the Amish in Johnson County, Iowa, expanded apace as if nothing adverse was happening. This is not to say that no Amish farmers lost their land, nor is it true that the depression damaged all non-Amish farmers. Nonetheless, the overall trend of ethnic turnover is clear.

Household structure exhibits little causal relationship to Amish expansion and non-Amish contraction between 1880 and 1895. The number of non-nuclear family members did not vary significantly among the ethnic groups.[54] The number of children per Amish household remained consistent throughout the period, meaning that Amish families had more children who needed to find land to farm.[55] The mean age of oldest and youngest children in the household shows a consistently younger age for the oldest child still at home in Amish households after 1880; that is, Amish children tended not to live at home as long and, presumably, were leaving home and establishing households at a younger age.

As the large cohort of Swartzendruber children was coming of age, the agricultural downturn made more land available, resulting in eight new family farms in the Amish community. The disappearance of the Hartman family from southern Johnson County and the steady growth of Swartzendruber households illustrates the larger trends of Amish differentiation and expansion in the nineteenth century. Most of the Swartzendruber families lived in Washington Township and became Amish-Mennonite. In 2000 no Old Order Amish family in the Kalona area was surnamed Swartzendruber.[56] Nonetheless, in 1910 the Swartzendrubers and other families remained participants in the Amish system of household formation despite their community's religious division into Old Order Amish and Amish-Mennonite groups.

Agricultural System

Along with household formation, the Amish agricultural system remained remarkably stable in Washington Township despite the growing religious and social differences between the Old Order Amish and the Amish-Mennonites. Amish settlers in Iowa established a discernibly different agricultural system between 1850 and 1880 (Chapter 2), and this system remained distinct from 1880 to 1910. Ethnic Amish farms—Old Order Amish, Amish-Mennonite, and former Amish—retained the "Pennsylvania Dutch style" of farming regardless of their religious orientation. The Amish farming system was the most easily established element of the Amish repertoire of community and the most tenacious.

One might have expected subtle differences between Old Order Amish and Amish-Mennonite farms to begin appearing during this period of religious differentiation. It seems that the Old Order Amish would remain more traditional in every aspect of socioeconomic life, while Amish-Mennonites would become more similar to the market-oriented farms surrounding them. One would expect the Old Order to exhibit more farm animals, less personal consumption, more investment in farm operations, more children per household, more butter, and more commitment to helping the next generation get started in farming. However, all measurements of available farm data show little difference between Old Order Amish and Amish-Mennonite farm households, but clear differences between ethnic Amish and non-Amish farms.

The federal agricultural censuses are not extant after 1880. However, tax assessor books for Washington Township are held by the Iowa Mennonite Archives. As many households as possible from the 1895 Iowa state census and the 1900 and 1910 federal censuses were matched with extant tax assessor records for 1896, 1899, and 1909. The assessor recorded farm animals and taxable property, including acres and value of farm land, but no information on field crops or farm production. This sketchy information is not really comparable to the massive data found for both Washington and Sharon townships in the 1880 agricultural census; nonetheless, statistical analysis offers some insight into the Amish farming system in relation to neighboring ethnic groups. For purposes of continuity, comparable variables from 1880, where available, are included in the analysis.

The ethnic population of Washington Township from 1880 to 1910 is depicted in Table 7.1. Most Old Order Amish lived in Sharon Township, since the Deer Creek districts in Washington Township were moving toward the Amish-Mennonite denomination during this period. Only 9 households are identified as Old Order in 1880, while 44 later became Amish-Mennonite.[57] The number of Old Order Amish households remains small, rising only to 15 in 1910, compared to 89 Amish-Mennonite households. There were no Welsh households in Washington Township, so the other ethnic categories are German and native-born American. The number of native-born households declined precipitously between 1880 and 1910, from 103 to 32.

Amish families had more children per household in each census year. The native-born grouping declines each census year, from 2.63 children in 1880 to 1.84 in 1910, while Amish families declined only from 3.72 to 3.31 children per household. While average farm size per farm household in Washington Township reveals that Amish farmers owned much more land than Germans and native-born farmers in 1880, an average of 175 acres versus 110 acres, the difference becomes statistically insignificant by 1910, 105 versus 101 acres. Amish household heads owned less and less farmland because they were more willing to subdivide farms in order to ensure their sons a livelihood. Amish farm sizes in the twentieth century tend to be much smaller than American farms, and it appears that the transition in Washington Township began to take place around the turn of the century. A 1972 study of Amish and non-Amish farms in Illinois revealed an average Amish farm size of 85 acres, while the average non-Amish farm was more than 500.[58] Despite their shrinking size, Amish farms were more valuable in 1910, at an average value of $6,171 versus the German average of $4,896.

As one would expect, even with taking farm size into account, Amish farms had more horses than neighboring German and native-born farms. From statistical parity in 1880, the difference becomes statistically significant in both 1900 and 1910. Amish farmers also raised more hogs. The number of hogs kept by all Washington Township farmers declined steeply between 1880 and 1910, but Amish farmers consistently raised more hogs, taking farm size into account.

Ethnic Amish farms were productive and diverse in comparison to other ethnic communities. Amish farmers tended to own more animals and more variety of livestock, in keeping with the Pennsylvania Dutch farming system that emphasizes the maintenance of soil fertility through manure. As already noted, Amish farmers subdivided their land to ensure the availability of farmland for the next generation, and the younger age of Amish household heads demonstrates their commitment to giving children a start in farming. Their larger families made finding more farmland an imperative, and pressure for more land also led to migration to other locations, as we will see in chapter 8. Amish farm households tended to be wealthier than neighboring farms.[59]

There are visible differences between ethnic Amish farms and non-Amish farms. However, despite increasing religious and social differentiation, there was little socioeconomic differentiation between Old Order Amish and Amish-Mennonite farms during this time period. Comparing Old Order Amish and Amish-Mennonite farms in Washington Township in 1895, 1900, and 1910 shows almost no statistically significant differences. Amish groups are more similar to each other than to non-Amish communities.

As was the case with household formation, the Amish experience in Johnson County contradicted the usual path of assimilation. The Amish agricultural system was so well established that it changed very slowly, even among the change-minded Amish-Mennonites. Studies of later periods have identified differences between Old Order Amish farms and the farms of their Mennonite cousins.[60] In Iowa these differences developed after 1910, likely with the farm mechanization and electrification movements during the following decades. The first hints of differentiation may appear in 1910, when Old Order Amish household heads show a much younger mean age than Amish-Mennonite farmers, 34.9 versus 42.0 years of age, but have similar farming resources.

Among the Amish in Iowa, religious change began to occur first, catalyzed by the trance preaching of Noah Troyer, resulting in a division between those willing to treat religious belief as a manipulable variable in a social system and those who held to the Old Order. Social and economic change occurred later, a reversal of the usual sequence traced by historians and sociologists.

In literature on immigrant assimilation, economic changes usually occur first, then religious and ideological changes.[61] The larger process of Amish differentiation during the nineteenth century might be termed counter-assimilation. Instead of becoming more like the dominant culture in agricultural production, participation in the land market, migration patterns, and the timing of reproducing the family farm, the Amish became more dissimilar. Theories of assimilation and acculturation have sustained the reverse order: economic assimilation first, then social and cultural, and finally cognitive. The Amish-Mennonite mechanism is counterintuitive, since they acculturated religiously but maintained economic distinctions. Furthermore, studies of rural immigrant and ethnic communities typically assume a period of establishing a spatially separate settlement, followed by varying rates of assimilation and loss of European characteristics.[62]

Anthropologist Sonya Salamon compared rural ethnic groups and identified land inheritance and household reproduction as the most critical factor in ethnic persistence. However, she utilized spatially discrete communities rather than several ethnic groups within one community.[63] The continuity of Amish ethnic identity within a mixed rural community makes their achievement all the more conspicuous. For the Amish-Mennonites in Iowa in the late nineteenth century, religion was the leading edge of acculturation. The Amish historically make no spiritual-temporal distinction; keeping religious beliefs and social expression congruent is part of their repertoire of community. When religious change fails to alter social patterns, the community is no longer Old Order Amish.

Religious conflict and pressure to find more land for offspring combined to lead a number of Johnson County Amish families to seek new locations during the 1890s and early 1900s. They followed the time-honored Amish pattern of migration, taking the Amish repertoire of community along to establish new settlements. Would, however, community be as portable for Amish-Mennonites?

This change of location opened wide new vistas for us boys. Wright County was a beautiful place. The level landscape stretched on and on for miles and miles. One's eyes sought vainly for an object on which to rest, often to find nothing but an empty horizon. The unbroken prairie lands were covered with native grasses and became in springtime, literally, a sea of flowers.

—Sanford Calvin Yoder, 1959

Chapter 8

Persistent Amish Migrations

The Amish move. It seems ingrained in their memory engrams, in their very patterns of existence—in short, in their repertoire of community. Migration is common sense, an expected behavior, essential to what it means to be Amish. Moses Rischin, the historian of American Jewish immigration, entitled a recent review article, "A Significant Part of History Deals with Mankind in Motion."[1] The same could be said of Amish history. The reality of constant motion contradicts popular-culture images of their never-changing stability.

During the late nineteenth century, the Amish repertoire of community became two distinct configurations, the Old Order Amish and the Amish-Mennonite. Both tradition-minded and change-minded groups struggled to preserve their distinctive identities within North American culture. The traditional practice of portable Amish community, embedded in the experience of

European persecution, expanded in North America to migration for a variety of reasons beyond necessity. Amish families and individuals moved to new communities to express personal choice of location, to seek better or cheaper land, to escape community conflict, to cement kinship ties, and to improve material conditions.

What should one make of Amish mobility? The task of describing Amish migration does not seem well served by immigration historiography. Over the past half-century, the explanations of immigration historians have moved through filiopietistic worship of the ancestors; Oscar Handlin's imagery of uprootedness, in which bewildered European peasants lost their Old World identities in American cities, making assimilation an inevitable process; John Bodnar's response to Handlin, *The Transplanted,* in which discrete European communities are recreated in the New World; and the world capitalist system of Wallerstein and others, in which the need for industrial labor and raw materials drove migration to cities and to the world's grasslands.[2] More recent historians have focused on networks and the construction of ethnicity in new locations. As Charles Tilly summarizes, "Networks migrate; categories stay put; and networks create new categories." Sets of people, linked by acquaintance, kinship, or work experience, formed units of migration. Old World identities did not translate directly to New World ethnicities, however. Groupings of immigrants acquired new identifications through interactions with others at their destinations.[3]

The Amish migrate in kinship and acquaintance networks, to be sure, but not from one place of origin to one destination. To return migration historiography to biological imagery, the Amish system of migration seems best described as strawberries, which create new plants with runners, spreading while retaining connections with other plants. To be sure, all Amish plantations are not genetically identical, but there is a freedom of movement among all the locations that would tend to modify the localism of reconstructed ethnicities based on immigrant networks in one location.[4] The Amish exhibit the ability to migrate to multiple locations, retain networks of support among those locations, and create similar communities.

The Amish community in Johnson County, Iowa, resulted from the Amish strawberry runner creeping westward in the middle of the nineteenth century. Settlers in the decade after the first three arrivals in 1846 came from Europe, Pennsylvania, Maryland, and Ohio. Almost immediately, the first settlers and their children began moving elsewhere, sometimes returning to eastern communities, sometimes moving within Iowa, and sometimes looking to Missouri, Kansas, Nebraska, Texas, Oklahoma, Oregon, and many other states.[5] Each new community formed a node of migration to still more locations. The ability to move and form new communities is part of being Amish.

An additional element was added to the Amish migration system during the nineteenth century. Migration became spatial and affiliative. Amish individuals and families could move to a different geographic location or to a different level of Amish-related group, or both. Somewhat like a unidirectional elevator, the ability to shift to another group helped stabilize the larger community system by offering, as it were, a safety valve for dissent and conflict.[6] The possibility of affiliative migration developed as a result of the Amish Great Schism of the mid- to late-nineteenth century, which produced two distinct Amish-related groups, the Old Order Amish and the Amish-Mennonites.[7] Both tradition-minded and change-minded groups confronted a culture marked by freedom of movement and relatively open land markets.

In the 1890s a sense of parental responsibility for children may have been the single most important reason, or excuse, for Amish settlers from Iowa to seek new localities. Once again, the Sleeping Preacher reflected and furthered a crucial component in the Amish configuration of community: retention of children.

Noah Troyer often expressed urgent concern for young people in his trance sermons. His desire to bring youth into the church appears in his sermon on 16 August 1878:

> Do not be like the old people who stand against the young people. I have seen people who stand right against the young people and would keep them out of the church. Don't you see there are some ministers who ought to have the knowledge who stand right against the young people because they will not come under the rules they have made[?] It is right to have established rules but such rules are not against the rules of Christ. There are people who will build the whole foundation of the church on little rules of their own.[8]

Troyer's message gave an explicit challenge to the Amish experience of *Ordnung*. One implication his hearers could have drawn was that parents must take responsibility to protect their children from what change-minded parents were beginning to perceive as dead Amish legalisms. Migration to a new community, and therefore adherence to a different *Ordnung*, might make it easier for children to accept the Amish way of life rather than reject it outright in favor of participating in American culture. The tradition of Amish movement expanded its meaning as various groupings of Amish sought to preserve multiple repertoires of community. Reflecting Noah Troyer's unintentional and personal dissociation, Amish pioneers sometimes created intentional dissociations of communities by distancing themselves from one another.

The Amish have been continuously aggressive in establishing new settlements. David Luthy's *The Amish in America: Settlements That Failed, 1840–1960* lists thirty-two states and a province in Mexico where at least one Amish settlement existed. Between 1960 and 1984, Old Order Amish pioneers founded 123 new communities in North America, and 71 in the decade between 1974 and 1984. In 1984 a total of 175 settlements existed in twenty states and one Canadian province.[9] By 1991 there were 215 Old Order Amish settlements in twenty-two American states and one province, Ontario, a total of 898 districts (congregations).[10] The pace of settlement in the nineteenth century was slightly less hectic, but the patterns of rapid population growth, expensive land in the older settlements, and the search for cheaper land in other areas have encouraged extensive roaming by Amish pioneers.

Amish and Mennonite inhabitants appear in records for at least thirty of Iowa's ninety-nine counties. Some "settlements" consisted of a family or two who bought land and awaited further immigration by others of their faith. Calls for more settlers and a minister filled the nineteenth-century pages of the *Herald of Truth* and the *Budget*. S. B. Wenger wrote in 1895 from South English, Iowa: "There are but two members of our faith here. We desire to have more of our people settle here and wish our friends and especially ministering brethren, either Mennonites or Amish, to stop with us." Wenger pointed out that the *Herald of Truth* had subscribers in twenty-six Iowa counties and called for organizing more churches for the scattered Amish and Mennonites in Iowa.[11]

Even though this book has concentrated on one Amish community, the overall impression should remain one of constant movement. Amish families and single persons moved into Johnson, Washington, and Iowa counties from other states and countries; and many moved from Iowa to Amish settlements elsewhere. Preacher Joseph Keim moved from Iowa to Illinois when he found himself in conflict with Jacob Swartzendruber. Christian J. Swartzendruber, son of Jacob, moved to Lyon County, Kansas, in 1869. Jacob F. Swartzendruber, his nephew, followed in 1873. Several other families moved from Iowa to Kansas, but all returned to the Kalona area by 1876, discouraged by a drought year made worse by grasshoppers, followed by an extremely wet year.[12]

Three families from Iowa lived briefly in Oregon during the early 1880s, Christian J. Swartzendruber, Jacob F. Swartzendruber, and William A. Kreider. All three returned to Iowa, and Christian was known ever after as "Oregon Chris."[13] Chris later lived in Fayette County, Illinois, and retired to Custer County, Oklahoma, where he died. It was not unusual for Amish families to move a number of times while remaining Old Order Amish. Most of the Amish families who settled in Iowa had lived somewhere else before moving to the Kalona area, and many of these families, or their children, moved on to try their luck in other locales.

High land prices, internal community conflict, and the 1893 depression made the 1890s a particularly busy decade of Amish migration from Johnson County. Sanford Yoder recorded a saying about the Amish and land that "an Amishman can determine the quality of soil by his sense of smell."[14] During the 1890s, many Amish farmers left the Kalona area to sniff out fertile land elsewhere in the United States.

Wright County, Iowa

One of the most exciting and promising new settlements formed from a migration of progressive families to Wright County, Iowa, in the north central part of the state (Figure 8.1).[15] In early October of 1892, the *Kalona News* reported that "Jos C. Gingerich, Will Kreider and Sam [Shem] Swartzendruber took a flying trapees *[sic]* going to the north-west, hunting land."[16] Apparently a good deal of folklore developed around this cross-country excursion in a spring wagon, since it was "considered a rather venturesome trip" at the time.[17] Melvin Gingerich mentioned "a week of camping experiences" before the group arrived in Wright County, and Sanford Yoder recalled that the expedition "furnished interesting material for discussion during many a Sunday afternoon visit between neighbors."[18]

Yoder recalled one tale in particular:

> One night, so the story goes, after the horses were taken care of and the men had bedded down in the wagon, a sudden wind and rainstorm arose which carried away part of the canvas covering, set the horses free, and started the vehicle on a precarious journey down the hill to what might well have been a very tragic destination. By the time the slumbering occupants got thoroughly awakened and realized what was going on, their improvised "Pullman" was gathering mo-

8.1. Small frame church building in Wright County, Iowa. The building was later moved to Daytonville, near Wellman in Washington County.

> mentum for its run down the grade. Uncle Shem, Uncle Will, and Uncle Joe, very scantily and indecorously clad, climbed out of the wagon, pell-mell, and finally brought it under control before it met with disaster. After some difficulty, they retrieved their horses and got things in hand for the continuation of their journey.[19]

Some fifty years later, Shem Swartzendruber's obituary mentioned that 1892 trip in a "covered springwagon" as one of the milestones of his life, along with his becoming a charter member of the new Amish-Mennonite Church in Wright County.[20]

The intrepid explorers decided they liked the raw, unimproved land in Wright County. Five families settled in Dayton Township during 1893: Solomon J. Swartzendruber, Shem Swartzendruber, Christian S. Yoder, William A. Kreider, and Solomon B. Yoder. Solomon J. Swartzendruber was the son of Bishop Joseph J. Swartzendruber, one of the original Amish settlers in Johnson County in 1846. "Sol" was born in Garrett County, Maryland, on 27

March 1856, shortly before his father returned to Iowa. He lived in McPherson County, Kansas, from 1882 to 1892, where he was ordained minister in 1889 and bishop a year later. After at least two visits to Iowa during the summer of 1892, Swartzendruber and Peter J. Miller returned to Iowa from Kansas in November of 1892, intending to "make Iowa their home in the future."[21] Swartzendruber quickly became involved in the plans for a new settlement in Wright County. After a swift trip and land purchase, he was already preparing to load a railroad car with his family's belongings in February.[22]

A series of extremely positive, almost euphoric, reports about the new settlement followed. Many years later, Sanford Yoder recalled his first impressions of the new country: "This change of location opened wide new vistas for us boys. Wright County was a beautiful place. The level landscape stretched on and on for miles and miles. One's eyes sought vainly for an object on which to rest, often to find nothing but an empty horizon. The unbroken prairie lands were covered with native grasses and became in springtime, literally, a sea of flowers."[23] Not even fierce winds and dust storms could dampen the new settlers' enthusiasm, nor could the necessity of taking their own building timber with them because of the lack of trees on the Wright County prairie.[24]

"Wright County Fever" reached a new pitch of excitement later in 1893. The interaction of aggressive land salesmanship and Amish interest resulted in a number of land transactions and the recruitment of new settlers for the fashionable new land. By the spring of 1894, as a Johnson County writer reported in the *Budget,* "A great many of our people are going to move to Wright county, Iowa, this coming spring."[25] With the 1894 influx of new settlers, the *Wright County Democrat,* taking notice of the Amish apparently for the first time, reported:

> The Amish settlement, south of this place, received a large accession this week and last from Johnson county. A number of car loads of stock, machinery and household goods have arrived. The Amish community is getting to be a strong one, and as they are a thrifty people, peaceable and law abiding, prompt and honest, they become valuable members of society. We hear that they will build a church this season in Dayton township, and that still other families will settle in its neighborhood. They are excellent citizens and should be welcomed to our county.[26]

The plan to build a church had to wait a few years, but it does indicate the enthusiasm and optimism of these first settlers; it also indicates a strong orientation toward the "meetinghouse Amish." Those who relocated to Wright County moved in order to practice their progressive Amish-Mennonite faith more freely. All the rapture with Wright County and the tensions in their own church community perhaps caused the Amish of southeast Iowa to wonder whether it would be their settlement that would eventually experience depopulation and dissolution.

Elias J. Miller rented a farm in Wright County and moved there in the spring of 1894. His brother Adam kept a diary of the exciting venture. He recorded his first entry in a blank notebook on February 25, less than two weeks before the brothers moved. The first entry begins, "Commenced keeping account of everything I do and everything that happens."[27]

Eli and Adam loaded their belongings on a railroad car at Wellman on March 5 and put their cattle on a car at Kalona the next day. On Wednesday, March 7, after walking to Kalona on the railroad, they boarded the Burlington, Cedar Rapids & Northern for the trip by rail to Wright County. It was the same week and same train that took Deacon Elias Swartzendruber, Abraham J. Swartzendruber, and Joseph C. Gingerich to the new land; all were cousins of Eli's wife, Mary.[28]

The Burlington-Cedar Rapids & Northern Railway ran east from Wellman and Kalona to Iowa Junction in the northeast corner of Washington County, then north through Iowa City and Cedar Rapids and northwest via Vinton and Iowa Falls to Clarion. The pair were well-lubricated for the trip: Adam recorded in his diary the purchase of tobacco, candy, and two pints of whiskey; he also logged two draughts of beer at Iowa City for 10 cents. When the party arrived in Clarion at 5 A.M., Adam bought breakfast at Sherwood restaurant for 25 cents. Then the group secured horses from a livery barn and proceeded to unload their railroad cars.[29]

Adam attended Amish church services at the Gillette school house the Sunday after his arrival; the services were entirely in German.[30] Two other youths, John Swartzendruber and Ed Gingerich, went home with him after church; later in the day, he took a buggy ride with Emma Gingerich and Fannie Albright. During his first week in Wright County, Miller hauled hay, rode a bicycle to visit Joe Gingerich, harrowed corn stalks, hauled manure, plowed a garden and planted potatoes, and traveled twice into Clarion.[31] That first week initiated Adam Miller into his routine of hard farm labor, socializing with other Amish youths, trips to town, and rural recreation.

During his first several months in Wright County, Adam kept in close contact with his friends around Wellman and Kalona. He sent at least thirteen letters and received eleven. On 21 May, he recorded his intention to join church; he had decided to quit tobacco on 16 May. For recreation, Miller played checkers with Joe Gingerich (March 28), made a fiddle (March 20), visited Eagle Grove and Clarion the same day and shared a pint of whiskey with three friends (March 19), and attended gatherings of Amish youth almost every Sunday afternoon as well as singings in the evening.

During the summer of 1894, Adam Miller worked at plowing corn and shocking oats. It seems that some of the excitement of relocating wore off in the heat of summer farm work. Miller recorded only two letters sent and three received during the three months of summer. He attended Sunday school or church services nine of the thirteen Sundays; however, he also wrote on June 17, "I was to church, refused to join church."

Miller also went swimming in Eagle Creek (June 3), attended a Ringling Brothers circus in Eagle Grove (June 6), went to a dance (June 22), joined the other Amish youths on a wagon ride (June 24), went fishing in the Iowa River and arrived back home at 2:30 A.M. (June 28), played baseball (July 22), and bought on credit a pair of "plow shoes" at Stanbery's store in Clarion for $1.35 (August 20). During a four-day period in late July, he helped four different Amish farmers shock oats.

During the rest of 1894, Miller recorded attendance at church or Sunday school only six of nineteen Sundays. On Sunday, November 4, he wrote, "Was to church house, didn't go in." Sunday afternoon gatherings of youth still drew his attention, but very little appears about Sunday evening singings. On Sundays when he apparently did not attend church, he still saw many of his Amish peers; on September 2 Miller wrote, "Nice day. Was at home. Sanford Yoder here all day. Went to Dan Ging[erich] in afternoon, all the young folks there. S. and S. Yoder here till late."

As for farm work, early September required fall plowing, followed by cane harvesting and road grading. He shucked corn nearly every day from mid-October to mid-November. Miller participated in a barn raising at Sol Swartzendruber's (October 4), and hauled loads of oats (September 25) and straw (December 28) into Clarion.

Miller also records a "kissing party" on 24 November at Christian Yoder's house. Melvin Gingerich described kissing games in his book, *The Mennonites in Iowa.* One version, known as the "Needle's Eye," often resulted in a young fellow kissing every girl at the party. Gingerich commented, "Whatever may be said about this game, it must be admitted that it was a good mixer," and he attributed the advent of such games among the Amish to the frontier milieu.[32]

In late December, during the slow season for farm work, Miller began attending the "Lyceum" every Friday evening at the Dayton Center school house. This literary society sponsored debates, and Miller attended every session but two from mid-December 1894 to March of 1895. Apparently he observed the proceedings at first, then later began to participate; however, in February he argued on the losing side four times in a row. The issues contested included "Batchelors *[sic]* should be taxed to keep old Maids" (8 February), for which Adam served as "leading speaker" on the negative side; "Free Trade is more harm to our country than Free Whisky and Tobacco" (15 February), which he argued in the affirmative; "Liquor has done more harm than War" (22 February), with Adam on the affirmative side; and "Tariff for revenue only is to the benefit of the people of our country" (23 February, a Thursday), with Miller taking the negative position.

Other winter activities included ice skating on Eagle Creek and White Fox Creek (1, 4, and 6 January); hunting rabbits (3 and 18 January); butchering hogs (17 January, 21 February); and a carpet-rag sewing (8 February). Miller won a "Boston bull dog revolver" with a 26 cent raffle ticket on 11 February, which he traded on 3 March for a "nickel fife" and an old violin. He bought an "E" string for the violin for 5 cents on 14 March in Clarion. Miller played fiddle for a dance at "Acy Kinson's" on 11 February and later attended a dance at "Dingman's" on 18 March. In March, Eli took six hogs to market that weighed an average of 208 pounds and brought $3.50 per hundred (16 March); later, he hauled 250 bushels of corn to the town of Holmes, receiving 40 cents per bushel (21 March).

The rich social life of Amish-Mennonite youths in Wright County included a worrisome (to church elders) resistance to joining the church. As the farmers tested the great plains environment for the Amish farming system, single Amish men and women tested the limits of church and community membership (Figure 8.2).

By 1895 the new Amish-Mennonite settlement in Wright County had grown rapidly. In only three years, at least eighteen family units and many single persons had made their homes in the new area. More importantly, the settlement had a full complement of Amish ministers in Bishop S. J. Swartzendruber, Preacher Jacob J. Swartzendruber, and Deacon Elias Swartzendruber. Both the *Kalona News* and the *Wellman Advance* began devoting part of their regu-

8.2. Hunting party of Amish youths, Wright County, Iowa, 1890s. This Amish-Mennonite community pushed the limits of Amish identity. Sanford C. Yoder stands third from the left in the rear.

lar correspondence sections to Wright County, as if the new Amish-Mennonite settlement were another local small town.[33]

Correspondents from Wright County to the *Weekly Budget* and southeast Iowa newspapers reported births, marriages, deaths, crop prospects, visits from relatives and ministers, weather, township meetings, and other paraphernalia of rural life. The *Weekly Budget* served an especially important role in keeping contact with friends and relatives in other Amish communities. Started in 1890 by J. C. Miller in Sugarcreek, Ohio, the *Budget* reached twenty post offices in Iowa by 1900. Out of a total circulation of 3,031, 179 subscribers were in Iowa: Kalona had 52, the town of Amish had 36, and Sharon Center had 23.[34] The Amish of Wright County were firmly connected with the organ of intersettlement communication because almost the entire community subscribed to, or wrote letters for, the *Budget* at one time or another.

Already in August of 1894, an astute observer from southeast Iowa remarked that the price of land was "getting rather high in proportion to the improvements," although he also considered the land in Wright County "first-class."[35] The depression of 1893 and a severe drought during the summer of 1894 took their toll economically. The financial depression forced Christian S. Yoder to sell his farm to newcomer Preacher Jacob J. Swartzendruber, and Yoder's son, Sanford, had to hire out to S. M. Bender "to help my parents get started again." Drought damaged the 1894 corn crop rather severely, and plentiful rain the following season brought huge crops and low prices. Those who could stored their grain to wait for higher prices in the future.[36]

The ardor of "Wright County Fever" began to cool. The Wright County correspondent for the *Wellman Advance* reported, "Our new comers are almost discouraged with this county, on account of the wind. Jonas Yoder says he would like it all right here, but it is a dreadful job to wash out his ears so often."[37] The flood of immigrants slowed to a bare trickle after 1895, as the extreme attractiveness of Wright County land began to wear off; hardly any new Amish settlers bought land after 1896.

Nonetheless, the small community put down roots and planned for further growth and development. The first minutes in the church record book are dated 26 March 1895; the group gathered to purchase land for a church and a cemetery and to elect trustees. The group agreed to buy land at $40 per acre from Daniel K. Yoder, from the southwest corner of his farm. S. M. Bender, Eli Miller, and John Gunden were elected trustees, assigned to lay out the cemetery and prepare for the church building.[38]

In May 1895 Adam Miller attended a huge ecumenical revival meeting in Eagle Grove, along with William Fisher (evidently not from the same family as John J. Fisher of the Amish community). The Sunday evening that Miller visited the "Camp Meeting," 26 May, a crowd reported at 2,000 or 2,500 attended the evangelistic service to hear "the brightest speaker on religious topics ever heard in our city," according to the breathless report to the *Wright County Monitor*.[39] That same evening, Miller shared a pint of whiskey with Ralph Fisher and Fred Smith. A month earlier, however, he had recorded the purchase of "Tobacco Antedott medicine" for 50 cents (25 April).

Miller did attend Amish services and Sunday school with greater frequency during April, May, and June. He wrote of going to church ten of the thirteen Sundays. One Sunday, 14 April, Adam and Tom Peachy drove to Sunday school in the "little buggy," while Eli and Mary took the "big buggy." The Sunday afternoon youth gatherings and evening singings continued, and Miller usually listed those present and where the events took place.

Adam Miller left Wright County on 22 November 1895 without recording any explanation for his move. The entry in Miller's diary for that day simply reads, "Left Wright Co Iowa for Jonson *[sic]* Co Iowa then to Elkhart Co Ind." Two years later, on 23 June 1897, lightning struck and killed Miller while he worked on fencing in Johnson County.[40]

Adam Miller's experiences in Johnson and Wright counties portray Amish-Mennonite migration undertaken to remain Amish. He recorded the pull of Amish tradition and the countervailing attractions of rural fairs and youth activities. In the turmoil of religious transition, Miller considered staying away from the church, but this would have meant forsaking the community as well. Miller did not bother to mention the main event of Wright County Amish-Mennonite religious conflict, nor did Sanford Yoder in his reminiscences of Wright County, *The Days of My Years.* From oral sources, Melvin Gingerich reported the dispute in this way:

> While the church was under construction, Bishop Solomon Swartzendruber made a business trip to Johnson County. While there he learned his brother Jacob Swartzendruber had left the Old Order Amish Mennonite Church without making the confession expected from him. He had joined the Warey church and was ordained preacher there but was dissatisfied and moved to Wright County. When Solomon returned to Wright County, he advised his brother to make peace with the Old Order brethren, but Jacob refused. The problem was taken up in church next, and Jacob was asked to leave the room while they discussed the matter. This he refused to do in spite of the entreaties of the bishop and deacon. After it was clear he would not leave the room, Solomon expelled him from church membership.

Gingerich commented, "This event was the death blow of that church."[41] None of the Amish residents of Wright County remained Old Order Amish, but the change-minded Amish-Mennonites could still disagree over how much of the traditional Amish community to retain.

Membership in the Wright County Amish-Mennonite Church peaked in 1902 at 38 members. Already in 1900, however, the pattern of relocation had begun that would eventually lead nearly all the community members away from Wright County. Two large waves of departure took place: 1900–1903 and 1906–1908. The first wave consisted of nearly all the original group of settlers, including Bishop Solomon J. Swartzendruber; the second wave was smaller, but included Preacher Jacob J. Swartzendruber.

Cheaper land in Nebraska, Minnesota, Missouri, Colorado, Texas, and

Michigan began to attract Amish settlers instead of north central Iowa. Christian C. Swartzendruber sold his land in June of 1900 and moved back to Johnson County; Isaac Swartzendruber sold his farm in July and moved to Iowa County.[42] Some of the older children began moving to other Amish settlements. Daniel J. Gingerich relocated to Oklahoma in November of 1900; M. S. Erb and Pete Swartzendruber moved to Minnesota in December; and Sanford Yoder and the brothers Amos and Simon Gingerich all left for greener pastures in southeast Iowa during this first wave of exits.[43]

Shem Swartzendruber and D. K. Yoder made a "prospecting trip" to Minnesota, North Dakota, Nebraska, Wisconsin, Arkansas, Oklahoma, and Missouri in March of 1901. Others considered leaving but stayed a few more years. Abraham J. Swartzendruber and William A. Kreider went on a "prospecting trip in Oklahoma."[44] Both remained in Wright County, although Swartzendruber, along with other locals, later "joined the throng of land seekers" who are "looking over the country" in Minnesota. Joel Guengerich went land hunting in Oklahoma, Kansas, and Nebraska.[45]

For such a small community, the flurry of departures in 1901 and the years following meant the effective end of the settlement. The church continued another nine years, but families continued to move away, and very few arrived to replace them. By the summer of 1904, the community was reduced to ten families. However, some families continued to plan for permanent settlement. Joseph C. Gingerich built a new house in May of 1902. Joel Swartzendruber put prodigious amounts of tile in his land, 935 rods in 1903 with plans for another 400 rods in 1904.[46] Still, by the spring of 1907, only seven families persevered. The church tax record for 1909 lists only five families.[47]

It seemed the Amish-Mennonite youth were in danger of drifting away completely from the church of their ancestors. The activities recorded by Adam Miller show hesitancy toward claiming the Amish configuration of ethnoreligious community. Sanford Yoder recalled his own feelings as a youth in Wright County, in the context of conversations with his terminally ill twin brother, Samuel:

> Among other things, we promised each other that we would become Christians, but when and where were problems that were not decided. We had a deep feeling that the church of our fathers was right in principle, and that it was from their faith that its people received their moral virtues and integrity. But as children and growing boys we had suffered so much ridicule and abuse because of

its customs and traditions which had no meaning to us, that we were reluctant to join its fellowship.[48]

Among other expedients to encourage their children to become members of the Amish-Mennonite church, leaders in Wright County secured evangelists to preach and convert recalcitrant youths. Religious conversion began to take the place of ordering community life on the basis of consensus and tradition. For example, Amish-Mennonite evangelist D. D. Miller from Middlebury, Indiana, was invited to hold a Bible Conference and special meetings from 10 to 14 October 1906. Elias Swartzendruber reported to the *Gospel Witness* that "four souls" had been baptized and "others also were under conviction." A report to the *Budget* stated that four were baptized and eight others had converted.[49]

Sanford Yoder entered high school in September of 1899, a year and a half after his twin died, and he graduated in May of 1901. When the Amish lad from Dayton Township entered school in town, at least two county newspapers took notice of the event.[50] If the tradition that Yoder was the first child born to Amish parents west of the Mississippi River to graduate from high school is correct,[51] then it was appropriate for local papers to record his entry. Yoder made his mark in the public high school. He and Maude Alexander were the champion Latin spellers of the tenth grade in March of 1900. By the end of his first year of high school, Yoder was serving as toastmaster at a reception given the seniors by the juniors, "introducing each speaker in a few well chosen words."[52] Yoder referred to his graduation from Clarion High School in May of 1901 as "the crowning achievement of my years in Wright County." He later became president of Goshen College, a Mennonite school in northern Indiana, thus continuing his commitment to education.

After he graduated from high school, Sanford Yoder was appointed a delegate to the Democratic "Representative Convention" in Wright County in July of 1901. Yoder nearly became a candidate for county superintendent of schools in Johnson County in 1905; and in that heavily Democratic county, he would have stood a good chance to win.[53]

The final four families departed from Wright County in late 1909 and early 1910. Samuel M. Bender moved to Parnell, Iowa, and Christian S. Yoder went to Chappell, Nebraska, to join his son, Sanford.[54] Joseph C. Gingerich moved to Wellman, Iowa, and Elias Swartzendruber moved to Morgan County, Missouri in February of 1910.[55]

One concrete result of the Wright County settlement was capital formation for further moves and land purchases, sometimes enabling settlers to return to their home communities and buy land there. Samuel M. Bender sold his 60-acre farm near Kalona in 1894 for $56 per acre; bought 160 acres in Dayton Township in February of 1895, most likely at a price under $50 per acre and perhaps as low as $35 or $40; and sold his quarter section of Wright County land in October of 1909 at $115 per acre. The value of Bender's land at least doubled and quite possibly trebled in fifteen years.[56]

John J. Fisher sold 200 acres in Washington Township on 1 March 1895 for $11,200, or $56 per acre. He sold another 120 acres the following year at $50 per acre. He bought 160 acres in Wright County in 1894 (price unknown), a second quarter section in 1901 at $56 per acre, and sold his 320 acres in 1902 at $79.[57]

One of the more spectacular price increases occurred for Joseph C. Gingerich. Gingerich sold 80 acres in Sharon Township in 1894 for $3,300, or $41.25 per acre. He bought 200 acres in Wright County in 1901 at $34.50 per acre and sold the same in 1909 at $100 per acre.[58]

Capital formation may have become a component of the Amish migration system during the late nineteenth century. William Kuvlesky reported a similar purpose for Amish settlements in Texas, perceived by the immigrants as a temporary expedient. "The move to Texas is an attempt by particular Amish to make a long-term adjustment to survive as economically viable parts of an older community they wish to be a part of."[59]

The church building in Dayton Township was dismantled in February of 1911 and shipped to Daytonville, Iowa, just northeast of Wellman; it served as a meetinghouse for the Daytonville Amish-Mennonite Church. It was dedicated to its new purpose on 18 June 1911, just thirteen years after it had been erected in Wright County.[60]

The cemetery remained a few more years. In October of 1912, Jonas Yoder traveled to Clarion from Wellman to build a fence around the graveyard. In 1941 the remaining six bodies, including Samuel Yoder, Sanford's twin brother who died in 1898, were removed from the cemetery and taken back to Johnson County.[61]

The Amish-Mennonite settlement in Wright County, Iowa, lasted seventeen years. It grew rapidly amid a great deal of excitement and optimism, reached a point of stagnation due to church conflict and rising land prices, and finally died out completely as the remaining families moved to other Amish-Mennonite settlements. Every family unit moved to another Amish-Mennonite community; only a very few individuals remained in Wright County. The overriding concern for children appears in the summary assessment of Deacon Elias Swartzendruber, who wrote about the experience in Wright County, "I have no regrets, because the family was saved for the church."[62]

Audrain County, Missouri

Another new settlement from Johnson County occurred in Audrain County, Missouri, near Centralia. More than twenty families moved there, but the community lasted only nineteen years and no longer existed by 1917.[63]

In the fall of 1897, four Amish land scouts set out in a horse and buggy and drove the 175 miles, at a pace of about 70 miles a day, to the region some 50 miles north of Jefferson City. Jacob D. Guengerich, John C. Gingerich, Jacob B. Miller, and Jacob Miller traveled south to Kirksville and then on to Larrabee in Audrain County. John C. Gingerich was not impressed and caught a train for Vandalia, Illinois, where his wife was visiting her sister. The other three "prospected" in several locations, and they found a favorable site near Centralia, where the land was level and inexpensive. The farmers living there came from Kentucky and Virginia and seemed to the Amish visitors "rather slipshod in their farming methods and practices." Land prices ranged from $20 to $40 per acre at a time when land averaged over $45 in Washington and Sharon townships. (In November 1897 Jacob G. Marner paid $5,500, $69 per acre, for 80 acres in Washington Township.) The Amish fathers wanted to find cheaper land so their children could establish homes of their own.[64]

In the spring of 1898, three Iowa families moved to Audrain County. Valentine Swartzendruber, grandson of Jacob and son of Frederick, bought a farm, while John C. Gingerich and Elmer J. Guengerich rented land. Other families followed over the next several years, including Shem Swartzendruber and Daniel K. Yoder from Wright County in 1901. Shem operated a threshing crew and sawmill. Most new settlers came from Iowa, but some moved in from Illinois, Michigan, and Texas.

The Amish farmers from Iowa were used to dairy farming, but the local farmers in Audrain County had cattle farms. They imported cattle by the train carload, raised corn for feed, and shipped the fattened animals to market. The Amish settlers were not impressed. Jacob D. Guengerich complained in a letter to the *Budget*, "Three fourth [*sic*] of the land is farmed by renters and their only aim seems to be make a living." He reported that livestock was not raised, only fed. And Guengerich wrote, with some incredulity, "They have very queer ideas here about rotating crops. They have great faith in resting land as they call it—letting it grow up in weeds and then burning off the weeds in the spring and putting it to corn again." It was said that one local farmer found his cattle manure so annoying that he stashed it in a corncrib.[65]

The Amish farmers no doubt thought primitive crop rotation methods and ignorance about manure had gone out of fashion in the eighteenth century. In contrast to the one-and-a-half story homes of the local farmers, the Amish householders built large barns and two-story houses. Guengerich expressed confidence in the community's long-term prospects, writing to the *Budget* in 1901, "All we need is a different mode of farming and more stock." And he disparaged his neighbors with the acerbic remark, "They dread everything that we call work."[66]

However, few Amish families stayed long. The settlement's first two years, 1898 and 1899, were extremely wet, and two drought years followed. The drought in 1901 made it necessary for local farmers to export their partially fattened cattle due to the lack of pasture and water.[67] A bumper crop in 1902 did not prevent families from moving away to escape the unpredictable and stormy weather. Before 1910 several families left the new settlement and moved to Oklahoma and Michigan, and there were never more than thirteen families in the community. Around 1913 more households exited and moved to Kansas, Ohio, and Michigan. There was also a conflict over the use of telephones. The families that moved away joined churches ranging from Old Order Amish to Mennonite, which might help explain the internal conflicts.[68] By 1916 only two families remained. The last family moved away in 1917.

In assessing the short-lived community, Daniel C. Esch commented, "I may safely say, we were all better off financially." Their land had increased in value, and almost all the Amish settlers had been able to buy land. Esch also claimed the local farmers had learned better agricultural methods from the northern farmers.[69]

Bee County, Texas

The first settlers in Bee County, Texas, were Mennonites from Illinois. Minister Peter Unzicker led a group from Illinois in 1905 to the area between San Antonio and Corpus Christi. Unzicker chose the site after a number of "prospecting" trips in the South. Unzicker bought 53.4 acres from the original

8.3. Small Amish-Mennonite church building near Tuleta, Texas. South Texas turned out to be an inhospitable environment for Amish farming practices.

Uranga grant, later the Chittim-Miller Ranch, and platted the town of Tuleta in 1906.[70] He named the town after a daughter of J. M. Chittim, who sold the land to Unzicker. In January 1906 there were six Mennonite families, with a total of 14 members. In 1907 Unzicker organized a Mennonite congregation in Tuleta, with 24 members. By 1913 there were 81 members, and the congregation peaked at 104 members a short time later.

The first schoolhouse in Tuleta, built in 1906, also served as a meetinghouse for Mennonite church services. Peter Unzicker, A. J. Miller, and A. E. Hostetler served as trustees of the school (Figure 8.3). Residents of the town also built an innovative educational institution, the Tuleta Agricultural High School, with Miss Amanda Stoltzfus as its first principal.[71] Amanda's father,

Christian H. Stoltzfus, had moved from Tennessee to Tuleta in 1909. Christian and four of his five sons established the Tuleta Mercantile Company, and Tuleta became a marketing center for the surrounding farming region. Stoltzfus had left the Amish and helped organize the Tuleta Presbyterian Church, but he and his family associated freely with the Mennonite group.[72]

A. Caswell Ellis from the University of Texas visited Tuleta in 1911. He reported three or four stores, a small hotel, a public park, a dozen residences, a church, and a new public school in the new hamlet. The local farmers, who were emphasizing diversity in their agricultural practices and were raising cows and hogs, had voted upon themselves the highest tax allowed by state law in order to build the new high school. Several farmers made sizable private contributions, and many locals helped build the $2,500 four-room school at a "grand rally" held on one day. The principal, Amanda Stoltzfus, helped draw the building plans. Stoltzfus, trained at Peabody Normal College, the University of Tennessee, and Columbia University, developed a curriculum of agriculture, manual training, and domestic service. A shop provided training in farm equipment use and repair. Twenty acres of land offered opportunities to learn the best methods of gardening and farming, and a place to experiment with crops and methods. The visitor expressed the wish that hundreds of Texas communities would follow the example of "this thrifty little community of Tuleta."[73]

Stoltzfus joined the Department of Extension at the University of Texas in 1914. The Tuleta public school, the first in Texas to operate an agricultural education program, had become "the most talked-about school in the state of Texas." Stoltzfus negotiated a provision in her contract with Texas that allowed her to supervise the Tuleta school. For example, she returned to her hometown in 1918 to report on the enthusiastic commencement parade through the town's streets.[74] Stoltzfus died on 11 October 1930. She earned high praise from the Texas General Faculty for her work in rural education and for her understanding of "the difficulties and hardships of the rural housewife." She led so many plays and games that she became known as the "play lady" of Texas. The faculty sent condolences to the Stoltzfus family.[75]

A few Amish-Mennonite families joined the Bee County settlement, including Abraham J. Swartzendruber from Wright County, Iowa. Before moving to Wright County, A. J. Swartzendruber had operated the Wassonville Mill in the southeast Iowa Amish community. He moved to Wright County in 1894 and engaged in farming, eventually buying land in Wall Lake Township, the farm furthest from the center of the Amish settlement. A corn shredder accident caused him to lose parts of two fingers in April 1899. In November 1900, he traded his land for a livery stable in Clarion, moved to town, and proceeded to improve and promote his business with a great deal of enthusiasm.[76]

Abraham J. ran an ad in each weekly issue of the *Wright County Monitor* for at least a year, advertising "First Class Turnouts, Reasonable Prices. Special attention given commercial men." Already in February 1901, he lit his business with electricity, prompting the *Monitor* to pronounce, "Abe is putting on a good many city airs for one so soon from the 'rural districts.'"[77] Swartzendruber bought 80 acres in Bee County for $2,000 on 2 November 1907. Swartzendruber died on 19 April 1919 and was buried in Bee County. His widow, Christina, sold their 80 acres in Bee County for $3,000 on 2 July 1921, and moved back to Washington County, Iowa.[78]

The Bee County farmers raised cotton, melons, corn, hay, broom corn, and sorghum. They were disappointed with the lack of rainfall and their inability to grow the same crops as they grew in the upper Midwest. However, while a Norwegian immigrant band grew discouraged and returned to Norway, the Amish and Mennonites persisted despite the semiarid climate.[79]

War conditions after 1915 and a severe drought in 1917 convinced most of the families to move back to the north. There were still 30 members in 1932, and Tuleta became the base for Mennonite mission outreach to Hispanic people in South Texas. For example, in 1938 a Mennonite Mission was organized in Normanna. After pastor E. S. Hallman retired to Akron, Pennsylvania, in 1950, the group dwindled to nine members by 1957, holding services only once a month.[80]

Moving to Stay

The new settlements in Wright County, Iowa; Audrain County, Missouri; and Bee County, Texas, resulted from change-minded Amish-Mennonite migrations. But Old Order Amish families also moved to preserve their tradition-minded community. In 1914 and 1915, several families moved to Buchanan County, Iowa, for cheap land and because they believed banning and shunning were not being enforced strictly enough in the Sharon churches.[81] Interconnected chains of Amish communities, like strawberries reproducing new plants, and disconnections among Amish affiliations, like elevators moving to different levels, both represent a degree of continuity with the Amish history

8.4. Washington Township grade school children, about 1910. Most of the children are Amish or Mennonite. Amish parents sent their children to public country schools until school consolidation and compulsory high school began to threaten their control of educational practices.

of aggressive migration. As the tendency to migrate interacted with situations of economic need and personal choice, new forms expressed old dispositions (Figure 8.4).

It is not unusual to meet elderly Old Order Amish who have lived in Arkansas, Oklahoma, Kansas, Missouri, and many other states. The Amish developed a trial-and-error method of community formation, as is shown by the large number of temporary Amish settlements spread throughout North America. Maurice Mook once pointed out that there were probably more extinct Amish settlements in Pennsylvania than permanent communities.[82] Ironically, the practice of using paternal authority to maintain Amish tradition, encouraged by the first Amish bishop in Iowa, Jacob Swartzendruber, became available later in the nineteenth century to dissociate from the Old Order Amish as well. Parents might protect children from too much change or too little change as a matter of familial and individual choice rather than having their central goal be the preservation of Amish community. The Amish repertoire of community changed most of all in the attempts to preserve it by self-conscious activism, including migration to new locales to seek new religious opportunities.

Conclusion

One Sunday morning in May 1917, Samuel D. Guengerich wrestled with his conscience. It was time for the biennial communion service at Upper Deer Creek Conservative Amish-Mennonite Church, and Guengerich was not sure he could consider himself unified with the other members of his congregation. He desired to partake, but he was worried about the drift toward "worldliness" in his community. Guengerich experienced once more the difficult equilibrium among individual choice, communal responsibility, and relations with the dominant American culture.

Guengerich's congregation had gone through several recent periods in which holding communion had been impossible. The worst had been the issue of telephones only five years earlier. Many members had wanted the convenience, but others had adamantly resisted the unprecedented innovation. In Lancaster County, Pennsylvania—so the story went—many Amish households purchased phones as soon as they became available. However, two people on a party line were overheard gossiping about someone else and had to make confession before the church. Then Amish members "decided that we just better not allow these phones."[1] But no such unmistakable guidance had appeared in Iowa.

Guengerich had finally taken the lead in 1912 and organized a petition for the ministers of the two Deer Creek congregations. He suggested that the top priority should be avoiding a schism; therefore, "the phones should be tolerated conditionally." Those who already owned or planned to own a telephone "should get out and stay out of the phone companies" and should only rent a phone. By avoiding business relationships with non-Amish companies, church members would "not be entwined in and connected with the world."[2] By the fall of 1914, the conservative bishop, William K. Miller, had moved to Buchanan County; the church reorganized the following spring and finally held communion. Telephones stayed.

This story illustrates how the struggle with technology and modernity, hardly an issue during the nineteenth century, began to take center stage in Amish communities and in scholarly attention paid to all Old Order groups.[3]

New technologies do make the Amish goal of separation from the world more complex to achieve. However, twentieth-century gadgets are merely the most recent obstacle to Amish unity, and Amish leaders continue with both conservatism and innovation. S. D. Guengerich followed both well-worn paths within the Amish repertoire of community.

In 1907 Guengerich had helped to reorganize the "German School Association of the Old Order of Amish Mennonites," originally incorporated in 1890 (Figure C.1). In this reorganization, Guengerich and his colleagues dropped the "Old Order" and added the purpose of encouraging young people "in charitable and benevolent work and institutions."[4] Ostensibly, the Sharon Old Order Amish districts and the Deer Creek Amish-Mennonite congregations were still struggling to remain together, but it had become clear that they were not going to succeed.

Guengerich could think back further than the telephone controversy—to church buildings, sleeping preachers, inheritance struggles, warfare, and even to colored dishes and household decoration. His weariness was understandable. Yet Guengerich could also reflect that each issue had been mediated through his Amish experience of community.

From the emotion-laden communal dreams of Bishop Jacob Swartzendruber, to the entranced, ambivalent visions of Sleeping Preacher Noah Troyer, to the nightmarish branching into several divergent denominational paths, the Amish configuration of community continued creating and adapting to the social and economic realities of rural America. The mental map of Amish community interacted with the social and physical environment to produce changes in both *habitus* and field. At times, the Amish community imposed its repertoire; at other times, the Amish found themselves forced to make adjustments. Perhaps the most significant element in the Amish configuration of community was flexibility.

Between the *habitus,* the cognitive principles carried by each individual, and the *field,* the social environment, stands a repertoire of community. Communities mediate between individuals and society, an aspect of social reality neglected by Pierre Bourdieu and other social theorists. The Amish shared a common "feel for the game," a set of communal principles that enfolded and impelled personal *habitus.* Individual Amish women and men did not face "the world" they distrusted as isolated persons, but they faced it as carriers and preservers of a communal configuration developed and nurtured over centuries.

The Amish experience in Iowa showed some components of the Amish

C.1. Elderly Samuel D. Guengerich entering his house.

repertoire of community to be far stronger than others. The agricultural system reached back to early modern Europe and remained the most stable. Paternal household authority and household formation were rooted nearly as deeply but needed adjustment in the new American environment. The Amish relationship to the American state had to be worked out during the American Revolution and the Civil War. Renting land in Europe barely prepared Amish landowners for the land market and inheritance systems in Iowa. No one could have anticipated the Sleeping Preacher and his challenge to the essential balance of individual and community. The peculiar combination of religious activism and economic stability turned out to be ephemeral. The Amish pattern of migration and portable community became a means of experimentation, capital formation, and exit.

The Amish encountered dangerous alternatives to their traditional repertoire: market farming; assertive women and children; unrestricted private property; contact with the state; revivalism and individual salvation; social and political activism; unlimited migration; and spiritualism. Amish leaders showed remarkable agility as they sought personal and social innovations to meet new situations and, at the same time, to preserve their cherished principles of community.

Other principles of the Amish configuration of community have become visible in the twentieth century: institutionalized teenage rebellion, or *rumspringe;* selective use of technology; small-scale farming; *gelassenheit,* or submission to the community; resistance to conscription in World Wars I and II; and maintaining social distinction through symbols of separation, such as the horse and buggy and plain clothing. The Amish have often chosen diverging paths to deal with these challenges. By 1930 there were four distinct denominations in Johnson County, all with Amish roots: Old Order Amish, Beachy Amish, Conservative Amish-Mennonite, and Mennonite. Even these divisions served a function by offering outlets to discontented members in the more tradition-minded groups.

Guengerich finally decided to attend his congregation on communion day, 13 May 1917. He heard sermons preached by Solomon J. Swartzendruber, grandson of Bishop Jacob Swartzendruber and former bishop in Wright County, and Gideon Yoder, son of Bishop Abner Yoder. The very same day, another Swartzendruber, Elmer G., was ordained by lot. Whatever he heard that morning convinced him to participate in the communion ceremony with his community. Writing in his diary later that Sunday afternoon, Guengerich expressed satisfaction that he had attended and taken *die Einigkeit,* or "Unity," with his congregation, even though it was clear that Upper Deer Creek was no longer Old Order Amish. He registered his customary irrepressible optimism about the future of his community.[5] Guengerich lived until 1929. He carried with him the first eighty-three years of his beloved Amish church in Iowa, and the repertoire of Amish community that he had toiled so long to preserve outlived him.

Appendix

Table A.1. Characteristics of Ethnic Households in Washington and Sharon Townships, Johnson County, Iowa, 1850–1910

	Amish-Native Born	*Amish-Foreign Born*	*German*	*Northeast States*	*Middle States*	*Southern States*	*Welsh Welsh*	*Other*	*All*
1850									
Heads	1	2	12	4	55	23	5	5	107
Farms	1	2	12	3	42	13	3	3	79
Age[a]	45.0	37.5	41.4	36.0	38.2	39.8	41.0	33.4	38.8
1860									
Heads	23	17	37	20	93	15	13	15	233
Farms	18	11	21	11	50	10	8	7	136
Age	36.0	47.8	38.5	44.7	38.4	45.5	42.1	45.3	40.5
1870									
Heads	70	15	82	13	124	14	15	14	349
Farms	62	13	59	8	98	12	13	10	277
Age	38.1	51.7	43.1	43.9	41.5	46.4	48.5	49.9	42.5
1880									
Heads	98	17	84	9	132	12	14	14	380
Farms	90	13	72	8	107	10	13	11	331
Age	40.3	58.4	47.3	50.6	46.3	51.1	50.2	49.9	46.0

	Old Order Amish	*Amish Mennonite*	*German Born*	*German Ancestry*	*Northeast States*	*Middle States*	*Southern States*	*Welsh*	*All*
1885[b]									
Heads	47	23	47	7	5	36	6	13	190
Farms	40	21	30	7	3	25	4	9	144
Age	44.1	40.7	47.3	36.9	46.0	42.4	52.8	52.5	45.1
1895									
Heads	69	77	62	19	3	112	8	13	386
Farms	61	63	41	19	3	87	7	12	314
Age	43.3	41.0	51.7	35.9	49.3	44.5	53.4	51.8	45.0
1900									
Heads	67	109	55	37	1	107	11	10	423
Farms	57	96	40	35	0	90	9	10	359
Age	46.5	40.8	53.8	37.5	—	44.5	47.1	52.8	45.0
1910									
Heads	69	111	27	46	0	79	9	6	374
Farms	61	103	20	43	0	64	8	6	316
Age	43.0	42.6	53.7	41.6	—	43.9	47.1	35.5	43.8

Source: U.S. Population and Agricultural Censuses, 1850, 1860, 1870, 1880, 1900, 1910; Iowa State Population Censuses, 1885, 1895.

Northeast States: Nativity in New England, including New York. Middle States: Nativity Mid-Atlantic or Midwestern states, Pennsylvania, Ohio, Maryland, Indiana, Illinois. Southern States: Nativity in Virginia, North Carolina, Kentucky, Tennessee.

[a] Of head of household. [b] Sharon Township only.

Table A.2. Number of Households and Farms by Ethnicity in Washington and Sharon Townships, Johnson County, Iowa, 1850–1910

	Amish	*German*	*Native*	*Welsh*	*Other*	*All*
1850						
Heads	3	12	82	5	5	107
Farms	3	12	58	3	3	79
Age[a]	40.0	41.4	38.5	41.0	33.4	38.8
1860						
Heads	40	37	128	13	15	233
Farms	29	21	71	8	7	136
Age	41.0	38.5	40.2	42.1	45.3	40.5
1870						
Heads	85	84	151	15	14	349
Farms	75	60	118	13	10	277
Age	40.5	42.7	42.1	48.5	49.9	42.5
1880						
Heads	115	84	153	14	14	380
Farms	103	72	125	13	11	331
Age	43.0	47.3	46.9	50.2	49.9	46.0
1885[b]						
Heads	70	54	47	13	6	190
Age	43.0	46.0	44.2	52.5	53.0	45.1
1895						
Heads	158	81	123	13	12	386
Age	42.0	48.0	45.2	51.8	53.6	45.0
1900						
Heads	188	92	119	10	14	423
Age	43.0	47.2	44.9	52.8	51.3	45.0
1910						
Heads	196	73	88	6	11	374
Age	43.0	46.1	44.2	35.5	50.0	43.8

Source: U.S. Population and Agricultural Census, 1850, 1860, 1870, 1880; U.S. Population Census, 1900, 1910; Iowa State Population Census, 1885, 1895

[a] Of heads of household. [b] Sharon Township only.

Notes

Abbreviations

AMC	Archives of the Mennonite Church, Goshen, Indiana
HoT	*Herald of Truth*
IMHSA	Iowa Mennonite Historical Society Archives, Kalona, Iowa
ME	*Mennonite Encyclopedia,* 4 Volumes, 1955–59
ME V	*Mennonite Encyclopedia,* Volume 5, 1990
MHB	*Mennonite Historical Bulletin*
MQR	*Mennonite Quarterly Review*
NA	National Archives, Washington, D.C.
Proceedings	Minutes of Amish Ministers' Meetings, 1862–76, 1878

Introduction

1. S. D. Guengerich, "A Brief History of the Amish Settlement in Johnson County, Iowa," *MQR* 3 (October 1929): 243–248.

2. On the problem of defining *community,* see Thomas Bender, *Community and Social Change in America* (Baltimore: Johns Hopkins University Press, 1978); and Peter Burke, *History and Social Theory* (Ithaca, N.Y.: Cornell University Press, 1992), 56–58. In 1955 George A. Hillery Jr. classified no fewer than ninety-four definitions of community and found little common ground among scholars in his "Definitions of Community: Areas of Agreement," *Rural Sociology* 20 (June 1955): 111–123.

3. Almost the entire corpus of important literature on the Amish focuses on the twentieth century, including the two best-known and widely read works, anthropologist John A. Hostetler's *Amish Society,* which, as the standard reference for over three decades, has gone through four editions (Baltimore: Johns Hopkins University Press, 1963, 1968, 1980, 1993); and sociologist Donald B. Kraybill's *The Riddle of Amish Culture* (Baltimore: Johns Hopkins University Press, 1989).

4. On boundaries and boundary maintenance, see Fredrik Barth, "Introduction," in *Ethnic Groups and Boundaries: The Social Organization of Culture Difference,* ed. Fredrik Barth (Boston: Little, Brown, 1969), 9–38. For a recent attempt to use more flexible terminologies but finally falling back on boundary maintenance, see Daphne Naomi Winland, "The Quest for Mennonite Peoplehood: Ethno-Religious Identity

and the Dilemma of Definitions," *Canadian Review of Sociology and Anthropology* 30 (February 1993): 110–138.

5. James Clifford, *The Predicament of Culture: Twentieth-Century Ethnography, Literature, and Art* (Cambridge: Harvard University Press, 1988), 644.

6. Pierre Bourdieu, "Les stratégies matrimoniales dans le système de reproduction," *Annales: Économies Sociétés Civilisations* 27 (July–October 1972): 1105–1127; translated as "Marriage Strategies as Strategies of Social Reproduction," in *Family and Society: Selections from the Annales: Economies, Sociétés, Civilisations,* ed. Robert Forster and Orest Ranum (Baltimore: Johns Hopkins University Press, 1976), 117–144. The article was summarized by James A. Henretta in "Social History as Lived and Written," *American Historical Review* 84 (December 1979): 1293–1322. See also Bourdieu's *The Logic of Practice* (1980; Cambridge: Polity Press, 1990).

7. Bourdieu, "Marriage Strategies," 141.

8. Burke, *History and Social Theory,* 120.

9. Pierre Bourdieu and Loïc J. D. Wacquant, *An Invitation to Reflexive Sociology* (Chicago: University of Chicago Press, 1992), 18.

10. Pierre Bourdieu, *Outline of a Theory of Practice* (Cambridge: Cambridge University Press, 1977), 72.

11. Bourdieu and Wacquant, *Invitation to Reflexive Sociology,* 17–18. Natalie Zemon Davis makes a similar point in *Fiction in the Archives: Pardon Tales and Their Tellers in Sixteenth-Century France* (Stanford: Stanford University Press, 1987).

12. Richard White, *The Middle Ground: Indians, Empires, and Republics in the Great Lakes Region, 1650–1815* (New York: Cambridge University Press, 1991).

13. Bourdieu, *Distinction: A Social Critique of the Judgement of Taste* (Cambridge: Harvard University Press, 1984), 101.

14. See, for example, *In Other Words: Essays towards a Reflexive Sociology* (Stanford: Stanford University Press, 1990), 9, 11.

Chapter 1. Configuring Amish Historical Experience

From Conrad Grebel's letter to Thomas Müntzer, 5 September 1524, in *The Sources of Swiss Anabaptism: The Grebel Letters and Related Documents,* ed. Leland Harder (Scottdale, Pa.: Herald Press, 1985), 290; transcription in J. C. Wenger, *Conrad Grebel's Programmatic Letters of 1524* (Scottdale, Pa.: Herald Press, 1970), 28.

1. For overviews of Amish history, see John A. Hostetler, *Amish Society,* 4th ed. (Baltimore: Johns Hopkins University Press, 1993); and Steven M. Nolt, *A History of the Amish* (Intercourse, Pa.: Good Books, 1992).

2. For a general overview of Anabaptism and the Radical Reformation, see Cornelius J. Dyck, ed., *An Introduction to Mennonite History: A Popular History of the Anabaptists and the Mennonites,* 3rd ed. (1967; Scottdale, Pa.: Herald Press, 1993);

George H. Williams, *The Radical Reformation,* 3rd ed., rev. and enlarged (1962; Kirksville, Mo.: Truman State University Press, 2000); and C. Arnold Snyder, *Anabaptist History and Theology, an Introduction* (Kitchener, Ontario: Pandora Press, 1995). The Amish descended from Swiss/South German Anabaptism. Dutch/North German and Moravian (Hutterian Brethren) Anabaptism are not under discussion in this book.

3. Harold S. Bender, "The Anabaptist Vision," *Church History* 13 (March 1944): 3–24; reprinted in *MQR* 18 (April 1944): 67–88. The article resulted from Bender's presidential address before the American Society of Church History in December 1943. See also the essays in Guy F. Hershberger, ed., *The Recovery of the Anabaptist Vision* (Scottdale, Pa.: Herald Press, 1957).

On the sources of Bender's essay, see Albert N. Keim, "History of The Anabaptist Vision," *MHB* 54 (October 1993): 1–7; and Albert N. Keim, *Harold S. Bender, 1897–1962* (Scottdale, Pa.: Herald Press, 1998).

4. James M. Stayer, *The German Peasants' War and Anabaptist Community of Goods* (Montreal: McGill-Queen's University Press, 1991); Werner O. Packull and James M. Stayer, eds., *The Anabaptists and Thomas Müntzer* (Dubuque, Iowa: Kendall/Hunt, 1980); Abraham Friesen, *Thomas Müntzer, a Destroyer of the Godless: The Making of a Sixteenth-Century Religious Revolutionary* (Berkeley: University of California Press, 1990); Hans-Jürgen Goertz, *Die Täufer: Geschichte und Deutung* (München: Beck, 1980); and the essays in Hans-Jürgen Goertz, ed., *Umstrittenes Täufertum* (Göttingen: Vandenhoek, 1975). See also James M. Stayer, Werner Packull, and Klaus Deppermann, "From Monogenesis to Polygenesis: The Historical Discussion of Anabaptist Origins," *MQR* 49 (April 1975): 83–121.

5. Klaus Deppermann, "The Anabaptists and the State Churches," trans. Ian Waite, in *Religion and Society in Early Modern Europe, 1500–1800,* ed. Kaspar von Greyerz (London: Allen & Unwin, 1984), 95–106.

6. *The Sources of Swiss Anabaptism: The Grebel Letters and Related Documents,* ed. Leland Harder (Scottdale, Pa.: Herald Press, 1985). See also Harold S. Bender, *Conrad Grebel c. 1498–1526: The Founder of the Swiss Brethren* (Goshen, Ind.: Mennonite Historical Society, 1950).

7. A brief account of these events can be found in Fritz Blanke, *Brothers in Christ* (Scottdale, Pa.: Mennonite Publishing House, 1961; German *Brüder in Christo,* published 1955 by Zwingli Press, Zürich).

8. An annotated version of the Schleitheim Confession appears in John H. Yoder, *The Legacy of Michael Sattler* (Scottdale, Pa.: Herald Press, 1973), 27–54.

9. Stayer, *German Peasants' War,* 4.

10. Ibid., 61–92, quote p. 83. Stayer has attempted to make the connections between Anabaptism and peasant radicalism even more explicit in his "Saxon Radicalism and Swiss Anabaptism: The Return of the Repressed," *MQR* 67 (January 1993):

5–30. See also James Stayer, "Anabaptists and Future Anabaptists in the Peasants' War," *MQR* 62 (April 1988): 99–139; Heinz Noflatscher, "Häresie und Empörung: Die frühen Täufer in Tirol und Zürich," *Der Schlern* 63 (1989): 619–639; published in English as "Heresy and Revolt: The Early Anabaptists in the Tyrol and in Zurich," *MQR* 68 (July 1994): 291–317; Roy L. Vice, "Valentin Ickelsamer's Odyssey from Rebellion to Quietism," *MQR* 69 (January 1995): 75–92. For rhetorical connections between the Peasants' War and Anabaptism, see Gerald J. Biesecker-Mast, "Social Movement Rhetorics of the Radical Reformation" (Ph.D. diss., University of Pittsburgh, 1995). For a recent summary of the debate, see Werner O. Packull, *Hutterite Beginnings: Communitarian Experiments during the Reformation* (Baltimore: Johns Hopkins University Press, 1995), 169–175.

11. On the Hutterites in Europe, see John A. Hostetler, *Hutterite Society* (Baltimore: Johns Hopkins University Press 1974), chaps. 1–4; and Leonard Gross, *The Golden Years of the Hutterites* (Scottdale, Pa.: Herald Press, 1980).

12. Klaus Deppermann, *Melchior Hoffman: Soziale Unruhen und apokalyptische Visionen in Zeitalter der Reformation* (Göttingen: Vandenhoeck and Ruprecht, 1979).

13. For an overview of Münster scholarship, see James M. Stayer, "Was Dr. Kuehler's Conception of Early Dutch Anabaptism Historically Sound? The Historical Discussion of Anabaptist Münster 450 Years Later," *MQR* 60 (July 1986): 261–288; and Ralf Klötzer, *Die Täuferherrschaft von Münster: Stadtreformation und Welterneuerung* (Münster: Aschendorff Verlag, 1992).

14. P[aul] S[chowalter], "Martyrs," *ME* III, 524; Claus-Peter Clasen, *Anabaptism: A Social History, 1525–1618* (Ithaca, N.Y.: Cornell University Press, 1972), esp. 358–422. Clasen documents 843 executions in Switzerland and the southern Germanic areas, excluding the Netherlands.

15. *Ausbund, das ist: Etliche schöne Christliche Lieder* (1564; Lancaster, Pa.: Lancaster Press, 1991). See also R[obert] F[riedmann], "Ausbund," *ME* I, 191–192; and Paul M. Yoder, Elizabeth Bender, Harvey Graber, and Nelson P. Springer, *Four Hundred Years with the Ausbund* (Scottdale, Pa.: Herald Press, 1964).

16. John Christian Wenger, ed., *The Complete Works of Menno Simons, c. 1496–1561*, trans. Leonard Verduin (Scottdale, Pa.: Herald Press, 1956); Cornelius J. Dyck, William E. Keeney, Alvin J. Beachy, trans. and eds., *The Writings of Dirk Philips, 1504–1568* (Scottdale, Pa.: Herald Press, 1992).

17. Thieleman J. van Braght, *Martyrs Mirror: The Story of Fifteen Centuries of Christian Martyrdom from the Time of Christ to A.D. 1660*, trans. Joseph F. Sohm, rev. ed. (Dutch 1660; Sohm trans. 1886; Scottdale, Pa.: Herald Press, 1998).

18. Philipp Jakob Spener, *Pia Desideria, oder herzliches Verlangen*, in *Philipp Jakob Spener Schriften*, ed. Erich Bayreuter (Hildesheim, N.Y.: Georg Olms Verlag, 1979), facsimile of 1680 edition in vol. 1, 123–548. For a useful introduction to Pietism, see Dale W. Brown, *Understanding Pietism* (Grand Rapids, Mich.: Eerdmans, 1978).

19. "Pietism," *ME* V, 703–704.

20. *Spener Schriften,* 231–234.

21. These are translated in Peter C. Erb, ed., *Pietists: Selected Writings* (New York: Paulist, 1983), 31–49.

22. Swiss Brethren (*Schweizer Brüder*) was the name the descendants of Anabaptists used for themselves in Switzerland, in contrast to North German and Dutch Anabaptists, who eventually accepted the name Mennonite, after Menno Simons.

23. F. Ernest Stoeffler, *The Rise of Evangelical Pietism* (Leiden: E. J. Brill, 1965).

24. Leo Schelbert, "Pietism Rejected: A Reinterpretation of Amish Origins," in *America and the Germans: An Assessment of a Three-Hundred-Year History,* Vol. 1, *Immigration, Language, Ethnicity,* ed. Frank Trommler and Joseph McVeigh (Philadelphia: University of Pennsylvania Press, 1985), 118–127. On the continuing interaction of Pietism and Anabaptism in Pennsylvania, see Stephen L. Longenecker, *Piety and Tolerance: Pennsylvania German Religion, 1700–1850* (Metuchen, N.J.: Scarecrow Press, 1994), esp. chap. 3, 47–70.

25. Ernst Müller included the text of a number of these official mandates in *Geschichte der Bernischen Täufer. Nach der Urkunden dargestellt* (Frauenfeld: J. Hubers Verlag, 1895); summarized in Delbert L. Gratz, *Bernese Anabaptists and Their American Descendants* (Goshen, Ind.: Mennonite Historical Society, 1953).

26. Summarized in Müller, *Geschichte der Bernischen Täufer,* 143–144.

27. Other issues included frequency of communion, footwashing, church discipline procedures, and offenses requiring excommunication. See the analysis of issues in John D. Roth, trans. and ed., *Letters of the Amish Division: A Sourcebook* (Goshen, Ind.: Mennonite Historical Society, 1993), 10–13.

28. Irvin B. Horst, trans. and ed., *Mennonite Confession of Faith* (Dordrecht) (Lancaster, Pa.: Lancaster Mennonite Historical Society, 1988). See also J[ohn] C. W[enger], "Dordrecht Confession of Faith," *ME* II, 92–93. Dutch Mennonites adopted the document at Dordrecht, Holland, at a reconciliation meeting on 21 April 1632.

29. A translation of "The Ohnenheim Attestation" appears in Roth, *Letters of the Amish Division,* 145–146. These practices from northern European Anabaptism differed from Swiss Brethren traditions.

30. Müller, *Geschichte der Bernischen Täufer,* 300.

31. See, for example, Milton Gascho, "The Amish Division of 1693–1697 in Switzerland and Alsace," *MQR* 11 (October 1937): 235–266. Robert Baecher has conducted extensive archival research in Switzerland and France and has uncovered important new information about Jacob Ammann and his family. Much of his research has been published in *Souvenance anabaptiste: Bulletin Annuel de l'Association Française d'Histoire Anabaptiste-Mennonite;* for summaries, see Robert Baecher, "Raisons et déroulement du schisme amish: Une perspective nouvelle," and "Le 'patriarche' de Sainte-Marie-aux-Mines," both essays in *Les Amish: Origine et par-*

ticularismes 1693–1993, ed. Lydie Hege and Christoph Wiebe (Ingersheim, France: Association Française d'Histoire Anabaptiste-Mennonite, 1996), 40–54 and 55–71.

32. Two recent attempts to track Amish migration in Europe are Horst Gerlach, *Mein Reich ist nicht von dieser Welt: 300 Jahre Amische, 1693–1993* (Kirchheimbolanden, Pfalz: Horst Gerlach, 1993); and Hermann Guth, *300 Jahre Amische Teilung, 1693–1993. Amische Mennoniten in Deutschland: Ihre Gemeinden, Ihre Höfe, Ihre Familien* (Saarbrücken: Hermann Guth, 1992). See also Horst Gerlach, "Mennonites in Rheinhesse and Migrations to America and Galicia," *Pennsylvania Mennonite Heritage* 9 (October 1986): 2–13; and "Amish Congregations in German and Adjacent Territories in the Eighteenth and Nineteenth Centuries," *Pennsylvania Mennonite Heritage* 13 (April 1990): 2–8.

33. Martin H. Schrag, *The European History (1525–1874) of the Swiss Mennonites from Volhynia* (North Newton, Kans.: Swiss Mennonite Cultural and Historical Association, 1974); Solomon Stucky, *The Heritage of the Swiss Volhynian Mennonites* (Waterloo, Ontario: Conrad Press, 1981). See also Jerold A. Stahly, "The Montbéliard Amish Move to Poland in 1791," *Mennonite Family History* 8 (January 1989): 13–17.

34. Hermann Guth, *The Amish-Mennonites of Waldeck and Wittgenstein* (Elverson, Pa.: Mennonite Family History, 1986), 10.

35. H[arold] S. B[ender], "Waldeck," *ME* IV, 873–874. Bender estimated that about half of the Johnson County, Iowa, Amish and Mennonites descended from the Waldeck Amish.

36. Guth, *Amish-Mennonites of Waldeck and Wittgenstein,* 42; Melvin Gingerich, "Mengeringhausen," *MHB* 32 (July 1971): 1–2. Frederick Swartzendruber, fourth child of Jacob and Barbara Oesch, wrote that Peter Guengerich bought the Gallows Mill before his death, meaning that the mill belonged to Barbara and her two sons when she married Jacob. See "A Frederick Schwarzendruber Letter [13 October 1893 to George Swartzendruber and Samuel Guengerich]," *MHB* 32 (July 1971): 2–3.

37. AMC, Daniel Bender Swartzendruber Collection, Hist. Mss. 1–144, Box 2, Folder 3.

38. Melvin Gingerich, *The Mennonites in Iowa, Marking the One Hundredth Anniversary of the Coming of the Mennonites to Iowa* (Iowa City: State Historical Society of Iowa, 1939), 123.

39. Daniel P. Guengerich, *An Account of the Voyage from Germany to America* (Kalona, Iowa: Jacob F. Swartzendruber, n.d.). Original in AMC, Daniel Bender Swartzendruber Collection, Hist. Mss. 1–144, Box 2, Folder 15.

40. In several chapters of this book, I use dreams as an indicator of social consciousness or shared memory. Recording a dream to preserve it is a social act, revealing a sense of significance and common recollection. No mystic group mind need be invoked to view dreams as valuable in the discovery of a communal repertoire. For recent research on collective memory, see Iwona Irwin-Zarecka, *Frames of Re-*

membrance: The Dynamics of Collective Memory (New Brunswick, N.J.: Transaction Publishers, 1994); James Fentress and Chris Wickham, *Social Memory* (Cambridge, Mass.: Blackwell, 1992); and David J. Middleton and Derek Edwards, eds., *Collective Remembering* (Newbury Park, Calif.: Sage, 1990).

41. Hostetler, *Amish Society,* 56–57.

42. Ibid., 65.

43. Amish and Mennonite settlement and early migrations within North America are described in Richard K. MacMaster, *Land, Piety, Peoplehood: The Establishment of Mennonite Communities in America, 1683–1790* (Scottdale, Pa.: Herald Press, 1985). For a sense of the amazing variety of locations, see David Luthy, *The Amish in America: Settlements That Failed, 1840–1960* (Aylmer, Ontario: Pathway Publishers, 1986). For an overview of Amish and Mennonite history in nineteenth-century North America, see Theron F. Schlabach, *Peace, Faith, Nation: Mennonites and Amish in Nineteenth-Century America* (Scottdale, Pa.: Herald Press, 1988).

44. Hostetler, *Amish Society,* 65.

45. J. F. Swartzendruber, "Mother's Story," *Christian Monitor* 14 (August 1922): 624–626; reprinted as "An Amish Migration," *Palimpsest* 17 (October 1936): 324–357. Pages cited from *Palimpsest* version.

46. Gingerich, *The Mennonites in Iowa, Marking the One Hundredth Anniversary,* 67–69; Melvin Gingerich, "John Carl Krehbiel (1811–1886): A Mennonite Pioneer in Iowa," *Mennonite Life* 15 (April 1960): 57–59.

47. Melvin Gingerich, *Mennonites in Iowa* (Kalona, Iowa: Mennonite Historical Society of Iowa, 1974) 20–21. This booklet is a revision and reprint of an entire issue of *Palimpsest* 40 (May 1959).

48. For extensive family information and local history on the Amish settlement centered in Johnson County, Iowa, see Katie Yoder Lind, *From Hazelbrush to Cornfields: The First One Hundred Years of the Amish-Mennonites in Johnson, Washington and Iowa Counties* (Kalona, Iowa: Mennonite Historical Society of Iowa, 1994).

49. For overviews of Iowa history, see Dorothy Schwieder, *Iowa: The Middle Land* (Ames: Iowa State University Press, 1996); and Leland L. Sage, *A History of Iowa* (Ames: Iowa State University Press, 1974).

50. Hansi Bontrager, *Eine Geschichte der ersten Ansiedlung der Amischen Mennoniten und die Gründung ihrer ersten Gemeinde im Staate Indiana, nebst einer kurzen Erklärung über die Spaltung die in dieser Gemeinde geschehen ist* ([Elkhart, Ind.: Mennonite Publishing Company], 1907); summarized in *Amish and Mennonites in Eastern Elkhart and Lagrange Counties, Indiana, 1841–1991* (Goshen, Ind.: Amish Heritage Committee, 1992).

51. Sage, *A History of Iowa,* 62–64; Gingerich, *The Mennonites in Iowa, Marking the One Hundredth Anniversary,* 114.

52. J. F. Swartzendruber, "An Amish Migration," 343–344.

53. J. D. Guengerich, "Early Frontier Life in Iowa," *Christian Monitor* 14 (June 1922), 561.

54. Ibid., 526.

55. Ibid., 562.

56. Samuel D. Guengerich, "A Brief History of the Amish Settlement in Johnson County, Iowa," *MQR* 3 (October 1929): 246.

57. J. F. Swartzendruber, "An Amish Migration," 345.

58. Ibid., 346.

59. Ibid., 353.

60. For a more complete description of these four ministerial offices, see Paton Yoder, "The Structure of the Amish Ministry in the Nineteenth Century," *MQR* 61 (July 1987): 280–297; and Paton Yoder, *Tradition and Transition: Amish Mennonites and Old Order Amish, 1800–1900* (Scottdale, Pa.: Herald Press, 1991), chap. 3.

61. Paton Yoder, "The Preaching Deacon Controversy Among Nineteenth-Century American Amish," *Pennsylvania Mennonite Heritage* 8 (January 1985): 2–9.

62. On ministerial duties and "keeping house," see Paton Yoder, *Tradition and Transition,* chap. 5; and J[oseph] F. B[eiler], "Ordnung," *MQR* 56 (October 1982): 382–384. Compare the specification of duties for all four ministerial offices in John S. Umble, "Amish Ordination Charges," *MQR* 13 (October 1939): 233–250.

63. Paton Yoder, *Tradition and Transition,* chaps. 7–10; Lorraine Roth, "The Amish Mennonite Division in Ontario, 1886–1891," *Ontario Mennonite History* 11 (March 1993): 1–7.

64. The term *sorting out* comes from Schlabach, *Peace, Faith, Nation,* 214.

Chapter 2. The Amish Agricultural System

Werner Weidmann, *Die Pfälzischer Landwirtschaft zu Beginn des Neunzehnten Jahrhunderts: Von der Französischen Revolution bis zum Deutschen Zollverein* (Saarbrücken: Institut für Landeskunde des Saarlandes, 1968), 281.

Wilhelm Heinrich Riehl, *Die Pfälzer* (Stuttgart and Augsburg, 1857), 288 (cited in Weidmann).

1. AMC, Daniel Bender Swartzendruber Collection, Hist. Mss. 1–144, Box 2, Folder 1. Swartzendruber recorded several of his dreams in tiny handwriting on scraps of paper. The dreams have been transcribed by Elizabeth Horsch Bender.

2. Jean Séguy, "The French Mennonites: Tradition and Change," *International Journal of Sociology and Social Policy* 2 (1982): 25.

3. Ibid., 26; Jean Séguy, "The Bernese Anabaptists in Sainte-Marie-aux-Mines," *Pennsylvania Mennonite Heritage* 3 (July 1980): 2–9.

4. Georg C. L. Schmidt, *Der Schweitzer Bauer im Zeitalter des Frühkapitalismus* (Bern: Paul Haupt, 1932), 91.

5. Séguy, "The French Mennonites," 26.

6. Alexandre Frédéric Jacques de Masson, marquis de Pezay, *Les soirées helvétiennes, alsaciennes, et franc-comtoises* (Amsterdam: Chez Delalain, Libraire, 1771), 41–42; cited by Jean Séguy, "Religion and Agricultural Success: The Vocational Life of the French Anabaptists from the Seventeenth to Nineteenth Centuries," *MQR* 47 (July 1973): 183.

7. Ibid., 45–47, 52–56.

8. Angelus, *Wanderungen eines Protestanten in Lothringen* (Strasbourg: C. F. Schmidt's Universitäts Buchhandlung, Friedrich Bull, 1880), 107.

9. Jean Vogt, *Recherches agraires rhenanes* (Strasbourg: Bibliothèque National Universitaire, 1963), 144–145.

10. B. H. Slicher van Bath, *The Agrarian History of Western Europe, A.D. 500–1850,* trans. Olive Ordish (1959; London: Edward Arnold, 1963), 254–299.

11. Summary taken from Jean Séguy, "Religion and Agricultural Success," 179–224, unless otherwise referenced. This article is chapter 7 of Séguy's dissertation at the University of Paris, 1970, later published as *Les assemblées anabaptistes-mennonites de France* (Paris: Moulton, 1977); the present article was published in French in *Archives de Sociologie des Religions* 28 (1969): 93–130, and translated by Michael Shank.

12. In addition to Séguy's discussion, see Dominique Varry, "Jacques Klopfenstein and the Almanacs of Belfort and Montbéliard in the Nineteenth Century," *MQR* 58 (July 1984): 241–257.

13. Pierre Marthelot, "Les Mennonites dans l'est de la France," *Revue de Géographie Alpine* 38 (1950): 484.

14. See, for example, Gabriel Richard, "Les anabaptistes ou mennonites en Lorraine," *Annales de l'Est,* 5th Series, 19 (1967): 131–177.

15. Jean Séguy, in collaboration with Robert Baecher, *Les Mennonites dans la révolution française* (Montbéliard: Éditions Mennonites, 1989).

16. Jean Vogt, "Anabaptistes et communautés rurales en Outre-Forêt," *Saisons D'Alsace,* 21 no. 59 (1976): 58–66.

17. Séguy, "The French Mennonites," 27.

18. Richard K. MacMaster, "Mennonites in the American Revolution," in *L'Amérique et la France: Deux Révolutions,* ed. Elise Marienstras (Paris: Sorbonne, 1990), 193–203; Richard K. MacMaster, with Samuel L. Horst and Robert F. Ulle, *Conscience in Crisis: Mennonites and Other Peace Churches in America, 1739–1789; Interpretation and Documents* (Scottdale, Pa.: Herald Press, 1979).

19. Séguy, "The French Mennonites," 29.

20. Horst Gerlach, trans. Noah G. Good, "Mennonites in Rheinhesse and Migrations to America and Galicia," *Pennsylvania Mennonite Heritage* 9 (October 1986): 4.

21. This sequence is discussed by Gerhard Hard, "Die Mennoniten und die

Agrarrevolution: Die Rolle der Wiedertäufer in der Agrargeschichte des Westrichs," *Saarbrücker Hefte* 18 (1963): 30–32; quotes on p. 30.

22. Ibid., 32.

23. Deborah H. Stinner, Ivan Glick, and Benjamin R. Stinner, "Forage Legumes and Cultural Sustainability: Lessons from History," *Agriculture, Ecosystems and Environment* 40 (1992): 233–248.

24. The observation on estates with separate *Knöpfler* and *Häftler* residents comes from Hard, "Die Mennoniten und Die Agrarrevolution," 36, who adds that intermarriage between the two groups was taboo (*verpönt*) and hardly ever occurred.

25. Among other places, Möllinger is named "Father of Palatinate Agriculture" in Wermer Weidmann, *Die Pfälzischer Landwirtschaft zu Beginn des Neunzehnten Jahrhunderts: Von der Französischen Revolution bis zum Deutschen Zollverein* (Saarbrücken: Institut für Landeskunde des Saarlandes, 1968), 281. For an extended discussion of Palatinate agriculture and Mennonite contributions, including a section on the specific activities of Möllinger and the Mennonite origins of potato distilleries, see Ernst Correll, *Das schweizerische Täufermennonitentum: Ein soziologischer Bericht* (Tübingen: J. C. B. Mohr, 1925), chap. 6; pages 110–129 have been translated by Marion Lois Huffines as "The Mennonite Agricultural Model in the German Palatinate," *Pennsylvania Mennonite Heritage* 14 (October 1991): 2–13. For the assertion that Jacob Dettweiler built the first distillery, see Hard, "Die Mennoniten und Die Agrarrevolution," 33.

26. Correll, "Mennonite Agricultural Model," 12, 7.

27. Hard, "Die Mennoniten und die Agrarrevolution," 39.

28. "Wo der Pflug durch goldene Auen geht, da schlägt auch der Mennonit sein Bethaus auf." Cited by Weidmann, *Die Pfälzischer Landwirtschaft*, 283, from Wilhelm Heinrich Riehl, *Die Pfälzer* (Stuttgart and Augsburg, 1857), 288.

29. On the complexities of land holding in central Europe, see Thomas Fox, "Land Tenure, Feudalism, and the State in Eighteenth-Century Hesse," in *Themes in Rural History of the Western World*, ed. Richard Herr (Ames: Iowa State University Press, 1993), 99–139.

30. On Mennonite agriculture in Prussia, see Johann Driedger, "Farming Among the Mennonites in West and East Prussia," *MQR* 31 (January 1957): 16–21; and Arkadiusz Rybak, trans. Peter J. Klassen, "The Significance of the Agricultural Achievements of the Mennonites in the Vistula-Nogat Delta," *MQR* 66 (April 1992): 214–220, which emphasizes drainage of delta swamps. On Mennonites in Russia, see especially James Urry, *None But Saints: The Transformation of Mennonite Life in Russia, 1789–1889* (Winnipeg: Hyperion, 1989).

31. Horst Gerlach, "Amish Congregations in German and Adjacent Territories in the Eighteenth and Nineteenth Centuries," *Pennsylvania Mennonite Heritage* 13 (April 1990): 2.

32. David Luthy, "Amish Beginnings: Three Centuries of Migration," *Mennonite Family History* 7 (July 1988): 114.

33. Wilhelm Abel discussed the ties of agrarian reform and political power in *Agrarkrisen und Agrarkonjunktur: Eine Geschichte der Land- und Ernährungswirtschaft Mitteleuropas seit dem hohen Mittelalter,* 3d ed. (1935; Hamburg: Paul Parey, 1978), 204–205.

34. Christopher Schultz, quoted in Dietmar Rothermund, *The Layman's Progress: Religious and Political Experience in Colonial Pennsylvania, 1740–1770* (Philadelphia: University of Pennsylvania Press, 1961), 62. On the migration of Amish and Mennonites to North America and the founding of communities in the British colonies, see Richard K. MacMaster, *Land, Piety, Peoplehood: The Establishment of Mennonite Communities in America, 1683–1790* (Scottdale, Pa.: Herald Press, 1985).

35. Benjamin Rush, *An Account of the Manners of the German Inhabitants of Pennsylvania,* published 1789 (Lancaster, Pa.: Pennsylvania German Society, 1910), 59–60. A useful compendium of contemporary comments can be found in Ira D. Landis, "Mennonite Agriculture in Colonial Lancaster County, Pennsylvania: The First Intensive Agriculture in America," *MQR* 19 (October 1945): 254–272.

36. For a sampling, see James T. Lemon, *The Best Poor Man's Country: A Geographical Study of Early Southeastern Pennsylvania* (Baltimore: Johns Hopkins, 1972); Amos Long Jr., *The Pennsylvania German Family Farm: A Regional Architectural and Folk Cultural Study of an American Agricultural Community* (Breinigsville, Pa.: Pennsylvania German Society, 1972); and Stevenson Whitcomb Fletcher, *Pennsylvania Agriculture and Country Life, 1840–1940* (Harrisburg: Pennsylvania Historical and Museum Commission, 1955). For the drawing of global distinctions between German and English farmers, see Richard H. Shryock, "British versus German Traditions in Colonial Agriculture," *Mississippi Valley Historical Review* 26 (1939): 39–54.

37. A[rthur] D. G[raeff], "Pennsylvania-German Culture," *ME* IV, 142–144.

38. For a popular account of Pennsylvania Dutch history and their gradual assimilation, see William T. Parsons, *The Pennsylvania Dutch: A Persistent Minority* (Boston: Twayne, 1976). See also Don Yoder, "The Pennsylvania Germans: Three Centuries of Identity Crisis," in *America and the Germans: An Assessment of a Three-Hundred-Year History,* Vol. 1, *Immigration, Language, Ethnicity,* ed. Frank Trommler and Joseph McVeigh (Philadelphia: University of Pennsylvania Press, 1985), 41–65.

39. Walter M. Kollmorgen published three significant studies of Amish agriculture as a continuing representative of traditional Pennsylvania Dutch farming: *Culture of a Contemporary Rural Community: The Old Order Amish of Lancaster County,* in *Pennsylvania,* Vol. 4, Rural Life Studies (Washington, D.C.: Government Printing Office, 1942); "The Pennsylvania German Farmer," in *The Pennsylvania Germans,* ed. Ralph Wood (Princeton: Princeton University Press, 1942), 29–55; and "The Agricultural Stability of the Old Order Amish and Old Order Mennonites of Lancaster

County, Pennsylvania," *American Journal of Sociology* 49 (November 1943): 233–241. For an interesting contemporary Amish account, see Gideon L. Fisher, *Farm Life and Its Changes* (Gordonville, Pa.: Pequea Publishers, 1978).

40. John A. Hostetler, "The Old Order Amish on the Great Plains: A Study in Cultural Vulnerability," in *Ethnicity on the Great Plains,* ed. Frederick C. Luebke (Lincoln: University of Nebraska Press, 1980), 92–108; David Luthy, *The Amish in America: Settlements that Failed, 1840–1960* (Aylmer, Ontario: Pathway Publishers, 1986).

41. General histories of agriculture in the American North and Midwest can be found in R. Douglas Hurt, *American Agriculture: A Brief History* (Ames: Iowa State University Press, 1994); David B. Danbom, *Born in the Country: A History of Rural America* (Baltimore: Johns Hopkins University Press, 1995); Jeremy Atack and Fred Bateman, *To Their Own Soil: Agriculture in the Antebellum North* (Ames: Iowa State University Press, 1987); Percy Wells Bidwell and John I. Falconer, *History of Agriculture in the Northern United States, 1620–1860* (New York: Peter Smith, 1941); Clarence H. Danhof, *Change in Agriculture: The Northern United States, 1820–1870* (Cambridge: Harvard University Press, 1969); Paul W. Gates, *The Farmer's Age: Agriculture, 1815–1860* (New York: Holt, Rinehart & Winston, 1960); John T. Schlebecker, *Whereby We Thrive: A History of American Farming, 1607–1972* (Ames: Iowa State University Press, 1975); and Gilbert C. Fite, *The Farmers' Frontier, 1865–1900* (New York: Holt, Rinehart & Winston, 1966). On migration streams to the upper Midwest, see John C. Hudson, "Migration to an American Frontier," *Annals of the Association of American Geographers* 66 (June 1976): 242–265; and Hudson, "North American Origins of Middlewestern Frontier Populations," *Annals of the Association of American Geographers* 78 (1988): 395–413.

On the making of rural and small-town frontier communities in the Midwest, see John Mack Faragher, *Sugar Creek: Life on the Illinois Prairie* (New Haven: Yale University Press, 1986); and Don Harrison Doyle, *The Social Order of a Frontier Community: Jacksonville, Illinois, 1825–1870* (Urbana: University of Illinois Press, 1978).

42. On the incorporation of farming regions into a national capitalist economy, see William Cronon, *Nature's Metropolis: Chicago and the Great West* (New York: W. W. Norton, 1991); James C. Malin, *History and Ecology: Studies of the Grassland,* ed. Robert P. Swierenga (Lincoln: University of Nebraska Press, 1984); Sue Headlee, *The Political Economy of the Family Farm: The Agrarian Roots of American Capitalism* (New York: Praeger, 1991); and Allan Kulikoff, *The Agrarian Origins of American Capitalism* (Charlottesville: University Press of Virginia, 1992).

43. On the emergence of the Midwestern corn belt, see Allan G. Bogue, *From Prairie to Cornbelt: Farming on the Illinois and Iowa Prairies in the Nineteenth Century* (Chicago: University of Chicago Press, 1963); and John C. Hudson, *Making the*

Corn Belt: A Geographical History of Middle-Western Agriculture (Bloomington: Indiana University Press, 1994).

For recent research on crop specialization in the Midwest, see several articles by Mary Eschelbach Gregson: "Specialization in Late-Nineteenth-Century Midwestern Agriculture: Missouri as a Test Case," *Agricultural History* 67 (Winter 1993): 16–35; "Rural Response to Increased Demand: Crop Choice in the Midwest, 1860–1880," *Journal of Economic History* 53 (June 1993): 332–345; and "Long-Term Trends in Agricultural Specialization in the United States: Some Preliminary Results," *Agricultural History* 70 (Winter 1996): 90–101.

On the persistence of yeoman farming in a capitalist economic framework, see James A. Henretta, "Families and Farms: Mentalité in Pre-Industrial America," *William and Mary Quarterly* 35 (January 1978): 3–32; Sonya Salamon, *Prairie Patrimony: Family, Farming, and Community in the Midwest* (Chapel Hill: University of North Carolina Press, 1992); and Terry K. Marsden, "Theoretical Issues in the Continuity of Petty Commodity Production," in *Rural Enterprise: Shifting Perspectives on Small-Scale Production,* ed. Sarah Whatmore, Philip Lowe, and Terry Marsden (London: David Fulton Publishers, 1991), 12–33. Henretta has been roundly criticized by partisans of rural capitalist transformation, but an element of economic "irrationality" seems to persist in farming when farmers perceive themselves following a way of life instead of pursuing a business. Consult the debate between Patrick H. Mooney and Susan Archer Mann, in Mooney, *My Own Boss? Class, Rationality, and the Family Farm* (Boulder, Colo.: Westview Press, 1988); and Mann, *Agrarian Capitalism in Theory and Practice* (Chapel Hill: University of North Carolina Press, 1990). For a recent summary of the issues, see Christopher Clark, "Rural America and the Transition to Capitalism," *Journal of the Early Republic* 16 (Summer 1996): 223–236.

44. Sharon Township was created in 1858; in 1850, the area was part of Liberty Township. I took the 1850 census listing and compared the names with land records and the 1860 census. Two clusters of names appeared in neither place, and I assume these thirty-seven households were outside the area that became Sharon Township. In all statistical operations with the 1850 census, I have excluded these households from the computer files. More information regarding the statistics on which this book is based can be found in my dissertation, "Alternate Dreams and Visions: The Amish Repertoire of Community on the Iowa Prairie, 1840–1910" (Ph.D. diss., University of Iowa, 1994).

45. This book often uses the household as a unit of analysis. On the opportunities and dangers of such an approach, see Robert M. Netting, Richard R. Wilk, and Eric J. Arnould, eds., *Households: Comparative and Historical Studies of the Domestic Group* (Berkeley: University of California Press, 1984); and Diana Wong, "The Limits of Using the Household as a Unit of Analysis," in *Households and the World-Economy,*

ed. Joan Smith, Immanuel Wallerstein, and Hans-Dieter Evers (Beverly Hills, Calif.: Sage, 1984), 56–63. On the relationship of household and agriculture, see Robert M. Netting, *Smallholders, Householders: Farm Families and the Ecology of Intensive Sustainable Agriculture* (Stanford: Stanford University Press, 1993).

One issue in household-level study is the obscuring of gender relations in household formation and maintenance. Because of the cultural practice of changing the female's family name upon marriage, it is more difficult to trace daughters than sons. A flurry of feminist critiques of the concept of the family in the social sciences appeared in the late 1970s and early 1980s, summarized in Barrie Thorne, ed., with Marilyn Yalom, *Rethinking the Family: Some Feminist Questions* (New York: Longman, 1982) and Diana Wong, "The Limits of Using the Household as a Unit of Analysis," 56–63. Given the structure of the census, it is difficult to escape the household as an analytical framework.

46. For the distinction, see Paton Yoder, "The Structure of the Amish Ministry in the Nineteenth Century," *MQR* 61 (July 1987): 280–297; and Paton Yoder, "The Preaching Deacon Controversy Among Nineteenth-Century American Amish," *Pennsylvania Mennonite Heritage* 8 (January 1985): 2–9.

47. Sanford C. Yoder, *The Days of My Years* (Scottdale, Pa.: Herald Press, 1959), 9.

48. Melvin Gingerich, *The Mennonites in Iowa, Marking the One Hundredth Anniversary of the Coming of the Mennonites to Iowa* (Iowa City: State Historical Society of Iowa, 1939), 310.

49. See Joan M. Jensen, *Loosening the Bonds: Mid-Atlantic Farm Women, 1750–1850* (New Haven: Yale University Press, 1986) for the virtual equation of butter production and women's labor in nineteenth-century American agriculture; and the even stronger claims by Virginia E. McCormick, "Butter and Egg Business: Implications From the Records of a Nineteenth-Century Ohio Farm Wife," *Ohio History* 100 (Winter/Spring 1991): 57–67.

50. The commodity and livestock prices used in comparisons come from one of three sources. I gave preference to prices printed in local newspapers, when available, because they reflect most directly the market in which local farmers participated. For 1859 (the 1860 census year), I consulted Atack and Bateman, *To Their Own Soil,* 233. For 1869 and 1879, I consulted U.S. Department of Agriculture Statistical Bulletin 15, "Prices of Farm Products Received by Producers: The North Central States" (Washington, D.C.: GPO, 1927), 120–121; and Norman V. Strand, *Prices of Farm Products in Iowa,* Iowa State College of Agriculture and Mechanic Arts, Research Bulletin no. 303 (Ames, Iowa: 1942).

51. *ME* II, 608.

52. Johnson County Land Records, Book 9, 583.

53. Johnson County Land Records, Book 30, 703.

Chapter 3. Preservationist Patriarchy

Harold S. Bender, trans. and ed., "Some Early American Amish Mennonite Disciplines," *MQR* 8 (April 1934): 95.

1. On the idea of the family as a microcosm of society, see John Demos, *The Little Commonwealth: Family Life in Plymouth Colony* (New York: Oxford University Press, 1970). On the family-state compact, see Sarah Hanley, "Engendering the State: Family Formation and State Building in Early Modern France," *French Historical Studies* 16 (1989): 4–27; and Hanley, "Social Sites of Political Practice in France: Lawsuits, Civil Rights, and the Separation of Powers in Domestic and State government, 1500–1800," *American Historical Review* 102 (February 1997): 27–52. On Republican Motherhood, see Linda K. Kerber, *Women of the Republic: Intellect and Ideology in Revolutionary America* (Chapel Hill: University of North Carolina Press, 1980); and Mary Beth Norton, *Liberty's Daughters: The Revolutionary Experience of American Women, 1750–1800* (Boston: Little, Brown, 1980).

2. The literature on gender and reform in the early American republic is voluminous. A few selections: Paul E. Johnson and Sean Wilentz, *The Kingdom of Matthias: A Story of Sex and Salvation in 19th-Century America* (New York: Oxford University Press, 1994); Mary P. Ryan, *Cradle of the Middle Class: The Family in Oneida County, New York, 1790–1865* (New York: Cambridge University Press, 1981); Mary P. Ryan, *Women in Public: Between Banners and Ballots, 1825–1880* (Baltimore: Johns Hopkins University Press, 1990); Paul E. Johnson, *A Shopkeeper's Millennium: Society and Revivals in Rochester, New York, 1815–1837* (New York: Hill & Wang, 1978); and Nancy A. Hewitt, *Women's Activism and Social Change: Rochester, New York, 1822–1872* (Ithaca, N.Y.: Cornell University Press, 1984). A useful summary can be found in Sean Wilentz, "Society, Politics, and the Market Revolution, 1815–1848," in *The New American History*, ed. Eric Foner (Philadelphia: Temple University Press, 1990), 51–71.

The Amish were hardly the only ones with religious doubts about early industrialism in the new American republic. See, for example, Jama Lazerow, *Religion and the Working Class in Antebellum America* (Washington, D.C.: Smithsonian Institution Press, 1995); Mark Y. Hanley, *Beyond a Christian Commonwealth: The Protestant Quarrel with the American Republic, 1830–1860* (Chapel Hill: University of North Carolina Press, 1994).

3. John A. Hostetler, *Amish Society*, 4th ed. (Baltimore: Johns Hopkins University Press, 1993), 59–65. Amish congregations traditionally meet in homes.

4. Richard K. MacMaster, with Samuel L. Horst and Robert F. Ulle, *Conscience in Crisis: Mennonites and Other Peace Churches in America, 1739–1789; Interpretation and Documents* (Scottdale, Pa.: Herald Press, 1979).

5. Jacksonian America has long been portrayed as a period of rapid social and eco-

nomic change. The Amish, despite their sense of isolation, were not immune from the atmosphere of upheaval. See Charles Grier Sellers, *The Market Revolution: Jacksonian America, 1815–1846* (New York: Oxford University Press, 1991).

6. Keith Sprunger, "God's Powerful Army of the Weak: Anabaptist Women of the Radical Reformation," in *Triumph Over Silence: Women in Protestant History,* ed. Richard L. Greaves (Westport, Conn.: Greenwood Press, 1985), 45–74. Phyllis Mack makes a similar observation about Quaker women in *Visionary Women: Ecstatic Prophecy in Seventeenth-Century England* (Berkeley: University of California Press, 1992), 4.

7. Joyce L. Irwin, *Womanhood in Radical Protestantism, 1525–1675* (New York: Edwin Mellen, 1979). On Quaker women, see especially Phyllis Mack, *Visionary Women.*

8. Wes Harrison, "The Role of Women in Anabaptist Thought and Practice: The Hutterite Experience of the Sixteenth and Seventeenth Centuries," *Sixteenth Century Journal* 23 (Spring 1992): 49–71, quote p. 50. See also John Klassen, "Women and the Family Among Dutch Anabaptist Martyrs," *MQR* 60 (October 1986): 548–571; M. Lucille Marr, "Anabaptist Women of the North: Peers in the Faith, Subordinates in Marriage," *MQR* 61 (October 1987): 347–362; Wayne Plenert, "The *Martyr's Mirror* and Anabaptist Women," *Mennonite Life* 30 (June 1975): 13–18; and Frieda Shoenberg Rozen, "The Permanent First Floor Tenant: Women and Gemeinschaft," *MQR* 51 (October 1977): 319–328. For a biographical collection of Anabaptist women, see C. Arnold Snyder and Linda A. Huebert Hecht, eds., *Profiles of Anabaptist Women: Sixteenth-Century Reforming Pioneers* (Waterloo, Ontario: Wilfred Laurier University Press, 1996).

9. Sprunger, "God's Powerful Army of the Weak," 46.

10. On the term *Hausvater* and the dominance of patriarchal social and economic structures in European history, see Otto Brunner, "Das 'Ganze Haus' und die alteuropäische 'Ökonomik,' " in *Neue Wege der Verfassungs- und Sozialgeschichte,* 2d ed. (1956; Göttingen: Vandenhoeck and Ruprecht, 1968), 103–127.

11. Gotthardt Frühsorge, "Die Begründung der 'väterlichen Gesellschaft' in der europäischen *oeconomia christiana.* Zur Rolle des Vaters in der 'Hausväterliterature' des 16. bis 18. Jahrhunderts in Deutschland," in *Das Vaterbild im Abendland I: Rom, Frühes Christentum, Mittelalter, Neuzeit, Gegenwart,* ed. Hubertus Tellenbach (Stuttgart: Verlag W. Kohlhammer, 1978), 10–123.

12. See Hans Medick, "Village Spinning Bees: Sexual Culture and Free Time among Rural Youth in Early Modern Germany," in *Interest and Emotion: Essays on the Study of Family and Kinship,* ed. Hans Medick and David Warren Sabean (New York: Cambridge University Press, 1984), 317–339, for an example of political and religious authorities working through *Hausvater* leadership to monitor and regulate youthful behavior.

13. Harold S. Bender, "The Discipline Adopted by the Strasbourg Conference of 1568," *MQR* 1 (January 1927): 57–66; Harold S. Bender, "An Amish Church Discipline of 1779," *MQR* 11 (April 1937): 163–168. A useful compendium of known Amish disciplines from Europe and North America is William R. McGrath, *Christian Discipline: How and Why the Anabaptists Made Church Standards* (Carrollton, Ohio: Amish Mennonite Publications, 1989).

14. Joseph F. Beiler, "Revolutionary War Records," *The Diary* 7 (March 1975): 71.

15. Hostetler, *Amish Society,* 68–70.

16. Ibid., 64.

17. Paton Yoder, *Tradition and Transition: Amish Mennonites and Old Order Amish, 1800–1900* (Scottdale, Pa.: Herald Press, 1991), 29–34; quote p. 29.

18. Helena M. Wall, *Fierce Communion: Family and Community in Early America* (Cambridge: Harvard University Press, 1990), ix, 8, 148.

19. For example, Robert N. Bellah et al., *Habits of the Heart: Individualism and Commitment in American Life* (Berkeley: University of California Press, 1985); and the essays in Richard O. Curry and Lawrence B. Goodheart, eds., *American Chameleon: Individualism in Trans-National Context* (Kent, Ohio: Kent State University Press, 1991).

20. John S. Umble, "Catalog of an Amish Bishop's Library," *MQR* 20 (July 1946): 230–241.

21. Harold S. Bender, "Some Early American Amish Mennonite Disciplines," *MQR* 8 (April 1934): 90–98. This article includes the disciplines of 1809, 1837, and 1865. A facsimile of Jacob Swartzendruber's copy, with J. F. Swartzendruber's note, may be found in *MQR* 20 (July 1946), following p. 239.

22. Melvin Gingerich, *The Mennonites in Iowa: Marking the One Hundredth Anniversary of the Coming of the Mennonites to Iowa* (Iowa City: the State Historical Society of Iowa, 1939), 244; from a notation in a notebook kept by Jacob Swartzendruber's grandson, Jacob Frederick Swartzendruber, in AMC, Daniel Bender Swartzendruber Collection, Hist. Mss. 1–144, Box 1, Folder 3. The grandson states explicitly that bundling was the reason Jacob Swartzendruber left Maryland and makes the claim for Iowa being one of the first Amish communities in America where bundling was not allowed.

23. Jacob Swartzendruber to Daniel P. Guengerich, after April 1858, AMC, Daniel Bender Swartzendruber Collection, Hist. Mss. 1–144, Box 1, Folder 23.

24. Miller evidently accused Swartzendruber of unspecified mistakes, and eventually Swartzendruber was obliged to make a confession before his congregation. Jacob Swartzendruber to Jonathan Yoder, Andrew Ropp, and Christian Ropp, 18 October 1866, AMC, Daniel Bender Swartzendruber Collection, Hist. Mss. 1–144, Box 2/5.

25. Swartzendruber's tribute to his deceased wife and notes on his remarriage

can be found in AMC, Daniel Bender Swartzendruber Collection, Hist. Mss. 1–144, Box 2, Folder 20.

26. Melvin Gingerich, "Two Old Letters from Iowa," *MHB* 31 (October 1970): 1–2. The letters are from C. B. Swartzendruver to S. D. Guengerich, dated 4 and 25 April 1892.

27. Harold S. Bender, trans. and ed., "An Amish Bishop's Conference Epistle of 1865," *MQR* 20 (July 1946): 222–229; original letters in AMC, Daniel Bender Swartzendruber Collection, Box 1, Folder 16.

28. The concern about public opinion seems somewhat ironic, given the Amish rhetoric of separation from the world. The language of boundaries was flexible, depending on whether the need was for economic well-being or internal policing.

29. Yoder, *Tradition and Transition,* 137–203; James Nelson Gingerich, "Ordinance or Ordering: *Ordnung* and the Amish Ministers' Meeting, 1862–1878," *MQR* 60 (April 1986): 180–199. Historians have come to see the Civil War era as crucial to the study of gender. See, among many examples, Elizabeth D. Leonard, *Yankee Women: Gender Battles in the Civil War* (New York: Norton, 1994); and Catherine Clinton and Nina Silber, eds., *Divided Houses: Gender and the Civil War* (New York: Oxford University Press, 1992).

30. *Verhandlungen der Diener-Versammlungen der Deutschen Täufer oder Amischen Mennoniten. . .* 1862–1876, 1878; translations and pagination from Paton Yoder and Steven R. Estes, *Proceedings of the Amish Ministers' Meetings, 1862–1878* (Goshen, Ind.: Mennonite Historical Society, 1999), 8; hereafter cited as *Proceedings.* The "articles of faith" phrase probably refers to the 1632 Dordrecht Confession of Faith.

31. *Proceedings,* 1862, 13.

32. *Proceedings,* 1863, 30, 32.

33. *Proceedings,* 1864, 47, 49.

34. *Proceedings,* 1864, 51–53.

35. *Proceedings,* 1864, 54–56.

36. Yoder, *Tradition and Transition,* 153–170.

37. Bender, "An Amish Bishop's Conference Epistle of 1865."

38. Ibid.

39. *Proceedings,* 1865, 63–64.

40. A term used by Jacob Swartzendruber in his letter to Jonathan Yoder, Andrew Ropp, and Christian Ropp; see note 24 above. *Proceedings,* 1865, 62.

41. An oral tradition reported by Melvin Gingerich, in *The Mennonites in Iowa,* 124. In the 1890s, Jacob Frederick Swartzendruber noted with disapproval the presence of porcelain dishes. See his copy book, AMC, Daniel Bender Swartzendruber Collection, Hist. Mss. 1–144, Box 1, Folder 3.

42. The original list may be found in AMC, Daniel Bender Swartzendruber Col-

lection, Hist. Mss. 1–144; work by Elmer G. Swartzendruber and Mary Gingerich on the identity of persons listed may be found in IMHSA.

43. Despite extensive research on the Amish family, little work has appeared on Amish women or gender relations. The only publications familiar to the author are Richard A. Wright, "A Comparative Analysis of Economic Roles within the Family: Amish and Contemporary American Women," *International Journal of Sociology of the Family* 7 (January–June 1977): 55–60; Julia Ericksen and Gary Klein, "Women's Roles and Family Production among the Old Order Amish," *Rural Sociology* 46 (Summer 1981): 282–296; Marc A. Olshan and Kimberly D. Schmidt, "Amish Women and the Feminist Conundrum," in *The Amish Struggle with Modernity* ed. Donald B. Kraybill and Marc A. Olshan (Hanover, N.H.: University Press of New England, 1994), 215–229; and, from an insider perspective, Alma Hershberger, *Amish Women* (Danville, Ohio: Art of Amish Taste, 1992).

A recent book by Sue Bender, despite its idiosyncrasies, often provides interesting insights into the world of Amish women: *Plain and Simple: A Woman's Journey to the Amish* (San Francisco: Harper & Row, 1989).

44. Emmanuel Hochstetler to Peter Swartzendruber, 29 November 1862, IMHSA; letter published in *Iowa Mennonite Historical Society Reflections* 5 (Summer 1991): 3–4.

45. Hostetler, *Amish Society,* 387–390.

46. Mahala Yoder Diary, typescript in AMC, Hist. Mss. 1–12 SC Long; the original diary is in private hands.

47. See Joan M. Jensen, *Loosening the Bonds: Mid-Atlantic Farm Women, 1750–1850* (New Haven: Yale University Press, 1986), and Virginia E. McCormick, "Butter and Egg Business: Implications From the Records of a Nineteenth-Century Ohio Farm Wife," *Ohio History* 100 (Winter/Spring 1991): 57–67, for the association of butter production and women's labor in nineteenth-century American agriculture.

48. Willard H. Smith, *Mennonites in Illinois* (Scottdale, Pa.: Herald Press, 1983), 132–133.

49. Gingerich, *Mennonites in Iowa,* 125–126, 129. The issue in 1868 in the Sharon Township congregation was communal responsibility in the disposition of private property; see Chapter 5.

50. David Beiler to Jacob Swartzendruber, AMC, Daniel Bender Swartzendruber Collection, Hist Mss 1–144, Box 1, Folder 12; Paton Yoder, *Tradition and Transition,* 99–112.

51. Sarah Whatmore has argued that patriarchal social relations stand at the core of the agricultural household. The Amish combination of paternal household leadership with religious values of separation and nonconformity would tend to support her thesis, although her work is more focused on the economic processes of consumption

and livelihood. See *Farming Women: Gender, Work and Family Enterprise* (London: Macmillan, 1991). Even more explicit about rural patriarchy, and more pessimistic, is Deborah Fink, *Open Country Iowa: Rural Women, Tradition and Change* (Albany: State University of New York Press, 1986); and *Agrarian Women: Wives and Mothers in Rural Nebraska, 1880–1940* (Chapel Hill: University of North Carolina Press, 1992). Nancy Grey Osterud, Mary Neth, and Joan Jensen represent an alternative view, emphasizing egalitarian social relations rather than economic or power inequalities in rural society, and the status granted to farm women because of their productive activities. See Osterud's *Bonds of Community: The Lives of Farm Women in Nineteenth-Century New York* (Ithaca, N.Y.: Cornell University Press, 1991); Neth's *Preserving the Family Farm: Farm Families and Communities in the Midwest, 1900–1940* (Baltimore: Johns Hopkins University Press, 1995); and Jensen's *Loosening the Bonds: Mid-Atlantic Farm Women, 1750–1850* (New Haven: Yale University Press, 1986). I do not dispute the high status of women in rural communities, and Amish women were no exception, but status does not equate to power. The power of farm wives to make decisions and control their own lives was seldom at the same level as that of their husbands.

52. Ellen K. Rothman, *Hands and Hearts: A History of Courtship in America* (New York: Basic Books), 44–49. On "night courting," or *nattefrieri,* among Norwegian immigrants in Wisconsin, see Jane Marie Pederson, *Between Memory and Reality: Family and Community in Rural Wisconsin, 1870–1970* (Madison: University of Wisconsin Press, 1992), 209–217.

Laurel Thatcher Ulrich has noted the possibility that bundling was "an attempt to preserve traditional parental *protection* of daughters in a marriage system which increasingly emphasized sexual attraction." *Good Wives: Image and Reality in the Lives of Women in Northern New England, 1650–1750* (New York: Oxford University Press, 1980), 122.

53. Henry Reed Stiles, *Bundling: Its Origin, Progress and Decline in America* (1871; New York: Book Collectors Association, 1934), 83–84. A more ribald flavor appears in Elmer Lewis Smith, *Bundling: A Curious Courtship Custom Among the Amish* (Akron, Pa.: Applied Arts Publishers, 1961).

Chapter 4. Struggles for Territory

In Harold S. Bender, trans. and ed., "An Amish Bishop's Conference Epistle of 1865," *MQR* 20 (July 1946): 229; original letter in AMC, Daniel Bender Swartzendruber Collection, Box 1, Folder 16.

1. Charles A. Beard and Mary R. Beard, *The Rise of American Civilization,* 2 vols. (New York: Macmillan, 1927), esp. vol. 2, chap. 18, "The Second American Revolution"; Louis M. Hacker, *The Triumph of American Capitalism: The Development of*

Forces in American History to the End of the Nineteenth Century (New York: Simon & Schuster, 1940), chaps. 24, 25, 26, and Appendix A; Patrick O'Brien, *The Economic Effects of the American Civil War* (Atlantic Highlands, N.J.: Humanities Press International, 1988). For a recent summary of the tangled debate over the economic impact of the Civil War, see Peter A. Coclanis, "The American Civil War in Economic Perspective: Basic Questions and Some Answers," *Southern Cultures* 2 (Winter 1996): 163–175. On rural and agricultural aspects, see Paul W. Gates, *Agriculture and the Civil War* (New York: Alfred A. Knopf, 1965), which essentially follows the Beard-Hacker interpretation.

2. See Richard F. Bensel, *Yankee Leviathan: The Origins of Central State Authority in America, 1859–1877* (New York: Cambridge University Press, 1990); Roger L. Ransom, *Conflict and Compromise: The Political Economy of Slavery, Emancipation, and the American Civil War* (New York: Cambridge University Press, 1989), 253–285; and Stuart Bruchey, *Enterprise: The Dynamic Economy of a Free People* (Cambridge: Harvard University Press, 1990), 254–260.

3. Maris A. Vinovskis, ed., *Toward a Social History of the American Civil War: Exploratory Essays* (New York: Cambridge University Press, 1990); Vinovskis, "Have Social Historians Lost the Civil War? Some Preliminary Demographic Speculations," *Journal of American History* 76 (June 1989): 34–58; Catherine Clinton and Nina Silber, eds., *Divided Houses: Gender and the Civil War* (New York: Oxford University Press, 1992); J. Matthew Gallman, *The North Fights the Civil War: The Home Front* (Chicago: I. R. Dee, 1994); Thomas P. Lowry, *The Story the Soldiers Wouldn't Tell: Sex in the Civil War* (Mechanicsburg, Pa.: Stackpole Books, 1994).

4. R. Douglas Hurt, *American Agriculture: A Brief History* (Ames: Iowa State University Press, 1994), 164.

5. AMC, Daniel Bender Swartzendruber Collection, Hist. Mss. 1–144, Box 2, Folder 1.

6. For an overview, see Paton Yoder, "The Amish View of the State," in *The Amish and the State*, ed. Donald B. Kraybill (Baltimore: Johns Hopkins University Press, 1993): 23–40.

7. Peter James Klassen, *The Economics of Anabaptism, 1525–1560* (The Hague: Mouton, 1964); see also Claus-Peter Clasen, *Anabaptism: A Social History, 1525–1618; Switzerland, Austria, Moravia, South and Central Germany* (Ithaca, N.Y.: Cornell University Press, 1972).

8. Richard K. MacMaster, *Land, Piety, Peoplehood: The Establishment of Mennonite Communities in America, 1683–1790* (Scottdale, Pa.: Herald Press, 1985), chap. 9; Richard K. MacMaster, with Samuel L. Horst and Robert F. Ulle, *Conscience in Crisis: Mennonites and Other Peace Churches in America, 1739–1789, Interpretation and Documents* (Scottdale, Pa.: Herald Press, 1979), 25–31.

9. MacMaster gave the following estimates for Pennsylvania: Quakers, 12.5 per-

cent; Mennonites, 8 percent; Dunkers, 2.5 percent; Moravians, 1.5 percent; and a few Schwenkfelders. The Amish population is included in the Mennonite figure (MacMaster, *Conscience in Crisis,* 51–52).

10. MacMaster, *Land, Piety, Peoplehood,* 236.

11. MacMaster, *Conscience in Crisis,* 130–131; MacMaster, *Land, Piety, Peoplehood,* 239–242.

12. MacMaster, *Land, Piety, Peoplehood,* 143–144.

13. MacMaster, *Conscience in Crisis,* 221.

14. Ibid., 266–267.

15. Quoted in MacMaster, *Land, Piety, Peoplehood,* 262.

16. MacMaster, *Conscience in Crisis,* 396–404, quote p. 404. See also Wilbur J. Bender, "Pacifism among the Mennonites, Amish Mennonites, and Schwenkfelders of Pennsylvania to 1783," *MQR* 1 (July 1927): 23–40; 2 (October 1927): 21–47; and Wilbur J. Bender, *Nonresistance in Colonial Pennsylvania* (Scottdale, Pa.: Herald Press, 1934).

17. Christian Z. Mast, "Imprisonment of the Amish in the Revolutionary War," *MHB* 13 (January 1952): 6–7; Christian Z. Mast and Robert E. Simpson, *Annals of the Conestoga Valley in Lancaster, Berks, and Chester Counties, Pennsylvania* (Scottdale, Pa.: Mennonite Publishing House, 1942), 268.

18. James O. Lehman, "The Mennonites of Maryland during the Revolutionary War," *MQR* 50 (July 1976): 211, 225–228.

19. MacMaster, *Land, Piety, Peoplehood,* 278–279; L. J. Burkholder, *A Brief History of the Mennonites in Ontario* (Toronto: n.p., 1935); Frank H. Epp, *Mennonites in Canada, 1786–1920: The History of a Separate People* (Toronto: Macmillan, 1974). Epp asserted, "The first permanent Mennonite settlements in Canada were founded as a direct result of the American Revolution" (p. 50).

20. For an overview, see Theron F. Schlabach, *Peace, Faith, Nation: Mennonites and Amish in Nineteenth-Century America* (Scottdale, Pa.: Herald Press, 1988), chap. 7.

21. James O. Lehman, "Conflicting Loyalties of the Christian Citizen: Lancaster Mennonites and the Early Civil War Era," *Pennsylvania Mennonite Heritage* 7 (April 1984): 2–15; and James O. Lehman, "Duties of the Mennonite Citizen: Controversy in the Lancaster Press Late in the Civil War," *Pennsylvania Mennonite Heritage* 7 (July 1984): 5–21.

22. *Proceedings,* 1863.

23. Alvin J. Beachy, "The Amish Settlement in Somerset County, Pennsylvania," *MQR* 28 (October 1954): 272.

24. John S. Umble, "Why Congregations Die: A Summary of the Causes for the Decline of Certain Ohio Congregations," *MHB* 8 (October 1947): 2. Umble also blamed pietist religious groups competing for converts, cheaper land elsewhere, and reactionary leadership enslaved to tradition.

25. Peter S. Hartman, "Civil War Reminiscences," *MQR* 3 (July 1929): 203–219.

26. Samuel A. Rhodes, "The Rebellion, the Cause of My Traveling Adventures to the North," diary excerpts in *MHB* 33 (July 1972): 2–3; L. J. Heatwole to [J. S.] Hartzler, 11 December 1918, published as "Brother Christian Good, Whose Gun Was 'Out of Order,'" *MHB* 33 (July 1972): 3. These stories and others are summarized in Samuel Horst, *Mennonites in the Confederacy: A Study in Civil War Pacifism* (Scottdale, Pa.: Herald Press, 1967).

27. Dorcas Steffen, "The Civil War and the Wayne County Mennonites," *MHB* 26 (July 1965): 2.

28. Letter reprinted in the *Budget*, 29 August 1917; and in *MHB* 38 (April 1977): 8.

29. John M. Brenneman, *Christianity and War: A Sermon Setting Forth the Sufferings of Christians, . . . by a Minister of the Old Mennonite Church* (Chicago: printed by Chas. Hess, 1863; reprints, 1868, 1915. German: *Das Christenthum und der Krieg*, Lancaster, Pa.: printed by Johann Bär's Söhnen, 1864; reprints 1868, 1920), 47.

30. John M. Brenneman, "A Civil War Petition to President Lincoln," *MHB* 34 (October 1973): 2–3.

31. Daniel Musser, *Non-Resistance Asserted: or the Kingdom of Christ and the Kingdom of This World Separated, and No Concord between Christ and Belial* (Lancaster, Pa.: Elias Barr, 1864), 43.

32. Ibid., 45.

33. Ibid., 46.

34. Levi Miller, "Daniel Musser and Leo Tolstoy," *MHB* 54 (April 1993): 1–7.

35. *History of Johnson County, Iowa* (Iowa City, Iowa: n.p., 1883), 522–523.

36. Samuel D. Guengerich Collection, AMC, Hist. Mss. 1-2-6, Box 11, Folder 1; documents also published in *MHB* 34 (April 1973): 6.

37. Harold S. Bender, trans. and ed., "An Amish Bishop's Conference Epistle of 1865," *MQR* 20 (July 1946): 225; original letter in AMC, Daniel Bender Swartzendruber Collection, Box 1, Folder 16.

38. Lehman, "Conflicting Loyalties of the Christian Citizen," 4.

39. Bender, "An Amish Bishop's Conference Epistle of 1865," 225.

40. The soldiers from Johnson County are listed in *History of Johnson County* (1883), 477–517.

41. Simeon Barnett, *History of the Twenty-Second Regiment, Iowa Volunteer Infantry* (Iowa City: N. H. Brainerd, 1865).

42. Jacob D. Guengerich to Samuel D. Guengerich, 3 May 1863; Noah Yoder to Samuel D. Guengerich, 5 August 1863; letters in possession of L. Glen Guengerich, Kalona, Iowa.

43. Mildred Throne, ed., "Reminiscences of Jacob C. Switzer of the 22nd Iowa," *Iowa Journal of History and Politics* 55 (October 1957): 321.

44. Emmanuel Hochstetler to Peter Swartzendruber, 29 November 1862, IMHSA; published in Iowa Mennonite Historical Society *Reflections* 5 (Summer 1991): 3–4.

45. Throne, "Reminiscences of Jacob C. Switzer," 326.

46. Barnett, *History of the Twenty-Second Regiment, Iowa Volunteer Infantry,* 8.

47. National Archives, Record Group 94, *Regimental Letter Order and Guard Report Book of the 22nd Iowa Infantry,* report dated May 27 and submitted by Captain B. Wilson.

48. Lieutenant S. C. Jones, *Reminiscences of the Twenty-Second Iowa Volunteer Infantry* (Iowa City: S. C. Jones, 1907), 40.

49. Throne, "Reminiscences of Jacob C. Switzer," 335–336.

50. Civil War Service Records, Emmanuel Hochstetler and Christian Hochstetler, NA.

51. Edith Wasson McElroy, *The Undying Procession: Iowa's Civil War Regiments* (Des Moines: State Historical Society of Iowa, 1964), 51.

52. Robert R. Dykstra, "Iowa: Bright Radical Star," in James C. Mohr, ed., *Radical Republicans in the North: State Politics during Reconstruction* (Baltimore: Johns Hopkins University Press, 1976), 170.

53. Ibid., 172. Dykstra also cites these figures in *Bright Radical Star: Black Freedom and White Supremacy on the Hawkeye Frontier* (Cambridge: Harvard University Press, 1993), 196. See also William F. Fox, *Regimental Losses in the American Civil War, 1861–1865* (Albany, N.Y.: Albany Publishing Company, 1889), 532–533.

54. *Proceedings of the Twenty-Second Regiment Iowa Volunteers at its First Reunion held at Iowa City, Iowa* (Iowa City, Iowa: Republican Publishing Company, 1887).

55. W. J. Bowen, Secretary, *List of Names and Addresses of Surviving Members of the Twenty-Second Iowa Volunteer Infantry, to September 15, 1903* [n.p., n.d.]; S. C. Jones, Secretary, *List of Names and Addresses of Surviving Members of the Twenty-Second Iowa Volunteer Infantry, to December 1, 1914* [n.p., n.d.].

56. Johnson County Land Records, Book 84, 451, 452.

57. Civil War Service Record, Phillip E. Shaver, NA.

58. Eli L. Yoder, "Wayne Co., Ohio, in 1861." Letter written 15 August 1861. *MHB* 34 (April 1973): 5.

Chapter 5. The Limits of Common Property

J. O. Kimmel to Abner Yoder, 27 March 1876, Abner Yoder Collection, IMHSA.

1. Peter James Klassen, *The Economics of Anabaptism, 1525–1560* (The Hague: Mouton, 1964). On the range of communalism from no private ownership of property to moderate communal claims on private property, see Bonnie J. McCay and

James M. Acheson, eds., *The Question of the Commons: The Culture and Ecology of Communal Resources* (Tucson: University of Arizona Press, 1990); and Hans-Jürgen Goertz, ed., *Alles Gehört Allen: Das Experiment Gütergemeinschaft vom 16. Jahrhundert bis Heute* (Munich: C. H. Beck, 1984).

2. Derek L. Phillips, *Looking Backward: A Critical Appraisal of Communitarian Thought* (Princeton: Princeton University Press, 1993); Christopher Clark, *The Communitarian Moment: The Radical Challenge of the Northampton Association* (Ithaca, N.Y.: Cornell University Press, 1995); Eric Foner, *Free Soil, Free Labor, Free Men: The Ideology of the Republican Party before the Civil War* (New York: Oxford University Press, 1970); Carol Kolmerten, *Women in Utopia: The Ideology of Gender in the American Owenite Communities* (Bloomington: Indiana University Press, 1990).

3. H[arold] S. B[ender], "Waldeck," *ME* 4, 873–874; Hermann Guth, *The Amish-Mennonites of Waldeck and Wittgenstein* (Elverson, Pa.: Mennonite Family History, 1986).

4. AMC, Daniel Bender Swartzendruber Collection, Hist. Mss. 1–144, Box 2, Folder 1.

5. Melvin Gingerich, *The Mennonites in Iowa: Marking the One Hundredth Anniversary of the Coming of the Mennonites to Iowa* (Iowa City: State Historical Society of Iowa, 1939), 130.

6. Johnson County Land Records, Book 14, 10.

7. Hugh F. Gingerich and Rachel W. Kreider, *Amish and Amish Mennonite Genealogies* (Gordonville, Pa.: Pequea Publishers, 1986), 170, 177; Johnson County Land Records, Book 12, 381; Book 14, 632.

8. Johnson County Probate Records.

9. Johnson County Land Records, Book 24, 305; Book 25, 121; Book 17, 398.

10. Ibid., Book 18, 256, 257.

11. Ibid., Book 24, 543.

12. Ibid., Book 29, 155; Book 29, 619; Book 37, 309.

13. The original copy of Jacob Swartzendruber's notes of worship meetings are deposited in AMC, Daniel Bender Swartzendruber Collection. A transcription and translation may be found in IMHSA.

14. *HoT,* July 1866, 56–57.

15. Gingerich, *Mennonites in Iowa,* 131; Abner Yoder Notebook, Abner Yoder Collection, IMHSA.

16. Willard H. Smith, *Mennonites In Illinois* (Scottdale, Pa.: Herald Press, 1983), 132–133; Johnson County Land Records, Book 24, 305.

17. Gingerich, *Mennonites in Iowa,* 125–126.

18. Johnson County Land Records, Book 30, 294; Book 70, 55.

19. Statistical analysis of the 1868 communion list excludes divided households, since there are too few for statistical operations.

20. Johnson County Land Records, Book 92, 119; Book 18, 449; Book 21, 439; Book 20, 220.

21. Ibid., Book 52, 614; Book 58, 406.

22. J. O. Kimmel to Abner Yoder, 27 March 1876, Abner Yoder Collection, IMHSA.

23. Somerset County, Pennsylvania, Probate Records, Book 4, 498. For a description of Pennsylvania German inheritance practices, see Jeannette Lasansky, *A Good Start: The Austeier or Dowry* (Lewisburg, Pa.: Oral Traditions Project, 1990). For a study of inheritance in American history, see Carole Shammas, Marylynn Salmon, and Michel Dahlin, *Inheritance in America from Colonial Times to the Present* (New Brunswick, N.J.: Rutgers University Press, 1987).

24. Somerset County, Pennsylvania, Probate Records, Book 1, 128; Book 2, 564.

25. Ibid., Book 8, 562; Book 9, 103.

26. Women holding property has been a problem for some patriarchal cultures. See Carol Karlsen, *The Devil in the Shape of a Woman: Witchcraft in Colonial New England* (New York: Norton, 1987).

27. Abner Yoder Collection, IMHSA.

28. Abner Yoder Notebook, Abner Yoder Collection, IMHSA.

29. J. O. Kimmel to Abner Yoder, 27 March 1876, Abner Yoder Collection, IMHSA.

30. Abner Yoder Notebook, Abner Yoder Collection, IMHSA.

31. Ibid.

32. Ibid.

33. Johnson County Land Records, Book 44, 85; Book 47, 442.

34. Christian D. Shetler to Samuel D. Guengerich, 6 April 1879, Samuel D. Guengerich Collection, IMHSA; published in *Nebraska Mennonite Historical Newsletter* 1 (March 1992): 2–3.

35. AMC, Daniel B. Swartzendruber Collection, Hist. Mss. 1–144, Box 2, Folder 5.

Chapter 6. Sleeping Preacher Strains

Sermons Delivered by Noah Troyer, Book 2, 14.

1. *Sermons Delivered by Noah Troyer, A Member of the Amish Mennonite Church of Johnson Co., Iowa, While in an Unconscious State. Second Book, Containing Six Sermons not before Published, Together with Several Articles from Other Writers* (Elkhart, Ind.: Mennonite Publishing Co., 1880), 10. Hereafter cited as *Sermons Delivered by Noah Troyer,* Book 2.

2. A point made by Ann Braude, in *Radical Spirits: Spiritualism and Women's Rights in Nineteenth-Century America* (Boston: Beacon Press, 1989), 3. For an over-

view of Spiritualism, see Robert Laurence Moore, *In Search of White Crows: Spiritualism, Parapsychology, and American Culture* (New York: Oxford University Press, 1977).

Several major novelists found Spiritualism irresistible and often made the connection with agitation to remove social and religious restrictions on women. See Henry James, *The Bostonians;* Nathaniel Hawthorne, *The Blithedale Romance;* William Dean Howells, *The Undiscovered Country;* and Harriet Beecher Stowe, *Old Town Folks,* among others.

3. Aarni Voipio, "Sleeping Preachers: A Study in Ecstatic Religiosity," *Annales Academiae Scientiarum Fennicae 75,* Series B (Helsinki, 1951).

4. William Pickens Drake, *X + Y = Z; or The Sleeping Preacher,* Centennial Edition (Owens Cross Roads, Ala.: Drake Publications, 1981). Reprint with additions of G. W. Mitchell, *X + Y = Z; or The Sleeping Preacher of North Alabama. Containing an Account of Most Wonderful Mysterious Mental Phenomena, Fully Authenticated by Living Witnesses* (New York: W. C. Smith, 1876).

5. For an overview, see Don Yoder, "Trance-Preaching in the United States," *Pennsylvania Folklife* 18 (Winter 1968/1969): 12–18; and Braude, *Radical Spirits.*

6. Franklin L. Yoder, "Noah Troyer—More Than a Curious Phenomenon?" Term paper at the University of Iowa, 2 December 1986, quoting two physicians, copy in IMHSA; Dr. Del Miller to Steven D. Reschly, 18 November 1992, copy in possession of author. On the nineteenth-century medical assessment of Spiritualism, see S. E. D. Shortt, "Physicians and Psychics: The Anglo-American Medical Response to Spiritualism, 1870–1890," *Journal of the History of Medicine and Allied Sciences* 39 (1984): 339–355; and Edward M. Brown, "Neurology and Spiritualism in the 1870s," *Bulletin of the History of Medicine* 47 (Winter 1983): 563–577.

7. Harry H. Hiller, "The Sleeping Preachers: An Historical Study of the Role of Charisma in Amish Society," *Pennsylvania Folklife* 18 (Winter 1968/1969): 30–31; Richard Noll, "Shamanism and Schizophrenia: A State-Specific Approach to the 'Schizophrenia Metaphor' of Shamanic States," *American Ethnologist* (1983): 443–457; Shomer Zwelling, "Spiritualist Perspectives on Antebellum Experience," *Journal of Psychohistory* 10 (1982): 3–25. Voipio, Hiller, and Yoder suggested self-hypnosis.

8. Ernest R. Hilgard, *Divided Consciousness: Multiple Controls in Human Thought and Action,* exp. ed. (1977; New York: John Wiley & Sons, 1986). See also Ian Hacking, *Rewriting the Soul: Multiple Personality and the Sciences of Memory* (Princeton: Princeton University Press, 1995).

9. *Diagnostic and Statistical Manual of Mental Disorders,* 4th ed. (DSM-IV) (Washington, D.C.: American Psychiatric Association, 1994), 477–491, 727–729.

10. Kenneth S. Bowers, "Dissociation in Hypnosis and Multiple Personality Disorder," *International Journal of Clinical and Experimental Hypnosis* 39 (1991): 155–176; Colleen Ward and Simon Kemp, "Religious Experiences, Altered States of

Consciousness, and Suggestibility: Cross-Cultural and Historical Perspectives," in *Human Suggestibility: Advances in Theory, Research, and Application,* ed. John F. Schumaker (New York: Routledge, 1991), 159–182; Erika Bourguignon and T. Evascu, "Altered States of Consciousness within a General Evolutionary Perspective: A Holocultural Analysis," *Behavior Science Research* 12 (1977): 197–216. See also Erika Bourguignon, ed., *Religion, Altered States of Consciousness, and Social Change* (Columbus: Ohio State University Press, 1973).

11. For the image of sleeping preacher as poet, giving expression to alternate visions of reality, see Julia Kasdorf, *The Sleeping Preacher* (Pittsburgh: University of Pittsburgh Press, 1992), especially the poem of the same title.

12. Braude, *Radical Spirits,* chap. 4 on Mediumship.

13. Ibid., 84, 129. See the interpretation of American individualism by Robert N. Bellah et al., *Habits of the Heart: Individualism and Commitment in American Life* (Berkeley: University of California Press, 1985), esp. chap. 9 on religion.

14. Johnson County Land Records, Book 39, 57; Book 32, 308.

15. Abner Yoder Notebook, Abner Yoder Collection, IMHSA.

16. *Sermons Delivered by Noah Troyer, the Noted Amishman, While in an Unconscious State. With A Brief Biographical Sketch of his Life* (Iowa City, Iowa: Daily Republican Job Print, 1879), 1–2. Hereafter cited as *Sermons Delivered by Noah Troyer,* Book 1.

17. "A Great Phenomenon," *Iowa City Daily Republican,* 15 June 1878, 4; HoT 15 (July 1878): 119.

18. Ibid.

19. Ibid.

20. Ibid.

21. No other eyewitness description of Troyer's preaching mentions a distended stomach, though most details recorded by the Iowa City reporter agree substantially with other accounts. Probably this first report of bloating and stomach cramps should not be overemphasized.

22. "A Great Phenomenon," *Iowa City Daily Republican,* 15 June 1878, 4.

23. *Sermons Delivered by Noah Troyer,* Book 1.

24. Ibid., 2.

25. *Predigten, vorgetragen durch Noah Troyer, ein Glied der Amischen Mennoniten Gemeinde in Johnson Co., Iowa, während er in einem Stand der Unbewußtheit war, nebst einer kurzen Beschreibung seines Lebens. Übersetzt aus dem Englischen durch John F. Funk.* (Elkhart, Ind.: Mennonite Publishing Co., 1879). Funk's English reprint did not alter the original copyright data.

26. *HoT* 17 (February 1880): 30.

27. Caroline Kinsinger to Abner Yoder, 27 January 1879, 25 May 1879; Phoebe Kinsinger to Abner Yoder, 2 August 1879; John M. Schrock to Abner Yoder, May 1880; all in Abner Yoder Collection, IMHSA.

28. *Sermons Delivered by Noah Troyer,* Book 2; translated into German as *Predigten, vorgetragen durch Noah Troyer, einem Gliede der Amischen Mennoniten Gemeinde in Johnson Co., Iowa, während er in einem Stande der Unbewußtheit war. Zweites Buch. Enthaltend sechs noch nie gedruckte Predigten, nebst etlichen von Andern geschriebenen Aufsätzen. Übersetzt aus dem Englischen* (Elkhart, Ind.: Mennonite Publishing Co., 1880); *HoT* 17 (April 1880): 70.

29. Chris E. Hershberger, "Regarding Noah Troyer, the Sleeping Preacher," Winter 1958–59, IMHSA.

30. John P. King, "An Account of Noah Troyer, and his Preaching in Indiana," *Sermons Delivered by Noah Troyer,* Book 2, 82–107.

31. *Sermons Delivered by Noah Troyer,* Book 2, 72.

32. On nineteenth-century Amish theology, see Paton Yoder, *Tradition and Transition: Amish Mennonites and Old Order Amish, 1800–1900* (Scottdale, Pa.: Herald Press, 1991), chaps. 4–5.

33. *Sermons Delivered by Noah Troyer,* Book 1, 4; Book 2, 17, 21.

34. Ibid., Book 1, 39–40.

35. Ibid., Book 1, 35.

36. Sanford C. Yoder, *The Days of My Years* (Scottdale, Pa.: Herald Press, 1959), 25–26.

37. Confirmed by the Abner Yoder Notebook, Abner Yoder Collection, IMHSA. The letter was dated 15 November 1874, and the Troyers were accepted as members in Johnson County, Iowa, on 22 November 1874.

38. *Sermons Delivered by Noah Troyer,* Book 2, 106.

39. *Sermons Delivered by Noah Troyer,* Book 1, 4, 11, 31.

40. *Sermons Delivered by Noah Troyer,* Book 2, 11, 30, 42.

41. "A Great Phenomenon," *Iowa City Daily Republican,* 15 June 1878, 4; *Sermons Delivered by Noah Troyer,* Book 2, 67, 70.

42. *Sermons Delivered by Noah Troyer,* Book 2, 54, 56.

43. Ibid., 68.

44. *Sermons Delivered by Noah Troyer,* Book 1, 18, 24.

45. *Sermons Delivered by Noah Troyer,* Book 2, 28, 45, 51.

46. *Iowa City Daily Republican,* 27 June 1878, 4; "The Amish Man Quit Preaching," *Iowa City Daily Republican,* 19 August 1878, 4.

47. "Additional Facts About Noah Troyer, the Man Who Preached while Asleep," *Iowa City Daily Republican,* 22 August 1878, 4.

48. *Iowa City Daily Republican,* 29 August 1878, 4; reprinted article from the *Washington [Iowa] Democrat.*

49. *Iowa City Daily Republican,* 7 September 1878, 4; 19 September 1878, 4; 25 September 1878, 4.

50. Ibid., 7 January 1879, 4.

51. Ibid., 22 July 1879, 1, 4.

52. "Noah Troyer Abroad," *Iowa City Daily Republican,* 24 November 1879, 4.

53. *Sermons Delivered by Noah Troyer,* Book 2, 74.

54. *HoT* 17 (January 1880): 10–11.

55. Ibid., 11.

56. "A Journey to Nebraska and Iowa," *HoT* 17 (January 1880): 12–13.

57. "Troyer—The Sleeping or Trance Preacher," *HoT* 17 (January 1880): 14.

58. John P. King, "Account of a Visit in the West," *HoT* 17 (July 1880): 131–132.

59. *HoT* 17 (September 1880): 165.

60. J. S. Coffman, "Noah Troyer," *HoT* 17 (October 1880): 180–181.

61. *Lewistown Gazette,* 20 September 1880; cited in S. Duane Kauffman, *Mifflin County Amish and Mennonite Story, 1791–1991* (Belleville, Pa.: Mifflin County Mennonite Historical Society, 1991), 132.

62. C. P. Steiner, "A Visit," *HoT* 17 (December 1880): 217.

63. "What Has Become of Noah Troyer?" *HoT* 18 (December 1881): 208. For a description of both preachers, see Hiller, "The Sleeping Preachers," 19–31. Kauffman began preaching in 1880, two years after Troyer, and lived until 1913. See Pius Hostetler, *Life, Preaching and Labors of John D. Kauffman: A Short Sketch of the Life, Preaching and Labors of John D. Kauffman* (Shelbyville, Ill.: Pius Hostetler, [1915]); and Jacob Christner, *Kauffman's Sermons* (Tampico, Ill.: Tornado Print, [1915]).

64. *HoT* 19 (15 January 1882): 23. Little information has survived concerning either Christian Zook or John Opliger, beyond the brief notices in *Herald of Truth.*

65. John F. Funk, "John D. Kauffman, The Sleeping Preacher," *HoT* 19 (15 March 1882): 81–83.

66. *HoT* (15 May 1882): 152.

67. *HoT* 20 (15 October 1883): 312; *HoT* 20 (1 May 1883): 136.

68. One strong challenge to ministers appeared in an anonymous article by A Voice from the Laity, "Why Not More Laborers?" *HoT* 19 (15 March 1882): 87. Defenses of traditional roles appeared in B. C. Kauffman, "A Voice from the Laity," *HoT* 19 (15 April 1882): 113–114; Wm. F. Holdeman, "Another Reply to 'A Voice from the Laity,'" *HoT* 19 (15 May 1882): 154; and Levi A. Ressler, "Ordaining Ministers," *HoT* 19 (15 July 1882): 214–215.

69. "A Mother's Responsibility," *HoT* 20 (15 February 1883): 59; "To Fathers and Mothers," *HoT* 20 (1 October 1883): 290; "Mother," *HoT* 20 (15 October 1883): 308–309; Noah Metzler, "Has a Woman the Right to Preach?" *HoT* 20 (15 March 1883): 85–86.

70. Abner Yoder Notebook, Abner Yoder Collection, IMHSA.

71. Ibid.

72. [Jacob F. Swartzendruber], "How the Sisters Shall Conduct Themselves," AMC, Hist. Mss. 1–144, Daniel Bender Swartzendruber Collection, Box 1, Folder 20.

73. Johnson County Land Records, Book 76, 89–91.

74. Yoder, *Days of My Years,* 24. Accounts of Troyer's death and funeral appear in *HoT* 23 (1 April 1886): 108; *Iowa City Daily Republican,* 4 March 1886, 3; *Iowa State Press* [Iowa City], 10 March 1886, 3; and *Washington County Press* [Washington, Iowa], 10 March 1886, 3.

75. *HoT* 23 (1 April 1886): 104; 23 (15 April 1886): 120; *Budget,* July 1910; copy in AMC, Hist. Mss. 1-1-10, John F. Funk Collection, Box 93, Folder 10.

76. H[arold] S. B[ender], "John D. Kauffman," *ME,* III, 157; M[elvin] G[ingerich], "Sleeping Preacher Churches," *ME,* IV, 543–544; Paul Erb, *South Central Frontiers: A History of the South Central Mennonite Conference* (Scottdale, Pa.: Herald Press, 1974), 80–81, 284, 394–396; Willard H. Smith, *Mennonites in Illinois* (Scottdale, Pa.: Herald Press, 1983), 158–161; Hope Kauffman Lind, *Apart and Together: Mennonites in Oregon and Neighboring States, 1876–1976* (Scottdale, Pa.: Herald Press, 1990), 45, 48–49, 55, 61.

Chapter 7. Unaccustomed Choices

Sermons Delivered by Noah Troyer, Book 2, 12.

1. AMC, Daniel Bender Swartzendruber Collection, Hist. Mss. 1–144, Box 1, Folder 3. Jacob Swartzendruber, his son Frederick, and his grandson Jacob Frederick all fulminated against excessively elaborate weddings. About this same time, Frederick published *Eine Ernste Betrachtung über die übertriebenen Mahlzeiten und Hochzeiten* (Elkhart, Ind.: Mennonite Publishing Co., 1895).

2. The best ethnographic description of this process is Abbie Gertrude Enders Huntington, "Dove at the Window: A Study of an Old Order Amish Community in Ohio" (Ph.D. diss., Yale University, 1956), 605–783.

3. Peter Berger defined the essence of modernity as the perception of choice and the ability to control one's own fate. See Peter L. Berger, *Pyramids of Sacrifice* (New York: Basic Books, 1974), 21; and, more generally, Peter L. Berger, Brigitte Berger, and Hansfried Killner, *The Homeless Mind: Modernization and Consciousness* (New York: Random House, 1973). Marc A. Olshan argued that the Amish are therefore modern because of their technological choices, in "Modernity, the Folk Society, and the Old Order Amish: An Alternative Interpretation," *Rural Sociology* 46 (Summer 1981): 297–309. However, there are limits on the degree of self-conscious choice that Old Order Amish persons can experience and still remain Old Order.

4. Theron F. Schlabach, "To Focus a Mennonite Vision," in *Kingdom, Cross, and Community: Essays on Mennonite Themes in Honor of Guy F. Hershberger,* ed. J. R. Burkholder and Calvin Redekop (Scottdale, Pa.: Herald Press, 1976), 15. Schlabach discusses the concept of "Quickening" most completely in *Gospel Versus Gospel: Mission and the Mennonite Church, 1863–1944* (Scottdale, Pa.: Herald Press, 1980),

chap. 1; and *A New Rhythm for Mennonites: The Mennonite Church and the Missionary Movement, 1860–1890* (Elkhart, Ind.: Mennonite Board of Missions, 1975).

5. Beulah Stauffer Hostetler, *American Mennonites and Protestant Movements: A Community Paradigm* (Scottdale, Pa.: Herald Press, 1987), chap. 7; Bernard J. Siegel, "Defensive Structuring and Environmental Stress," *American Journal of Sociology* 76 (July 1970): 11–32. Hans-Ulrich Wehler coined the intriguing term *defensive modernization* to characterize agrarian, administrative, and military reforms carried out in Prussia and other German states between 1789 and 1815. The ruling class, aspiring to security against the French Revolution and Napoleon, allowed a great deal of change in order to secure their larger agenda. See Wehler, *Deutsche Gesellschaftsgeschichte,* vol. 1, 1700–1815 (Munich: Beck, 1987).

6. Kirsten Hastrup, *Culture and History in Medieval Iceland* (Oxford: Oxford University Press, 1985), 230. Cited by Peter Burke, *History and Social Theory* (Ithaca, N.Y.: Cornell University Press, 1992), 158.

7. Marshall Sahlins, *Islands of History* (Chicago: University of Chicago Press, 1985). Sahlins's work on Hawaii was sharply refuted by Ceylonese anthropologist Gananath Obeyesekere, *The Apotheosis of Captain Cook: European Mythmaking in the Pacific* (Princeton: Princeton University Press, 1992); and defended by Sahlins, *How 'Natives' Think, About Captain Cook, For Example* (Chicago: University of Chicago Press, 1995). See the judicious discussion of both sides by Clifford Geertz, "Culture War," *New York Review of Books* 42 (30 November 1995): 4–6.

8. H. Ottenberg, "Ibo Receptivity to Change," and H. K. Schneider, "Pakot Resistance to Change," both in *Continuity and Change in African Cultures,* ed. W. R. Bascom and M. J. Herskovits (Chicago: University of Chicago Press, 1959), 130–143 and 144–167. Cited by Peter Burke, *History and Social Theory,* 160.

9. Russell Krabill, "The Coming of the Amish Mennonites to Elkhart County, Indiana," *MHB* 52 (January 1991): 3.

10. Paton Yoder, *Tradition and Transition: Amish Mennonites and Old Order Amish, 1800–1900* (Scottdale, Pa.: Herald Press, 1991), chap. 7.

11. David Beiler, *Eine Vermahnung oder Andenken* (n.p. [1928]), 3; trans. and ed. John S. Umble, "Memoirs of an Amish Bishop," *MQR* 22 (April 1948): 101.

12. David A. Treyer, *Hinterlassene Schriften* (Navarre, Ohio: Wayne County Amish, 1920), 56.

13. Werner Sollors, ed., *The Invention of Ethnicity* (New York: Oxford University Press, 1989). See also Kathleen Neils Conzen, "German-Americans and the Invention of Ethnicity," in *America and the Germans: An Assessment of a Three-Hundred-Year History,* vol. 1, *Immigration, Language, Ethnicity,* ed. Frank Trommler and Joseph McVeigh (Philadelphia: University of Pennsylvania Press, 1985), 131–147; and Conzen, "The Invention of Ethnicity: A Perspective from the U.S.A.," *Journal of American Ethnic History* 12 (1992): 3–41. More generally, see Eric Hobsbawm and Terence

Ranger, eds., *The Invention of Tradition* (Cambridge: Cambridge University Press, 1983).

14. *Sermons Delivered by Noah Troyer,* Book 2, 48.

15. In his dissertation Melvin Gingerich lists, apparently from oral sources, the following household heads as being in the dissenting group: John Gingerich, Jacob Boller, John Troyer, Deacon David Yoder, Noah Troyer, Joseph S. Yoder, and Moses P. Miller. Melvin Gingerich, "The Mennonites in Iowa" (Ph.D. diss., University of Iowa, 1938), 138.

16. Abner Yoder Notebook, Abner Yoder Collection, IMHSA.

17. Brief biographies of Samuel D. Guengerich appear in A. Lloyd Swartzendruber, "Samuel D. Guengerich," *MHB* 11 (October 1950): 1, 3; and David Luthy, "Samuel D. Guengerich (1836–1929): Teacher and Publisher," *Family Life* (January 1993): 22–25.

18. Samuel D. Guengerich Diary, Samuel D. Guengerich Collection, IMHSA.

19. Guengerich's seven teaching certificates are in the Samuel D. Guengerich Collection, AMC.

20. Samuel D. Guengerich collection, AMC; both letters translated and published in *MHB,* 35 (October 1974): 4–5.

21. Elmer G. Swartzendruber, "Featuring the Life of Samuel D. Guengerich," *Living Echoes* 2 (February 1983): 2.

22. Samuel D. Guengerich Collection, AMC, Hist. Mss. 1-2-6, Box 11, Folder 1; documents also published in *MHB* 34 (April 1973): 6.

23. Samuel D. Guengerich Diary, 18 June 1865, Samuel D. Guengerich Collection, IMHSA.

24. Johnson County Land Records, Book 20, 484; Book 30, 235.

25. Samuel D. Guengerich Diary, 16 July 1865, Samuel D. Guengerich Collection, IMHSA.

26. Melvin Gingerich, "One-Hundred Years of Sunday School at Kalona, Iowa, 1871–1971," *MHB* 32 (April 1971): 3.

27. Samuel D. Guengerich, "Etwas über die Nothwendigkeit eines gehörigen Religionsunterrichts," *Herold der Wahrheit,* July 1877.

28. "Sunday School in Deer Creek," *HoT* 19 (1 July 1882): 201; "Sunday School in Iowa," *HoT* 20 (15 October 1883): 310.

29. *HoT* 15 (January 1878): 10; 15 (February 1878): 28.

30. H[arold] S. B[ender], "Christlicher Jugendfreund," *ME* I, 585.

31. *Katechismus für kleine Kinder, zum Gebrauch für Schulen, Sonntagschulen und Familien* (Elkhart, Ind.: Mennonite Publishing Co., 1888; repr. 1903, 1916).

32. "The German School Association of the Iowa Old Order Amish Mennonites," *MHB* 16 (July 1955): 7–8; papers of incorporation in Johnson County Land Records, Book 65, 384.

33. Samuel D. Guengerich, *Deutsche Gemeinde Schulen: Ihren Zweck, Nutzen und Nothwendigkeit zum Glaubens-Unterricht, deutlich dargestellt* (Amish, Iowa: Samuel D. Guengerich, 1897).

34. Samuel and Barbara Guengerich to John F. Funk, 27 March 1874, published in *MHB* 35 (October 1974): 3.

35. Peter Brenneman et al. to Amos Herr, 17 May 1875, *MHB* 35 (October 1874): 3–4.

36. Samuel D. Guengerich Diary, Samuel D. Guengerich Collection, IMHSA.

37. Samuel D. Guengerich, "A Brief History of the Origin and Development of the So-Called Amish Mennonite Congregation of Johnson County, Iowa, Also Giving a Short History of their Early Settlement in the State of Iowa," typescript in IMHSA, 24.

38. Guengerich, "A Brief History," 26.

39. Samuel D. Guengerich to Joel and Elizabeth Beachy, 9 December 1881, Samuel D. Guengerich Collection, IMHSA.

40. Samuel D. Guengerich to Joel and Elizabeth Beachy, 26 April 1888; Barbara Guengerich to Joel and Elizabeth Beachy, 14 December 1890, Samuel D. Guengerich Collection, IMHSA.

41. Barbara Guengerich to Caroline [her sister], 18 October 1891, Samuel D. Guengerich Collection, IMHSA.

42. Document in Elmer G. Swartzendruber Collection, IMHSA; AMC, Daniel Bender Swartzendruber Collection, Hist. Mss. 1–144, Box 2, Folder 14.

43. Sanford C. Yoder, *Days of My Years* (Scottdale, Pa.: Herald Press, 1959), 34.

44. John D. Hershberger notebook, photocopy in IMHSA.

45. Ibid.

46. On the telephone issue, see the relatively brief mentions in Melvin Gingerich, *The Mennonites in Iowa, Marking the One Hundredth Anniversary of the Coming of the Mennonites to Iowa* (Iowa City: State Historical Society of Iowa, 1939), 258, 311–312. On the divisiveness of telephones in plain groups in Pennsylvania, see Diane Zimmerman Umble, *Holding the Line: The Telephone in Old Order Mennonite and Amish Life* (Baltimore: Johns Hopkins University Press, 1996).

47. Account book in Samuel D. Guengerich Collection, IMHSA.

48. Code of Iowa 1897, Section 333, and Senate Journal 1896; Letters dated 21 January and 4 April 1896, Samuel D. Guengerich Collection, IMHSA.

49. A point made by Luthy, "Samuel D. Guengerich," 25.

50. This is taking into consideration only those who remained within Washington and Sharon townships, of course. Some Amish-Mennonites moved to Wellman, Kalona, and other nearby towns and took up businesses or worked as wage laborers.

51. "History of Sharon Methodist Church and Community, 1907–1957" (n.p.,

n.d.); and records of the South Sharon United Methodist Church, Kalona Historical Society Archives, Kalona, Iowa.

52. Steven D. Reschly, "From *Amish* Mennoniten to Amish *Mennonites:* A Clarion Call in Wright County, Iowa, 1892–1910" (master's thesis, University of Northern Iowa, 1987), chart on 132.

53. On the persistence of ethnic characteristics across several generations, see Gary Foster, Richard Hummel, and Robert Whittenbarger, "Ethnic Echoes through 100 Years of Midwestern Agriculture," *Rural Sociology* 52 (Fall 1987): 365–378. A critique and discussion ensued in the summer 1989 issue of *Rural Sociology:* Marwan Khawaja, "Ethnic Echoes through 100 Years of Midwestern Agriculture: Commentary on Foster et al.," 246–255; Gary S. Foster, Richard Hummel, and Robert Whittenbarger, "Ethnic Echoes: A Rejoinder to Khawaja," 256–261; and Sonya Salamon, "The Uses of Ethnicity to Explain Agricultural Structure: A Rejoinder to Khawaja," 262–265.

54. Nancy Grey Osterud comments on the uniformity of household formation strategies and structures in the Nanticoke Valley of New York, in *Bonds of Community: The Lives of Farm Women in Nineteenth-Century New York* (Ithaca, N.Y.: Cornell University Press, 1991), 56–62, 134–135.

55. Thomas J. Meyers has discovered that the families of Amish household heads employed in factories contain a significantly lower number of children than farm households in contemporary northern Indiana. By 1910, however, there were no differences in number of children among Old Order Amish, Amish-Mennonite, and former Amish households in Johnson County. See Thomas J. Meyers, "Population Growth and its Consequences in the Elkhart-Lagrange Old Order Amish Settlement," *MQR* 65 (July 1991): 317.

56. D. Miller, *Iowa Amish Directory* (Millersburg, Ohio: Abana Book Services, 1992).

57. It is somewhat anachronistic to use the terms "Old Order Amish" and "Amish-Mennonite" in 1880, since the Deer Creek districts did not construct meetinghouses until 1890. These numbers in 1880 indicate households that later became Amish-Mennonite or remained Old Order Amish and are intended for purposes of comparison with the later census figures.

58. John A. Dukeman, *Way of Life of Illinois Amish-Mennonite Community and its Effects on Agriculture and Banking in Central Illinois* (New Brunswick, N.J.: Stonier Graduate School of Banking, Rutgers University, 1972), 43.

59. Metin M. Coşgel compared Amish and non-Amish farm households in Sharon and Washington townships from 1850 to 1880 and concluded that Amish farms were not as productive as non-Amish farms. He adopted a non-Amish standard of productivity, the ratio of outputs to inputs, to prove this hypothesis. The reason

he identified is the "bequest motive"—in other words, forming new households was more important than profit. However, almost every variable examined in chapters 2 and 7 of this book show that Amish farmers were highly successful economically in addition to their efficient approaches to community reproduction. See Coşgel, "Religious Culture and Economic Performance: Agricultural Productivity of the Amish, 1850–1880," *Journal of Economic History* 53 (June 1993): 319–331.

60. Steven D. Reschly and Katherine Jellison, "Production Patterns, Consumption Strategies, and Gender Relations in Amish and Non-Amish Farm Households in Lancaster County, Pennsylvania, 1935–1936," *Agricultural History* 67 (Spring 1993): 134–162; James E. Landing, "Personal Decision Expressed in Agriculture," *Bulletin of the Illinois Geographical Society* 12 (December 1969): 69–77.

61. The classic statement on assimilation remains Milton M. Gordon, *Assimilation in American Life: The Role of Race, Religion, and National Origins* (New York: Oxford University Press, 1964). For recent treatments, see Elliott R. Barkan, "Race, Religion, and Nationality in American Society: A Model of Ethnicity—from Contact to Assimilation," *Journal of American Ethnic History* 14 (Winter 1995): 38—75; Russell A. Kazal, "Revisiting Assimilation: The Rise, Fall, and Reappraisal of a Concept in American Ethnic History," *American Historical Review* 100 (April 1995): 1–14.

62. See, for example, Robert C. Ostergren, *A Community Transplanted: The Trans-Atlantic Experience of a Swedish Immigrant Settlement in the Upper Middle West, 1835–1915* (Madison: University of Wisconsin Press, 1988); Jon Gjerde, *From Peasants to Farmers: The Migration from Balestrand, Norway, to the Upper Middle West* (New York: Cambridge University Press, 1985); and Kathleen Neils Conzen, "Peasant Pioneers: Generational Succession Among German Farmers in Frontier Minnesota," in *The Countryside in the Age of Capitalist Transformation,* ed. Jonathan Hahn and Steven Prude (Chapel Hill: University of North Carolina Press, 1985), 259–292.

63. Sonya Salamon, *Prairie Patrimony: Family, Farming, and Community in the Midwest* (Chapel Hill: University of North Carolina Press, 1992). See also Salamon's earlier articles, "Ethnic Differences in Farm Family Land Transfers," *Rural Sociology* 45 (Summer 1980): 290–308; "Ethnic Communities and the Structure of Agriculture," *Rural Sociology* 50 (Fall 1985): 323–340; and "Ethnic Determinants of Farm Community Character," in *Farm Work and Fieldwork: American Agriculture in Anthropological Perspective,* ed. Michael Chibnik (Ithaca, N.Y.: Cornell University Press, 1987), 167–188.

Chapter 8. Persistent Amish Migrations

The Days of My Years (Scottdale, Pa.: Herald Press, 1959), 35.

1. *Journal of American Ethnic History* 15 (Spring 1996): 44–51.

2. Oscar Handlin, *The Uprooted* (Boston: Little, Brown, 1951); John Bodnar, *The*

Transplanted: A History of Immigrants in Urban America (Bloomington: Indiana University Press, 1985); Immanuel Wallerstein, *The Modern World-System* (New York: Academic Press, 1974); Dirk Hoerder, *Labor Migration in the Atlantic Economies: The European and North American Working Classes During the Period of Industrialization* (Westport, Conn.: Greenwood Press, 1985); James C. Malin, *History and Ecology: Studies of the Grassland,* ed. Robert P. Swierenga (Lincoln: University of Nebraska Press, 1984). For exemplary studies of transplanted communities, see Robert C. Ostergren, *A Community Transplanted: The Trans-Atlantic Experience of a Swedish Immigrant Settlement in the Upper Middle West, 1835–1915* (Madison: University of Wisconsin Press, 1988); Jon Gjerde, *From Peasants to Farmers: The Migration from Balestrand, Norway, to the Upper Middle West* (New York: Cambridge University Press, 1985); Walter D. Kamphoefner, *The Westfalians: From Germany to Missouri* (Princeton: Princeton University Press, 1987); and Royden K. Loewen, *Family, Church, and Market: A Mennonite Community in the Old and New Worlds, 1850–1930* (Urbana: University of Illinois Press, 1993).

3. Charles Tilly, "Transplanted Networks," in *Immigration Reconsidered: History, Sociology, and Politics,* ed. Virginia Yans-McLaughlin (New York: Oxford University Press, 1990), 79–95; quote p. 84.

4. See Kathleen Neils Conzen, "Mainstreams and Side Channels: The Localization of Immigrant Cultures," *Journal of American Ethnic History* 11 (Fall 1991): 5–20.

5. For arrivals and exits from Iowa, see Katie Yoder Lind, *From Hazelbrush to Cornfields: The First One Hundred Years of the Amish-Mennonites in Johnson, Washington, and Iowa Counties* (Kalona: Mennonite Historical Society of Iowa, 1994).

6. This concept is suggested by Leo Driedger, "The Anabaptist Identification Ladder: Plain-Urbane Continuity in Diversity," *MQR* 51 (October 1977): 278–291.

7. Paton Yoder, *Tradition and Transition: Amish Mennonites and Old Order Amish, 1800–1900* (Scottdale, Pa.: Herald Press, 1991).

8. *Sermons Delivered by Noah Troyer,* Book 1, 18.

9. David Luthy, *The Amish in America: Settlements that Failed, 1840–1960* (Aylmer, Ontario: Pathway Publishers, 1986); David Luthy, *Amish Settlements Across America* (Aylmer, Ontario: Pathway Publishers, 1985), 1, 6. See also David Luthy, "Why Some Amish Communities Fail: Extinct Settlements, 1961–1996," *Family Life* (December 1996): 20–23; (January 1997): 17–20.

10. David Luthy, "Amish Settlements Across America: 1991," *Family Life* (April 1992): 19–24.

11. S. B. Wenger, "Correspondence," *HoT* 32 (1 May 1895): 137.

12. Luthy, *Amish in America,* 123–28.

13. Ibid., 393–96.

14. Sanford C. Yoder, "The Amish in Wright County," *The Palimpsest* 43 (September 1962): 405.

15. On the Wright County Amish-Mennonite settlement, see Steven D. Reschly, "From *Amisch* Mennoniten to Amish *Mennonites:* A Clarion Call in Wright County, Iowa, 1892–1910" (master's thesis, University of Northern Iowa, 1987); and Melvin Gingerich, *The Mennonites in Iowa, Marking the One Hundredth Anniversary of the Coming of the Mennonites to Iowa* (Iowa City: State Historical Society of Iowa, 1939), 333–336.

16. "Amish Center," *Kalona News* 1 (7 October 1892): 1.

17. Yoder, *Days of My Years,* 35.

18. Gingerich, *Mennonites in Iowa,* 333; Yoder, *Days of My Years,* 35.

19. Yoder, *Days of My Years,* 35–36.

20. *Gospel Herald* 35 (14 May 1942): 159.

21. *Budget* 3 (30 June 1892): 1; *Kalona News* 1 (26 August 1892): 1; *Kalona News* 2 (18 November 1892): 1.

22. "Local Items," *Wellman Advance* 4 (10 February 1893): 4.

23. Yoder, *Days of My Years,* 36.

24. Shem Swartzendruber took wood in early 1893, according to *Kalona News,* 2 (3 February 1893): 1; and John Gunden shipped wood to Wright County in August of 1893, as reported in *Wellman Advance* 4 (25 August 1893): 8.

25. J. E. Miller, "Hawkeye Gleamings," *Budget* 4 (15 February 1894): 1.

26. "Clarion News," *Wright County Democrat* 10 (7 March 1894): 4.

27. Miller wrote his journal in English, using pencil and a lined notebook. The journal and a typed transcription are in IMHSA.

28. *Kalona News* 3 (9 March 1894): 4; *Wellman Advance* 5 (9 March 1894): 4; Adam Miller diary, 5, 6, 7 March 1894.

29. Adam Miller diary, 7, 8 March 1894.

30. Ibid., 11 March 1894; Samuel Kreider, "Reminiscences," in *The Frederick and Sarah (Yoder) Swartzendruber History,* ed. Amos Gingerich (Parnell, Iowa: n.p., 1958), 110.

31. Adam Miller diary, 12 to 18 March 1894.

32. Gingerich, *Mennonites in Iowa,* 234–235.

33. The first separate headings for Wright County appeared in *Kalona News* 4 (26 April 1895): 5; and *Wellman Advance* 6 (2 May 1895): 1.

34. *Budget* 10 (7 June 1900): 1. A brief history of the Amish newspaper, with many sample letters, appears in Elmer S. Yoder, *I Saw It in THE BUDGET* (Hartville, Ohio: Diakonia Ministries, 1990).

35. *Wellman Advance* 5 (17 August 1894): 8.

36. Yoder, *Days of My Years,* 40, 43; *Wright County Monitor* 25 (10 October 1894): 5.

37. "Wright County," *Wellman Advance* 6 (13 June 1895): 4.

38. The church record book from Wright County can no longer be located. Long-

hand notes taken by Melvin Gingerich are extant in AMC, Iowa-Nebraska Conference Collection, II-6-1, Box 11, Folder 7.

39. "Eagle Grove," *Wright County Monitor* 26 (29 May 1895): 5.

40. Accounts of the accident appear in "Death by Lightning," *Wellman Advance* 8 (24 June 1897): 4; and "Killed by Lightning," *Kalona News* 6 (25 June 1897): 5.

41. Gingerich, *Mennonites in Iowa,* 335.

42. "Personal Mention," *Wright County Monitor* 31 (27 June 1900): 5; Elvina Gingerich, "Correspondence," *Budget* 11 (12 July 1900): 1.

43. "Personal Mention, *Wright County Monitor* 31 (14 November 1900): 5; *Budget* 11 (20 December 1900): 2. Sanford left in August of 1901, "Personal Mention," *Wright County Monitor* 32 (21 August 1901): 5; Amos left to teach school near Iowa City in October of 1902, "Personal Mention," *Wright County Monitor* 33 (29 October 1902): 5; and Simon departed for Johnson County in April of 1903, *Budget* 13 (9 April 1903): 1.

44. "Personal Mention," *Wright County Monitor* 32 (20 March 1901): 5; *Budget* 11 (4 April 1901): 1; "Personal Mention," *Wright County Monitor* 32 (28 August 1901): 5.

45. "Personal Mention," *Wright County Monitor* 32 (20 November 1901): 5; "Personal Mention," *Wright County Monitor* 32 (2 October 1901): 5.

46. "Personal Mention," *Wright County Monitor* 33 (28 May 1902): 5; "Personal Gossip," *Wright County Monitor* 34 (23 December 1903): 5.

47. "Field Notes," *Gospel Witness* 3 (15 May 1907): 104; Wright County Church Records, tax list for 1909.

48. Yoder, *Days of My Years,* 49.

49. "Field Notes," *Gospel Witness* 2 (17 October 1906): 458; Elias Swartzendruber, letter in *Gospel Witness* 2 (24 October 1906): 472; *Budget* 17 (1 November 1906): 1.

50. "School Notes," *Wright County Monitor* 30 (13 September 1899): 5; "Florence Factors," *Eagle Grove Eagle* 5 (13 September 1899): 4.

51. An assertion made, among other places, on Yoder's funeral service bulletin, in February of 1975. AMC, Sanford C. Yoder collection, Hist. Mss. 1–162, Box 27, Folder 11.

52. "School Notes," *Wright County Monitor* 31 (21 March 1900): 8; "School Notes," *Wright County Monitor* 31 (30 May 1900): 5.

53. Sanford C. Yoder, "The Amish in Wright County," *Palimpsest* 43 (September 1962): 430; "Democratic Convention," *Wright County Monitor* 32 (17 July 1901): 5; Yoder, *Days of My Years,* 56–57.

54. "The City in Brief," *Wright County Monitor* 40 (22 December 1909): 5. Yoder moved on 3 February 1910, *Wright County Monitor* 41 (9 February 1910): 5.

55. "The City in Brief," *Wright County Monitor* 41 (5 January 1910): 5; "Field Notes," *Gospel Herald* 2 (3 February 1910): 712.

56. *Kalona News* 3 (14 September 1894): 5. Land that sold in August of 1895 at

$50 per acre in Dayton Township was described by a local newspaper editor as "the best sale we have heard of so far this season." *Wright County Monitor* 26 (28 August 1895): 5. The same issue stated that land was selling in Wall Lake Township at $26 to $32 per acre. *Wright County Monitor* 40 (13 October 1909): 5. The editor described the transaction as "the top price paid for farm land in this locality."

57. Johnson County Land Records, Book 75, pp. 79, 497; "Real Estate Transfers," *Wright County Monitor* 33 (15 March 1902): 1.

58. Johnson County Land Records, Book 72, 248; "Real Estate Transfers," *Wright County Monitor* 32 (10 April 1901): 1; "Real Estate Transfers," *Wright County Monitor* 39 (4 March 1908): 1.

59. William P. Kuvlesky, "The Texas Amish: Social Adaptation" (Paper presented at the Rural Sociological Society, 1990), 17.

60. Gingerich, *Mennonites in Iowa,* 322; "Field Notes," *Gospel Herald* 4 (29 June 1911): 200.

61. *Wright County Monitor,* 2 October 1912; "Old Cemetery Is Moved Monday," *Wright County Monitor,* 16 October 1941.

62. Gingerich, *Frederick and Sarah (Yoder) Swartzendruber History,* 137.

63. *ME* I, 181. Brief accounts appear in Daniel C. Esch, "The Amish Mennonite Colony in Audrain County, Missouri," *Gospel Herald* 32 (15 February 1940): 986–987; L. Glen Guengerich, "The Amish Mennonite Colony in Audrain Co. Missouri," *MHB* 7 (June 1946): 1–2, 4; Paul Erb, *South Central Frontiers: A History of the South Central Mennonite Conference* (Scottdale, Pa.: Herald Press, 1974), 63–65; and Luthy, *Amish in America,* 244–250.

64. Johnson County Land Records, Book 77, 277; Guengerich, "Amish Mennonite Colony in Audrain Co. Missouri," 1.

65. *Budget,* 7 June 1900, 4; Guengerich, "The Amish Mennonite Colony in Audrain Co. Missouri," 1.

66. *Budget,* 18 April 1901, 4.

67. Luthy, *Amish in America,* 246.

68. Ibid., 250.

69. Esch, "Amish Mennonite Colony in Audrain County, Missouri," 987.

70. Erb, *South Central Frontiers,* 378–379; Willard H. Smith, *Mennonites in Illinois* (Scottdale, Pa.: Herald Press, 1983), 197; Plat of Tuleta by Peter Unzicker, dated 1 October 1906, in Bee County Land Records, Book L-2, 610.

71. Bee County Land Records, Book 54, 504. Photos of the two buildings are printed in Camp Ezell, *Historical Study of Bee County, Texas* (Beeville, Tex.: Beeville Publishing Co., 1973), 263.

72. Interview with John Christian Stoltzfus, grandson of Christian H. Stoltzfus, 21 October 1991.

73. A. Caswell Ellis, "Tuleta Rural Agricultural High School," *Farm and Ranch* 30 (27 May 1911): 2.

74. "Tuleta Community is Established in 1906," *Beeville Bee-Picayune* 72 (16 October 1958): 1–4; Amanda Stoltzfus, "Opening of Tuleta School and Community Fair," *Farm and Ranch* 37 (3 August 1918): 10–11.

75. "Meeting of the General Faculty [of the University of Texas]," 25 November 1930, Center for American History, University of Texas, Austin, Texas.

76. "Local Items," *Wellman Advance* 4 (11 November 1892): 4; *Wright County Democrat* 15 (5 April 1899): 4; "Personal Mention," *Wright County Monitor* 31 (7 November 1900): 5.

77. "Personal Mention," *Wright County Monitor* 32 (6 February 1901): 5.

78. Bee County Land Records, Book P-2, 202; Bee County Land Records, Book 59, 64–65.

79. *Budget* 18 (5 September 1907): 1; 19 (9 July 1908): 1; Interview with John Christian Stoltzfus.

80. *ME* IV, 753; Mennonite Church listing in the County Church Directory, *Beeville Bee-Picayune* 72 (16 October 1958): B-5.

81. Gingerich, *Mennonites in Iowa,* 310–311.

82. Maurice A. Mook, "Extinct Amish Mennonite Communities in Pennsylvania," *MQR* 30 (October 1956): 267–276.

Conclusion

1. Donald B. Kraybill, *The Riddle of Amish Culture* (Baltimore: Johns Hopkins University Press, 1989), 143.

2. Elmer G. Swartzendruber Collection, IMHSA.

3. A great many articles and books use modernization theory to explain Amish history and culture. A recent example is Donald B. Kraybill and Marc A. Olshan, eds., *The Amish Struggle with Modernity* (Hanover, N.H.: University Press of New England, 1994).

4. Johnson County Land Records, Book 65, 384; Book 96, 560.

5. Samuel D. Guengerich Collection, IMHSA.

Name Index

Note: Page numbers in *italics* denote illustrations.

Subject Index

Page numbers in *italics* denote illustrations; those in BOLDFACE denote tables.

Other Center Books in Anabaptist Studies

The Amish and the State
edited by Donald B. Kraybill

Amish Enterprise: From Plows to Profits
Donald B. Kraybill and Steven M. Nolt

Amish Roots: A Treasury of History, Wisdom, and Love
edited by John A. Hostetler

Amish Society, Fourth Edition
John A. Hostetler

Brethren Society: The Cultural Transformation of a "Peculiar People"
Carl F. Bowman

Holding the Line: The Telephone in Old Order Mennonite and Amish Life
Diane Zimmerman Umble

Hutterite Beginnings: Communitarian Experiments during the Reformation
Werner O. Packull

Hutterite Society
John A. Hostetler

Mennonite Entrepreneurs
Calvin Redekop, Stephen C. Ainlay, and Robert Siemens

Old Order Amish: Their Enduring Way of Life
Lucian Niemeyer and Donald B. Kraybill

The Riddle of Amish Culture
Donald B. Kraybill

Two Kingdoms, Two Loyalties: Mennonite Pacifism in Modern America
Perry Bush

About the Author

Steven D. Reschly grew up in a Mennonite, formerly Amish, community in southeast Iowa, about 25 miles from the Amish and Mennonites who are the subject of this book. He received a B.A. in history from Goshen College, a master of divinity from Goshen Biblical Seminary, an M.A. in history from the University of Northern Iowa, and a Ph.D. in American history from the University of Iowa. He has served as a Mennonite minister and as chairman of the Mennonite Historical Committee. Dr. Reschly is an assistant professor of history at Truman State University in Kirksville, Missouri.

Library of Congress Cataloging-in-Publication Data
Reschly, Steven D.
The Amish on the Iowa prairie, 1840 to 1910 / Steven D. Reschly.
p. cm.
Originally presented as the author's thesis (Master's)—University of Northern Iowa.
Includes bibliographical references (p.) and index.
ISBN 0-8018-6388-0 (acid-free paper)
1. Amish—Iowa—history. I. Title.
F630.M45 .R47 2000
977.7'0088287—dc21 99-050723